WHEN WE SAY WE'RE HOME

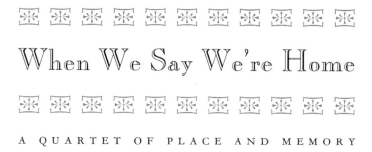

When We Say We're Home

A QUARTET OF PLACE AND MEMORY

W. Scott Olsen, Dawn Marano, Douglas Carlson, Wendy Bishop

Foreword by Judith Kitchen

THE UNIVERSITY OF UTAH PRESS

SALT LAKE CITY

Printed on acid-free paper

"Fire and Ice" by Robert Frost appears with
the permission of Henry Holt & Company.

LIBRARY OF CONGRESS
CATALOGING-IN-PUBLICATION DATA

When we say we're home :
a quartet of place and memory /
W. Scott Olsen, editor ;
Dawn Marano, Douglas Carlson, Wendy Bishop :
p.   cm.
ISBN 0-87480-591-0 (alk. paper).—
ISBN 0-87480-592-9 (pbk. : alk. paper)
1. Home.   2. Family life.   3. Dwellings
4. Geographical perception.
I. Olsen, W. Scott, 1958–
GT2420.W44 1999
392.3'6—dc21
98-54376

CONTENTS

૭૭૭૭૭

WHEN WE SAY WE'RE HOME

Judith Kitchen

WHAT IS HOME? I live in my new husband's old house in a town I came
to more than twenty years ago by accident. It's only ninety miles from
where I grew up, but it took me two other states, two countries, and ten
houses (seven rented, three owned) to get here. The landscape here on the
flat plains of Lake Ontario could not be more different from my hometown perched at the edges of the Appalachians. A change in landscape
means a change in history—the carnage of Sullivan's march versus the
westward expansion of the Erie Canal. And when I go back there—only an
hour and a half on a new four-lane highway—nothing is as it was. My
childhood home was severely flooded in the wake of Hurricane Agnes in
1972. It looks the same on the outside, but I know that inside it's been rad-
ically altered. I resist the urge to knock on the door and ask the owners to
let me look around. The village center is gone, victim of the same devastating force of nature. Even the river has been moved.

Sometimes, on an early winter evening, we drive out into the blue dusk,
and a house, set back from the road, will throw its lights out over the snow,
drawing us into its interior spaces. That house becomes my eleventh
home—the home of my imagination. My experience is not unique. In fact,
it has a peculiarly American resonance. In a culture as rootless, as energetic,
as ours, the concept of "home" is problematic. We inherit the idea of a vast
landscape most of us have never fully seen. We are nostalgic for a past we
have been busy eradicating.

When We Say We're Home: A Quartet of Place and Memory addresses the
question of home through four personal explorations. The writers presented here (W. Scott Olsen, Dawn Marano, Douglas Carlson, and Wendy
Bishop) each play a different instrument; their stories, their voices, their
styles, are distinct. But the book should be read as the "quartet" of its sub-
title, looking for the harmonies and counterpoints as well as differences.
The individual voices, with their overlapping concerns, amplify each other,
giving rise to larger, more global issues.

And these voices are not alone. This book adds to a vigorous national dialogue. Many of us sense that there's something important at stake, something as important as the land itself. Like me, like the early pioneers, like the earliest inhabitants of this continent, these four writers have not stayed put. None of them is living where he or she grew up. They find themselves "going West" into a West that is all too attractive to all too many people. They want—and need—to preserve its wilderness. Seeking to stake a claim somewhere *new,* someplace *else,* these writers must first observe themselves as outsiders. The house of the present is building *on* the past—a conflation of place and memory. This shift of perspective involves both landscape and history—a history that includes the cultural, political, and geological layers that give shape to the present. W. Scott Olsen's wide sky and open prairie—its weather and its physical properties—determined the orientation of the house he built. Dawn Marano's personal history sometimes collides with the communal Mormon history of her adopted home in Salt Lake City. Douglas Carlson's Chautauqua County carries its Iroquois origins in its very name. And Wendy Bishop, after youthful wanderings, matures into a Florida suburb very like the California she left behind. But the challenge is internal as much as external. These writers are looking for what Scott Russell Sanders has described as a feeling of "rightness, at-homeness, a knitting of self and world." They have moved physically, and now must move spiritually as well. They have to turn "place" into "home."

How they do this varies. Olsen, beginning a career and a family, deliberately settles into a community. Marano embarks on a course of active study (aided both by a new husband who equips her to enter the terrain and by a number of women who share their knowledge). Carlson, clearly the most rooted, makes the effort to shake himself loose from old ties, only to find new connections. Bishop, struggling to make a home for her children, almost by accident finds her daily ritual has become a way of life. In each case, however, becoming a part of a community involves a meaningful encounter with nature—with its snowstorms, its floods and erosions, its very indifference. Home, it appears here, is more than a sense of belonging. It's all the various ways we fit ourselves into a landscape, meet its demands, give it a human significance. In the end, these writers make a place for the *self.* The exterior landscapes become internal necessities.

Ancient inland sea to architect's office, Ácoma to Biosphere II, wolf hunt in the Kabob swamp to wild-horse roundup in Theodore Roosevelt

National Park, kiva to hot tub, the tensions inherent in the conjunction of the human and the natural make for engaging reading, even controversy. While each writer is aware of environmental and ecological concerns, this book is mostly a human document, wryly aware of human inconsistencies. Often these writers feel most at home when they have been severed from responsibilities, set adrift in alien territory. Olsen recognizes an interior landscape in a New Zealand of mountain passes and penguins coming in from the sea at sunset, even as he confronts the decision of whether or not to bungee jump. Marano's carefully planned fishing trips (complete with marinated pork tenderloins and shrimp scampi) are a fiasco of forgotten necessities as well as a celebration of newfound skills. Carlson discovers in Yellowstone the meaning of his daily commute in upstate New York. Bishop perceives in her chaotic movement through time and space an equally fluid movement through *class*—labeling herself a member of "Category X: bohemian, self-cultivated, intellectual."

When we *say* we're home . . . When what we say becomes a *story* . . . Story, then, is one way of knowing you're home. And home will provide us with its own stories. The present needs the past. These four writers—from the North, South, East, and West—raise important issues, including the concept of home, acquiring roots, the stewardship of the environment, development of social policy, and questions of identity. But most of all, they tell their individual stories of how they made peace with their own contradictory impulses. They make us think about ourselves and the spaces we inhabit.

When We Say We're Home

W. SCOTT OLSEN

LET ME BEGIN—with a question.

What do you *mean,* when you say you're home?

To mean is oftentimes the same verb as *to intend,* so let me ask it that way, too.

What do you *intend,* when you say you're home?

I don't mean the normal stuff. I don't mean walls and windows. I don't mean bathrooms and closets, or if the floors are carpet or hardwood, or if the shingles on the roof are black, or brown, or primary red. And I certainly don't mean a street address. Home has nothing to do with a deed that's been registered with a clerk.

There's something else going on when we say we're home. The word itself is larger than a simple location. In my dictionary, the word means a dwelling place, the place of one's nurturing, the place in which one's affections center, or where one finds rest, refuge, or satisfaction. The word means your country, as well as your grave.

Really, though, this much isn't news. We tell ourselves all the time that we know the difference between a house and a home. We say we know the real distance between our parents' homes and our own, between history and the present tense. We claim we know how far it must always be to just leave the driveway.

But my wife, my two kids, my dog, and I have just built a new house. I've been thinking a lot about the things that hold it up, that make it work, that make it look nice. And I've been thinking about the peculiar hope we have for the places we live. The way we unpack first the whole sums of who we are. Not about the *fact,* but about the *ways* a house becomes a home.

What I've been feeling, you see, and what I've been thinking about, is Desire. About the desire to talk, to reach over the distance and loneliness imposed on us at the moment of self-awareness, about the wanting we feel for communion every day. And something deeper, too. About the desire we share for the mysterious—about the wanting we have for what we call the sacred.

But if I'm going to tell you that what I mean when I say I'm home is a kind of desire—if I'm going to tell you that what I intend when I say I'm home is some step closer to the sacred—first, I need to tell you a true story, about something else.

❧

Not really so very long ago, just after the New Year changed, my family and I set out to make what is normally a ten-hour drive from Kansas City, where we had stopped to visit my brother, to Fargo, North Dakota, which is very nearly where we live. The afternoon was a bit chilly and overcast in Kansas City, but nothing out of the ordinary for early January. Nothing on the radio warned us of an oncoming adventure or hardship. As we drove north, past Saint Joseph, past Tarkio, past Omaha and Council Bluffs, we fully expected to find our driveway before the day was over.

Near Sioux City, the radio news began to change. An unexpected combination of two parts of the jet stream, the announcers said. Heavy snow, they said. Strong wind. Blizzard warnings were being posted for all of South Dakota. My wife and I listened to this news while our two children slept in the backseat, while our dog and the too large collection of carelessly packed clothes and Christmas presents rocked in the space behind the kids.

I live on the east side of Fargo, on the Minnesota side of the Dakota border, and heavy weather is nothing new for me, my family, or my neighbors. Thunderstorms, hail storms, and tornadoes can descend out of the summertime evenings, and winter temperatures without windchill are often twenty-five or thirty degrees below zero. The windchill can taste eighty degrees below, killing your flesh before you know you're cold, and heavy snow is just a fact of life.

The threat in the radio news was not so much the depth of the bad weather, but the fact that we were exposed, on the road, poorly equipped for this turn of the page. In Sioux City I asked a gas station attendant what he'd heard about the road heading north. He said the storm was still a ways off, that the last he heard was the roads were still okay. Light snow was falling here, pleasant looking in the lights of the gas station, so we decided to keep going.

And this, of course, was a mistake.

Not far north of Sioux City, the wind leaped up around us, and the snow fell as hard as heavy rain. The highway became impossible to see—we drove by the reflected light of tenth-of-a-mile markers, creeping from one to another. And we began to pass pickup trucks and cars in the median and off the shoulder, then semitrucks that had become likewise stuck. My wife and I were thankful for a heavy car with four-wheel drive, and worried.

I cannot tell you how many hours or miles it was before we got to Vermilion, South Dakota, where we discovered a gas station convenience shop filled with more than one hundred people, infants whose diapers were being changed in the aisle between the root beer and salsa, men and women wanting to be anywhere other than where they were, but too afraid or filled with good sense to try and leave. After some time on the phone, we did hear of a hotel seven miles away, a tremendous distance in this storm, with vacant rooms—so we put together a caravan of cars and crawled into town. Once in our hotel room we opened the curtains and watched the theater of heavy weather until sleep was upon us.

The next morning, I phoned the South Dakota Highway Patrol and asked a bad question.

"Is I-29 heading north open?" I asked.

"Yes," said the officer on the telephone, "it is."

What I failed to ask, of course, was "How far?"

We drove, slowly, over ice and compacted snow, past wrecks clearly fatal, from Vermilion to Watertown, South Dakota, where we found the barriers still drawn across the highway, eighteen-wheelers parked on the highway behind the barriers as if awaiting the start of the Indy 500, and hotel lobbies filled with people who had been waiting for a room for two days already, since an ice storm here preceded the blizzard. Perhaps we were lucky, but again a room opened for us, a place where we could rest with the kids and the dog, and wait while the highway crews forced their way through fifteen- and twenty-foot drifts, but only after probing them gently with long steel rods in search of cars and perhaps bodies.

The next day, the roads were still not open, and every one of us who could booked our rooms for another night. But in the middle of the afternoon, some people rose, looked at maps and out the windows, and decided to find another route. Highway 212, they said, east to Winona, then north to Alexandria, then west into Fargo. Three hundred miles to make the

120-mile line. Or west, others said, to the road that joins with Jamestown, then east into Fargo. Again, two hundred extra miles against the promise of getting home. And these people lived in Fargo, in Grand Forks, in Winnipeg, Canada, and in places even farther away. They warmed up their cars, were bid farewell by the community of people sharing news of fact and rumor and personal history in the hotel lobby, and set off.

And it occurred to me, as they drove off into the becoming twilight, the situation had suddenly achieved metaphoric weight. We were at the place of Story, and Poem. There were things to be learned about the human spirit here, about the desire to get home, about the bravery of the spirit when faced with elemental threats, about urgency and family and risk. As I looked at the impatient and idling trucks still waiting at the highway barrier, I discovered they too could be seen as metaphor, the rush of commerce and money halted only so long by something so trivial as a storm. We had all the rhetorical elements. We had a dramatic setting, a cast of major and minor characters, dialogue, the comic relief provided by the hotel clerks, and now, with part of the cast heading away toward certain danger and uncertain success, we had transcended anecdote and moved into something larger. As these people pulled away from the hotel, I felt somehow richer, knowing their efforts were possible, heroic and human both.

For an hour or two after the climax, those of us still in the hotel wandered through the denouement. We ate supper, mingled, phoned for highway reports, watched television, bathed the kids, drank too much coffee. And then something remarkable happened. The men and women who had driven east were on the telephone with the desk clerk. They had been in accidents, all of them, too far away to try and get back to our hotel, but they wanted to let us know! Perhaps not surprisingly, a short while later the people who had struck out west were on the phone. They too had failed to find an open path, and they too wanted to share the news.

And it occurred to me then, having moved beyond metaphor, perhaps not even really beginning until metaphor had been achieved, intuitively, in the backs of our heads, the hotel had become a homeplace. We had a shared story now, a story about weather and risk and fear and hope. The location of the story we shared was a hotel lobby. And the effect of any story shared is a kind of family, a kind of care.

Just one night earlier than this, at the gas station convenience store, the hundred people dripping snow and fear onto the vinyl floor were friends, good friends, at the moment of entering. We smiled at each other, waited our turns at the pay phone, and each of us gave our version of the story we already knew. Each of us listened to the other, to one story of slow driving through wind and whiteout piled up on the back of another version of the same story. And as each story came out, the larger picture began to appear. We could begin to see the night as it really was.

There is no meaning to nature. The storm was simply a lot of snow and a lot of wind in the same place at the same time. The storm did not *intend* anything. But people need meaning. As we heard the very small differences between how each of us came to the gas station lights, those small differences became the essential matter, the lesson about the many different ways we can be.

We had a shared story from the beginning, and just as a family will retell old stories at dinnertime, looking for the new or varied detail that will lead to some other insight, we told our adventures to give this homeplace life. When the caravan of cars and trucks and four-by-fours left that gas station and sought other places in town, it really did feel like leaving home.

And so it was the next night, too. These people were calling back, reclaiming a connection with those of us left wondering, as they had been, about the world beyond a hotel lobby. They felt a connection, and thus a responsibility, to share the new understanding of their continued experience.

The next morning, the sun came out, the highway barriers had been drawn back, and we made our way to our more permanent home. Our neighbors and friends knew we'd been stuck, and like family, their story of the few days passed and our story of those days needed to be joined, and shared, more than once.

⁊

What do you *mean* when you say you are home? What do you *intend?* For me, what I'm learning is that *home* and *desire* are nearly synonymous. Desire, according to psychology, is born at the moment an infant discovers it is not its mother, at the moment when loneliness is first perceived, at the moment when we are first filled with a wanting to foreclose a distance between ourselves and another. This distance, between self and other, between object and subject, between me and you, has been called a Potential Space. We cannot fill this space, ever. Yet we spend our lives and talents pouring what we can into it. We are forever trying to explain ourselves to ourselves, reaching over to ask, "Was it like this for you, too?" And those moments when the space becomes smaller, those are the location of home.

There are other ways of looking at desire, or home—comparisons just as rich. The central event of the Catholic mass, for example, is the sacrament of communion. Each parishioner walks to the wafer and cup and accepts a moment of the Mysterious. We don't argue about transubstantiation anymore, so let us say this central, defining act is an act of metaphor, an act of Story, and Poem. Yet, even here, the work isn't over. To be fully participant, to find the greatest value in the intimate accepting of the mysterious, to be most completely at home in the congregation, you need to explain something. You need to tell your story, and have it joined, at least in the ears of one listener, to the stories of the others.

What used to be called confession is now the sacrament of reconciliation, a change I, a non-Catholic, especially admire. Think about it this way. To be reconciled with a community does not require just admission of guilt or wrongdoing. Instead, it requires you to say, in effect, "Me too. I too belong to this community. I too have an individual's spark, and with it a wanting to know I'm not alone. I am like these other people, perhaps more like them in private than in public, and I will admit to my obligations here."

A home is an act of desire, an act of reconciliation, a way either to illuminate those parts of living and thinking and feeling that are invisible because they are routine, and through this illumination find a way to celebrate the ordinary and make it transcendent, or to articulate and give voice to what most often remains private, and through this confession to make a way for others who have wondered. A home is a way to keep firm the details of our own lives and whatever meanings we can draw from them.

A home is the witnessed development of an idea, or a hope. When those drivers who tried and failed to make it home called back to the hotel, the news they offered was not only the poor conditions of the road, but also the particular and idiosyncratic quality of having tried to drive them. Their news offered a fuller picture of the hotel lobby, those of us listening to the desk clerk, what else was possible outside the wooden double doors. The news they offered came from the other side of metaphor, news sent back home, to make, for however short a time, the space between us smaller.

My wife, my children, my dog, and I are living in a new home now. And not just a home we found. Not somebody else's ideas about how light should enter a room, or how open the spaces should be. With an architect, a kind of magician who turns hopefulness and desire into the ink of blueprints, and builders who transformed ink into wood and glass and Sheetrock and carpet, each of us intending to own the same home in our differing ways, we mean something new.

The stories are coming already. There is the story of our daughter's first slumber party—six seven-year-old girls trying to fall asleep in the same room. There is the story of our four-year-old son, almost every night, singing at the top of his voice while playing catch in the shower, throwing a washcloth as high as he can and then not slipping as he reaches for it through the falling water. There is the story of a difference of opinion— our dog versus the grass seed. There are stories of full moonlight, of hard rain, of crimson sunsets and midnight hail. And there are all the stories of everything else, too.

What do I mean when I say I'm home? I mean a place where the distance between us is shorter, where the smallest details can offer the most joy or insight or even trouble. A home is the archive, the safekeeping place of real histories. A home is where we love.

Home Stories

I.

My sister leaps from a small apple tree and lands on a garter snake.

It is midsummertime, and she is young, first or second grade, and so she is barefoot. My parents and I are also in this yard, though I cannot remember exactly where. Two unmanageable puppies named Sandy and Ranger, which we will own only for a few weeks, roll in the grass. What I remember is that all of us are together, and watching.

The snake curls around my sister's foot. And it's clear, somehow immediately, that there is no danger to either my sister or the snake.

Nobody moves. Not my parents. Not the dogs. Not me. My sister is frozen, mouth open but soundless, arms out to each side, her eyes enormous. The snake, pinned, keeps its tiny, intimate grasp on her ankle and sole. Its eyes look up at her, certainly wondering.

This is theater, I think, though not in those words. This is *the moment.* As long as it's suspended, there is magic. Anything, *anything,* can happen.

I remember smiling. I remember having enough time to smile, slowly. The pleasure of the sustained tableau growing. And to be honest, I cannot remember who moved first.

2.

I am nowhere near this one, but I know it well.

It is summertime, and my family is at a lake in Missouri. The day is filled with sunshine and humidity. My parents are relaxing on the dock by our house. The afternoon quiets in our cove, but clearly there is a fair bit of traffic on the lake. Large boats and small, heading toward or away from waterskiing, toward or away from docks attached to bars and restaurants, toward or away from work and routine, pass the house and dock. None of us four kids are home.

My parents say they could see our small boat from some distance, and they knew there was something wrong. The way it was coming at us, my father says, was too direct, too fast. My youngest brother, Chris, was driving the boat, and the boat was full-throttle for home.

There is a way to drive a boat that will gentle the waves. Take the waves at an angle, or trim the propeller so very little of the boat rests in the water, or some combination of the two. But it was clear my brother Chris had no interest in this art. What waves got underneath his bow became spray.

My parents say Chris entered the cove too fast, turned the boat sharply so its side slid up to the dock, and only then did they see my other brother, older than Chris, whose name is Kurt. He stood up in the back of the boat and lifted his arm so it crossed his belly. Between his elbow and wrist, the arm took an unexpected turn downward and stretched the skin.

Kurt smiled at my parents before he spoke. "Do you think it's broken?"

What followed was the usual rush to the hospital, the X rays, the cast. But none of these things are why I hold onto this story. Nothing about a broken arm, even with the added drama of a jostling boat ride across an unsmooth lake, is really all that illuminating. I love this story for what happened before the manic crossing. I love this story for the *how it happened.*

Imagine my brother Kurt, the one with the curly hair and the "why not?" grin, standing on the roof of a dock. Imagine his friends, high-school-age women and men, tanning on the dock's platform, or resting on flotation cushions in the water. Each of them talking, laughing, sharing the simple joy of an untroubled summer afternoon by water. In the water below my brother's rooftop, imagine an inner tube. An overly large, black, truck-sized, unoccupied ring. And imagine my brother wondering, "Can I dive through that?"

I wasn't there, so I can't tell you how it really happened. But in my imagination he leaves the roof of the dock the first time without telling his friends what he plans. He trusts each of them will look up as he jumps. Perhaps they will gasp as they see his arms rise above his head, his head lower toward the center of the tube.

On this first jump, although he would never say it this way, he was beautiful. The leap into wondering, the precision of his aim, the straightness of his body from fingertip to toe. And then the cold rush of blackness in deep lake water. When his head surfaced, I'm sure his friends were amazed.

An encore was required, of course. And now knowing he could do it, my brother obliged. Another time he dove, beautifully, while they watched. And then another. Perhaps it was ten or a dozen more dives, each of them equally thrilling, much like the leaping of a figure skater, before some small thing changed.

Perhaps a boat on the far side of the lake made a wake my brother did not see, and lifted the ring, pushed it to one side or another, while my confident brother was in midair. Perhaps the underwater kicking of one of his friends made a current no one could see. And perhaps the beauty of it all simply faded. Perhaps art became mundane and turned toward sideshow. I wasn't there. I can't tell you how it really happened. And the stories are different, depending on whom you ask.

The easy part is to say my brother broke his arm stupidly, trying to dive from the roof of a dock through the middle of a floating inner tube. The difficult part is trying to imagine him standing on that roof, looking at that ring, wondering if he was good enough to pull this one off, and then leaping without any assurance at all that he was.

3.

Here's another one from the New Year's blizzard.

In Watertown, South Dakota, we needed a room, and there were none to be had. The interstate highways were closed, and the weather still loomed close and heavy. Two days' worth of stranded men and women, college students, truck drivers, families returning from holiday reunions lined up behind counters at the hotels, credit cards ready.

At one hotel, the least likely one of them all to have a room because it's so near the interstate, I leaned on the counter and smiled at the desk clerk. This is a routine I know. For six years, my years in graduate school, I worked as a night auditor for hotels. Eleven at night until seven in the morning, balancing the daily receipts, checking people in, or out, recording the wake-up calls and listening to the stories of people who were tired, or running, or crazy. I smiled at the clerk, a gray-haired woman named Shirley, and we talked about life behind the desk. After a short while, I asked her about the real situation regarding the rooms.

"We might have one," she said. "It's not a guaranteed reservation. But it's expensive."

"I don't care," I said. "I have two kids in the car. And my wife is worried."

"Okay," she said.

At six o'clock in the evening, when the people with the reservation failed to show up—no one knew what part of the storm they were lost in, and they had not called—Shirley gave us the room, at a little more than one hundred dollars a night. Unpacking the car, already a mess of its own, we carried the suitcases and blankets and toys past the people in the lobby who had not been offered space, each of them looking at us. Shirley wasn't at all happy when she saw our dog come through the lobby. The other desk clerk, however, pointed out that our dog is small (as if that makes a real difference), and, well, she'd already let several others in with pets.

In the room, we unpacked what we could stand to see again—this one-day trip was now into day three—turned on the television, and tried to relax. But the television didn't help—the dramas there more clearly irrelevant and silly when compared to the drama outside our window, or the exasperation of those sleeping in lobby chairs. The toys had been played with too much already. And it was too early for any of us to find sleep. There was no restaurant or coffee shop in this hotel, and even the small pool had been closed for repairs. We couldn't wander the halls or rest in the breakfast room; we were afraid the dog would bark. Lucky enough to have a room, we felt trapped inside it.

A benefit of paying so much for this room was that the room was a suite, and it included a large hot tub in the living room. Kate and Andrew were ecstatic. They had never been in a hot tub before. My wife and I were happy for this easy entertainment.

The kids got undressed while we filled the tub. They got in, swam, splashed, made noise while outside the hard light of street lamps reflected off ice and snow and then through the window. We were glad for this space, despite feeling the closeness of those walls, the limits of what we had packed. At some point, I wandered over to the wall, where a switch for the jets in the tub was placed.

"Hey kids," I said, hand on the switch. "Want to see something?"

My wife, on the couch, smiled. We both thought we knew what was coming.

Andrew and Kate looked up at me and, together, seeing my hand on the switch, said, "Yes!"

I turned the switch and walked toward the children, then kneeled. The bubbles filled the tub as the pumps pushed the water hard. Kate's smile changed, from anticipation, to question, to glee. Andrew, however, was on the move. His small body not heavy enough to resist the push of the jets, his bottom was racing around the perimeter of the tub, each circumference made a bit faster than the one just before. His eyes grew large as he worked to understand what was happening, and finally his mouth opened.

"Dad!" Five or more syllables to call me, another circuit around the tub.

Kate was laughing. Maureen looked at Andrew, then at me, her eyebrows near the top of her head.

I heard a blast of the hard wind hit the room's window as I rose and turned toward the wall and the switch. Of course, I was going to shut off the motors. But not quite, I must admit, with all possible speed.

A Desire for Home

My wife, Maureen, and I both crouched at our bedroom window, peering over the windowsill. The sun was already lower than the treetops, house lights were beginning to show on porches and through curtains, and we knew, if we weren't careful, we'd be seen. We were, after all, spying on our neighbors. The neighbors we liked. The neighbors we greeted on summer evenings. The neighbors who were selling their house.

A woman named Linda, our real estate agent, paced the sidewalk in front of their house, the shadows of the old and thick elm trees that lined the street falling on her shoulders and hair. She had just given them our offer. They were talking it over. Maureen and I peered, stared, concentrated on the dining room windows of the house next door, the thin fabric that served as window covering there, hoping to see Mark and Susan, hoping to see their faces and read something from them, hoping we'd suddenly develop the ability to read lips and tone of voice long-distance, through walls and windows.

The house next door was for sale, and Maureen and I wanted it. We'd been renting the small white stucco house—a good find in a pleasant neighborhood next to campus—when the house next to it came up for sale. Mark and Susan were moving only a few blocks away, to a house and a lot on the banks of the Red River, because the college was thinking about putting a parking lot on the other side of their house. The idea of a college parking lot didn't strike Maureen or me as a particularly bad idea; after all, it would be empty all summer—and in winter it would be too cold to be any type of hangout. It would be a better option than the party houses that then lined Seventh Avenue.

And we weren't just thinking about location. The house next door was, for both of us, a perfect house. The floors downstairs were dark hardwood oak. The staircase was oak. The floors upstairs were bright maple. The house had a sunroom, with windows on four sides. The living and dining rooms had crown molding where the ceiling met the walls. The kitchen was quaint, with rosemaling, a Norwegian folk art, painted on the cabinet faces. At the staircase landing, where the stairs turned and doubled back on themselves, there was a door leading outside, to a small deck, where we imagined glasses of wine on calm summer nights, quiet talk, even—perhaps—a bit of romance.

The house had wood siding, hand-cut cedar shakes. There was a bedroom for us, a bedroom I could use as a study, and a bedroom that nearly ached for a child. There was a wood-burning fireplace, a real one, with a brick face and a heavy oak mantle. And there was a garage, set back a ways, with its original wood-plank floor.

The house was old, even then, built in 1929, which for us made it even more attractive. There were things we could do for this house, projects, ways to love the structure itself. We imagined ourselves already in the house, and we imagined ourselves in the house forever. We talked about the ways we would move in the house, where we would be in the evenings. We talked about how, with just the one bathroom, we would get ready in the mornings. We did not yet have children, but we talked about them, too. How they would come down the stairs, where they would play, how we would sit at the dining room table.

Linda walked toward us on the sidewalk, then turned and paced the other direction. The front door opened, she smiled and went in again. Maureen and I leaned a bit harder against the windowsill. All we could hear was the sound of our own breathing.

I don't remember the details of the next few hours, or days, but we got the house. Mark and Susan moved over to the river, and Maureen and I invited a bunch of friends to help on a sunny weekend afternoon carry stacks of plates, loose piles of books, odd bulky couches and beds out the door, across one driveway, and then in the other door. And suddenly there we were. We had bought our first house.

And here's a fact that's important. I wanted this house, this first house for us, to also be our last house. Maureen was born, grew up, went to college, got married—and home for her was always the same place. The house on top of the hill in Jefferson City, Missouri. The house with the swimming pool in back, and a small apple-tree grove. The house that contained every story their family had.

I liked the *taste* of that idea, the way that kind of rootedness rolled around in my imagination and desire. I liked what it meant toward the idea of going home, of belonging to a place, of seeing old people you knew when they were very much younger. I liked the kind of ownership this meant. Not really ownership of a building, but ownership of a part of a growing story.

My own family was far from nomadic, but it's fair to say we'd moved as well. The first memories I have of my own living, dim and scattered as they are, are memories of the second house I lived in. Two houses in Kansas City, then a move to Chicago and a house in Northbrook, then a house in Long Grove, then a long time in Lake Forest. Then a house in Osage Beach, Missouri. Then another house in Osage Beach, and then another. Then a house in Charlottesville, Virginia. Then a house in Kansas City again. Then a farm outside Charlottesville, in a place called Free Union. Six houses my parents called home dated after I left for college. Going home meant seeing my parents, oftentimes my brothers or sister, and hearing their stories, but never quite rejoining my own.

This old house, new for us, was for me a chance to practice the responsibility of permanence. Maureen said I was crazy.

Still, we got right to it. We put a new floor in the kitchen. We braced the rafters in the attic. We tore up the bright-red plush carpet that was everywhere, and we had the oak and maple floors sanded and stained. We bought rugs, and furniture. We saved for central air-conditioning—and as it was being installed discovered we needed a new furnace as well. We planted a flowering tree, a gift from a friend, in the backyard. We mowed the grass, trimmed the hedge, shoveled the snow. We got to know our neighbors well, and to like them all very much. There were birds in the trees and bushes, sparrows and nuthatches and robins and hummingbirds and mourning doves and, once or twice, cardinals. Rabbits and squirrels ran through the yard, and vegetables grew in the small garden we kept on the south side of the house. The house was, in so many ways, perfect.

In time, we had a daughter, Kate, and then a son, Andrew. Midnight feedings in front of the television in the sunroom. Endless loops around the tables and chairs as they were being rocked to sleep. Our friends in the neighborhood had children nearly the same ages as ours. As they all grew older, they played in the small park across the street from our house—on the swings and slide—and ran from one house to another. In summertime, children named Kaia, and Megan, and Erin, and Anne, and Sam, and Lucas, and Stephanie, and Emily, and Katie ran through sprinklers in the backyard, climbed the tree in the front yard, rode their bicycles in the shade of the elm trees. Sometimes we would walk less than half a block to campus, and then go visit the pond. In wintertime, when we were finished with the snowblower and shovels, we would build ice caves in the snow mounds—twists and turns so you would never come out the same hole you entered. We would throw snowballs at each other, or hide our heads in our coats because the wind was strong and the temperature dangerous.

We were in a good house, in a good neighborhood, surrounded by people we liked, and trusted, and whose children got along with ours. We knew the man who read our electric and natural gas meters, and the woman who delivered our mail. We watched each others' houses when vacations were possible. We helped, and we shared, and if there was a chance to wave at each other, or stop to speak, we waved, and stopped.

Even then, however, the house wasn't *really* perfect.

The garage held only one car. On deep-cold mornings, temperatures of ten or twenty or nearly thirty degrees below zero, heading out to start the other car made dreams of a larger, and attached, garage as wonderful as dreams of Tahiti.

The basement, made of cinder-block walls and a concrete floor, leaked water in the springtime, or after any hard rain. Small streams of water running from the corner by the garden, or from the corner by the washing machine and dryer, or the corner pressed up to the edge of the front yard by the driveway. Streams that ran across the floor and then down a drain without problem, but streams our dog would run through, streams that would get into anything left on the floor.

The cedar shakes that sided the house were the originals, and they were dry. Some of them had broken—just very few, but enough for us to see them always. And squirrels had been chewing their way through. We could hear them in the sunroom walls, could imagine their small claws as they gripped the studs and climbed, and while we had no worry they would enter the house—our dog would see to that—we still worried the hole they'd made would lead to something larger.

But these problems weren't the reason we sold the house. These problems could be fixed, and most of them were, because fixing an old and beautiful house is a source of wonder and joy. We sold the house because we'd fallen in love with an idea.

It started, I think, in the living room. One day, I don't really know when, Maureen looked at the back wall, the table there, the three small piano windows over the table, and imagined something else.

"We should put a door there," she said. Or something very close to that.

"A door?" I asked.

"French doors, big ones, so we can see the backyard. And a deck, or a porch or something."

Our backyard was wonderful to look at. With the garage on one side, a thick hedge more than seven feet tall on the other, and a dense row of trees at the back, it sheltered birds all summer, turned brilliant in fall. In winter, the limbs and branches caught snow and sunlight; we caught ourselves at windows just staring. And in spring, each new bud was a happy moment. There was good reason to want to see the backyard more.

The idea caught on. If we pushed out the living room with French doors and a porch, then we could push out the kitchen as well. Over the kitchen, we could add on to the bathroom. We could move the garage forward, make it large enough to hold two cars, connect it to the house, and build a new study over it since the room I'd once used was now Andrew's bedroom. We could jack up the whole house on stilts, rip out the old foundation and put in a fancy new one, then lower the house back down. We could add a swimming pool, a greenhouse, a heliport, a virgin forest, a lake, or at least a lake view. Once we got started, it seemed, we had lots of ideas.

The ideas were good ones. But somewhere in our dreaming we crossed a line, even though we didn't know it yet. French doors were the first hint that the house needed—or, more exactly, that we wanted—something beyond repair. The first hint that we wanted something else.

⁊

Four o'clock on a Tuesday afternoon and I'm sitting at a round conference table in a square room, three floors above the street, in the offices of a company called Image Group, talking with Richard Moorhead, an architect, the man who took what we said we wanted and imagined a house—the house we built and now live in. The perfect house, for us.

There are pictures on the walls here. A solitary home on a prairie hill-side. A hospital. A courthouse addition. A sunroom and patio. And the home of some people we know. There are notebooks filled with photographs on the shelf behind me, too. Each of them witness to what this company can do, to the scope of this way of seeing.

Richard is the type of man who is overworked, and overjoyed at being so. He appears tall because he's so thin, and always on the brink of laughter, or exposition. He's one of those people who seems, often, to be thinking of something else, or simply waiting for the conversation to provide an opening for the idea he's been turning.

What I want to know, of course, is impossible. I want to know how he did it. I want to know how he took what he listened to, the ways Maureen and I explained our love for the old house, as well as what we found lacking there, and added to that what we said we wanted for the new house, and came up with an idea. I want to know, when his pen first matched ink to paper, what he saw in the back of his head. But I cannot ask him about magic—even the ordinary magic of imagining something as intimate as a new house—so I ask the other questions, to circle in.

"How," I ask him, "did you get started with all this? When did you know *this* is what you wanted to do?"

"Well," he says, "I think, like so many people, it was by default. Growing up in Fargo, in fact, I wanted to be an artist. A painter, drawer, sculptor, whatever. And I remember being clearly told by my parents that was no way to earn a living. But showing some interest in that direction, knowing there would be no choice of education other than North Dakota State University—that was just mind-set: stay at home and go to school—the closest program to satisfy parents who wouldn't let me go to an art program was architecture."

"Was there a point you knew you'd stay with it—that this was, indeed, right?"

"Yeah, yeah," he says. "As with most architectural programs, the first year was just getting used to college or university, and the second year was when you started to get into the program and, I mean, it was absolute. I took a drawing course or two, mechanical drafting, in my freshman year—second year was love at first sight."

"Second year?"

"The second year of architectural then, and maybe even still now, was basic design, a course I was fortunate enough to teach several years later. And it just works out. It's so universal. You've heard me, I think, talk about my youngest son's education in Rhode Island. It's just the whole premise that you can teach design and then go off and be an architect or a painter or a jeweler or do whatever. Design is a universal language; it's that broad and deep."

⁓

There are things we said we wanted:

We wanted a kitchen that faced southeast, to catch the morning light.

We wanted hardwood floors.

We wanted space for the kids to run, to play, to make a mess in their joy and not have parents one step behind them, demanding a tidier world.

We wanted windows. Lots of windows.

We wanted porches. Front and back.

We wanted a place to work—apart from each other.

We wanted private space.

We wanted openness, as few walls as possible.

We wanted bathrooms.

We wanted windows. Lots of windows. We wanted every room to be cross-lit. Windows in more than one wall.

We wanted places to put our stuff.

We wanted a yard, big enough for children to breathe.

We wanted a two-car garage, attached, with space to open the doors.

We wanted windows. Lots of windows.

At some point we decided not to put the French doors in the old house, to skip the good ideas there. And so we were sitting in a restaurant called the Tree Top with Richard, going over the things we wanted.

"You know what I really want?" I asked.

"What?" he said.

"I want five hundred thousand dollars, so we can get everything else on the list."

He laughed, then told us we didn't need that much. With good design, he said, we could have nearly everything we wanted, and stay close to budget. He started to talk then about additive design, ideas he'd picked up from looking at old houses on Nantucket. He drew boxes on a piece of paper, then drew other boxes pressed against them. I nodded, trying to fit these boxes into what Maureen and I had begun to imagine, but I wasn't paying attention. In the back of my head, I was grinning.

Windows. We were getting lots of windows.

❧

I wish I had a better memory. Important moments go by, and I don't know enough to hang on to them until much later, after they've faded. Sometimes I can't recover them at all. This is the case with the lot our house now stands upon. I cannot remember when we first saw it. I cannot remember when we first stopped the car, got out, walked the length of it to see how the sun looked from the corners. But I do know that once we found it, we walked there quite a lot.

It's pie-shaped, narrow at the street, opening to the south and west. To one side, a small ditch and then green space owned by a church, and then the church and its parking lot. To the back, which is twice the depth of our old house lot, a somewhat larger ditch and then a field where, in two seasons, we've watched wheat turn golden and sugar beets grow large. The other sides border lots where our neighbors will build their own homes. But our lot was turned just right, we imagined—our neighbors could build anything at all and not block the sun coming into what we hoped would be a kitchen space. It would be years before the field was taken by developers and turned into another subdivision, and even then the distance would not foreclose the sky.

Every day we turned our car south on Eighth Street, crossed over the interstate highway, pulled into a circle of pavement fronted by a map showing where the lots would be. For now, just dirt. Pigweed and foxtail. Field mice, jackrabbits, and fox. Nowhere else was it so clear that Columbus had it wrong—the earth is, in fact, very flat. And nowhere else was it so clear that the sky is beautiful, that the clouds are theater, that sunlight and moonlight are proof of something large.

"Here?" we asked each other.

We walked the lot with friends, with relatives, and with Richard.

"Here," we said.

❧

"That first job, working for Clark and Holman here in Fargo," Richard tells me, "was a wonderful, wonderful job. I mean it was one of those things where they probably would have hired anybody who walked off the street. They were just desperate to get help because they had so much work. And in that first year, I had the good fortune to just learn so much. I learned more in that one year than many people can hope to learn in a career. In the office at that time were North High School, Metropolitan Savings and Loan, and Dakota Hospital. All three projects, all on the drawing boards, all at one time, and they were just swamped. And I largely did North High School as a wet-behind-the-ears kid right out of school. It was *my* project. I took it from a very broad and incredibly powerful concept to the point where it was done.

"Tracey and I got married about a year later, and Tracey continually reminded me it was a hateful time to go on a honeymoon because I *really* needed to get back to watch the progress day-to-day on this school project, which was just starting construction."

☙

Then we had to rush. A county program we needed for the mortgage said we had to have the foundation in, and capped, by New Year's Eve. Fall was turning toward snow, and we didn't have plans. We didn't know how far back from the road. We didn't know how many feet from one side to the other, from front to back. We needed a shape. We needed a hole in the earth. We needed men to come with equipment to dig, to build, to pour, to wait, to remove, to build some more. Time was a problem now.

And then the snow came hard. Lots of it. And early. The weather turned very cold. By mid-December, nearly a foot of snow stood on our lot. When the city snowplow, an only occasional visitor through the loop where no families yet lived, made walls of snow over the gutters, the wind drew up drifts even taller. Six feet. Then ten feet tall. Driving into what would be our neighborhood, the place we imagined our children playing, where we hoped to place a home that would hold all the stories we had and those still to come, now required four-wheel drive, courage, a working heater, hope.

"You're lucky," said Rod. Rod Ulven, the "U" of D&U Construction—Hal Dickelman, his partner, is the "D"—was on the phone, talking about what days he could get someone out to push the snow back, to strip the lot, to break through the frost, and then to dig the hole. "The snow," he said, "has pretty much insulated the ground from the real cold weather. There's no more than six or ten inches of frost, I bet. It costs extra to break through frost—this way it won't cost you so much."

Lucky. We felt lucky then. We welcomed the new snow. What we didn't know yet was that we had seen only two of the seven blizzards that winter. We didn't know that we'd receive more snow than any year here in recorded time. We didn't know that we'd face what people called the Flood of the Century. We didn't know we'd be standing in lines with strangers, handing sandbags one after another, to save the homes of people we didn't know. We didn't know that come springtime, the snow that was saving us money would cost other people their homes, their businesses, and, in some cases, their lives.

Sitting around the round conference table, we looked at drawings. We had to get a shape for the basement. We could finesse the details of the first and second floors later. We had all winter, and then all spring. Finally, we had the rough shape and size. One rectangle pressed against the other. We went out to the lot, stood where we measured the front door would be, where the garage would be, where the hole would begin.

Go, we said. Dig the hole. We had to make the deadline. It didn't matter that we hadn't sold the old house, that we didn't have anyone with ready ink. Standing in fresh snow, the wind blowing it to our faces and into our hair, we were thankful for the insulation.

The big machines showed up and cleared the lot. Walls of snow stood against the ditches. Rod and Hal pounded stakes into the ground—marked the lot for excavation. Maureen and Richard and I drank champagne and broke bread as the earth was opened. Rod and Hal took sips, then turned toward their work.

"This is good bread," said Rod.

"This is going to be a marvelous house," said Richard.

The forecast said more snow.

⌘

"It was clear," he says, still at the table on a bright January afternoon, a little more than a year since we began digging, "that I had to practice."

I had asked him about his time teaching at North Dakota State University.

"I couldn't teach just a few hours a day. I really have to create. I couldn't just tell it. So—about that same time, I really had to get out and see all that

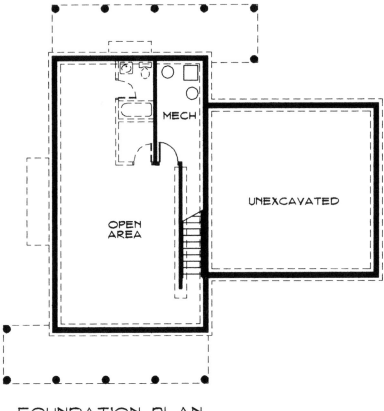

FOUNDATION PLAN

was out there to see—I thumbed my nose at Fargo, North Dakota, and took off."

There are stories about working in Minneapolis, then a move to Washington, D.C.

"Is it now," I ask, "or later that you came to the kind of style that perhaps you're more comfortable with?"

"My education," he says, "as with everybody's education in the early '60s, was absolute diehard modernist, international class, straight, flat roofs, crisp, less is more. That was the dictum, that's what I believe. That's consistency. If your budget didn't allow anything fancy, then you couldn't do anything fancy. You couldn't put a different color around the front door and say that's to celebrate entrance. But it's got to be a whole work of art, that's what it's really all about. In Washington, D.C., and more specifically Georgetown and Alexandria, I came to understand that we threw the baby out with the bathwater. There were many, many, many good ideas. We were taught that to be a really creative architect you had to invent a new style every Monday morning, and there was so much more, and Washington's a wonderful place to see this, so much more to know and understand about what's already happened than to think that anybody can be so brilliant as to come up with anything better overnight."

"So were you just wandering around the streets in Georgetown looking at buildings?"

"No, it was just an opportunity to think. One of the bicentennial goals was to have three or four really hallmark projects, and one of them was a University of the District of Columbia. We did a master plan for the new university in town, and it was so intense that we were just closeted for a period of about six weeks. When we got our first break, met our first huge deadline that really defined this master plan, I had the opportunity and need to get away and so went down to the University of Virginia, and saw what a *real* campus was all about. It could have taught me so much more had I gone there first."

"Would the sensibilities of the employers at that time have bought that aesthetic?"

"They would have had a hard time with that—although this was a designed-by-a-committee sort of thing, as a master plan, which is a very complex thing, not an individual creative work—but more important than the sensibility of the employers, our *clients* would have bought it, and should have had it. That was exactly what the client wanted. So, along with making me realize there were better ideas out there to learn *from,* I learned that the client isn't someone you have an adversarial relationship with. What the client wants and needs just might be right too."

ᔐ

We have a videotape of the building of our house. First the large machines to level the earth. Then the claw to dig it up. Then the concrete company to build the forms for the footings. Ten, maybe fifteen men in our hole in the ground when the revolving concrete truck shows up, beeps its way backward toward the opening. Sunshine reflects from the snow and ice fields, bright and hard.

Standing at the far edge of the hole, I see the foreman look up at me.

"Owner's here," he calls to his men.

I wonder how close the truck could come to the edge, angled as it was. How much weight the edge could hold before the frozen dirt and clay gave way. Men put the chute together, point it at the wood forms for the footings. One man gives signals to the other man driving the truck. The truck comes closer, then closer. One wheel reaches the edge and goes past it, just a bit. The concrete begins to race down the chute toward men with shovels.

"What do you do," I ask the foreman, "when a truck starts to fall in a hole?"

I am sure, seeing this, it has happened before.

"Run," he says.

The fluid concrete steams from truck to form.

That night, and the next night too, after dark, we drive from the old house to the hole in the ground and stare at the opening, at the footings now covered with insulating blankets, and try to imagine what will come next—how a house will rise from this. We crawl down a ladder and step carefully over the blankets. We've been told there are tricks of the eye to learn while a house goes up. The hole looks too small. The stud walls look too big. Sheetrock makes the rooms get small again.

Standing in the bottom of what would be our new basement, our feet below where even the floor would be, we wonder about size nonetheless. This looks small, we tell each other, pacing out where the rooms might be.

Two days later, the concrete men are back, to build the forms for the foundation walls. And new snow comes with them, with wind. On the videotape, the beginnings of the third blizzard cloud the picture—snow racing horizontal from left to right, from west to east. The men have sweatshirt hoods and mad-bomber hats pulled tight to their heads. Jackets zipped up tight. A boom truck pumps concrete from the revolving mixer to the back of the foundation. Men walk the open and filling walls, guiding and shaking the thick stuff all the way down.

"Is this," I ask one of the men, "one of the worst weather days you guys have had to work in, or does this even count?"

He looks at me hard.

"This *is* the worst," he says.

The blizzard comes and leaves. Bright new snow banked against the foundations walls both inside and out. Rod and Hal build the cap for the foundation, hang a furnace from the rafters to keep it all from freezing through. It is still before New Year's Eve. Maureen and Kate and Andrew and I walk around on the cap, pace off where the rooms will be, look at morning sun dogs from where we think the bedrooms and kitchen will be, and laugh about moving in early. Kate and Andrew say sleeping bags would be just fine by them.

Confident, we pack the car for a holiday trip to Missouri. And, although we didn't know it yet, a very long drive home.

✍

"What brought you back to town?" I ask.

"This is a story I like to tell, and I've probably told you before, but, I'll tell it again. When I was working in Minneapolis, I was working on a hospital project down in Des Moines, Iowa. The hospital administrator, I swear to God, came up and put his arm around me and said, 'We are really so glad to have you here. We thought about hiring a more fashionable architect, who we know could have built us a much handsomer building, but we picked you because we knew that you would do it technically correct.'

"Just a few short years later, then I was working in Washington because I wanted to work for a design firm, and the chairman of the biology department, who was the chairman of the building committee, put his arm around me, walking down the road, and says, "You know, we've thought about hiring somebody else for the science center; but we really wanted to make sure that we would hire somebody who could be sensitive to this Colonial Gothic campus and we really don't give a rip about how well it works."

Richard smiles. We both laugh.

"He didn't say that. But the intimation was that he really wanted to make sure that this thing could beautifully tie in and work with the facility. Both men bought the image of the firm. Of a substantial, technical hospital-architecture firm in Minneapolis, and this caring, sensitive design firm in Washington. But they got the same *guy*. They got the guy, and the guy has belief in the balance of that it's got to work, but it's got to look right, and they're both important. And what art is, is making the whole thing come together.

"Well, so back to the question—what brought me back to here. In Washington, we did projects like the Kennedy grave, the Executive Office

Building, right across from the White House. A project we were working on was the Senate Office Building. These were absolutely wonderful, exciting projects. These are projects where the client screams out to make this as wonderful as you can. But what I realized after a relatively short period of time in Washington is, as wonderful as that commission was, they were first and foremost a three-hundred-man firm. Which means it's a corporate style. Which means the decisions are made by somebody else over here. The designer very rarely has a chance to make a case to the client, so there's a bureaucracy within the process that doesn't really lend itself to a real creative process.

"I tried to explain this to both companies, and I'm surprised they didn't pay much attention. I explained it to them by saying, 'Well, there's these two guys down in Fargo, North Dakota. I don't know if you've ever heard of Fargo, but they really know how to work with a client. They know how to get this balance of design, technical, and function and serve what the client's needs are. You might be able to learn something by how these people put buildings together.' They said they weren't much interested.

"But one day, out of the blue, I was in need of a product I specified for North High School, and I couldn't find it in any of the catalogs. So I called back here and they said, 'By the way, would you like to come back and be a partner in the firm?' It must have been just absolutely the right day."

ৎৢ

I'm told there was a napkin. A paper napkin, from underneath a glass of wine in a restaurant. And on this napkin, the first sketch of our house. Denise Drake, an interior designer and partner with Richard, looked at Maureen and me one day, and her voice took on the tone of a secret about to be revealed. Something big.

"I've seen the napkin," she said.

"The napkin?"

"Your house."

"What's it like?"

"Oh no, I can't say yet. All the spaces aren't quite right yet. But it's coming together now. It's very, very nice."

Denise and her husband, Kim Kemmer, and their daughter live in, and love, a house Richard designed. It stands out from its neighbors, which look, in their neighborhood, as well as in ours, like the same idea done over and over. A full three stories tall, and narrow, it has a strong echo of a grain elevator to it, which on the prairie is a fine echo to have. There's a porch out front, a deck on the back overlooking a small stream. As much as was possible, each floor is just one large room.

Kim works with Maureen at the advertising agency, and so they'd talked about the process of building a house. More important, they talked about the *idea* of building a house. The idea that drives the way a house behaves.

We knew what our basement would look like, and where the garage would be. And we'd had long talks about how we wanted the house to act. More than what finishes we wanted, or anything at all having to do with material, what we wanted was a house that allowed a certain kind of living, a certain style of being a family. We knew the kids would have the basement to run. We said the first floor should be social space, open space, a place to talk and smile across rooms. The kitchen, we said, should accept the fact that it's the best place on a normal family day, and the place when friends are over that most people want to gather. And the fireplace, we said, should burn wood. The second floor was for bedrooms, for laundry, for a study, for being alone, for work, for settling into a chair with a very large book, or settling into bed and resting against an offered arm.

We wanted to see the napkin.

But the snow would not go away. Blizzards five and six came through town. Snowfall reached the most-ever record. People looked at their calendars, at the approach of spring, at the approach of warmer air, and then they turned to look at the river. It was time to worry.

Our old house was six blocks from the river. And it backed up to a low coolie. A dike at a park five blocks away protected our entire neighborhood, and the college.

We'd seen sandbags go up before. In our eleven years in town, two or three times the river had moved up the backyards of friends and threatened their basements. Everyone knew the routine. A pile of sand in the driveway, a line of neighbors and students to bag and carry and place, cookies and soda as a thank-you. But we never had cause to worry about our own house before. We never had cause to worry about the dike.

This time it wasn't just a few people along the river who wondered if they would stay dry. Flood stage for the Red River in Fargo is measured at seventeen feet. The forecasts said the river would near, and possibly pass, forty feet. We could lose both towns entirely.

The air grew warm. The snow began to melt. The river began to open. The river began to rise. Every night on the news we heard the stories from upstream. The towns of Wahpeton and Breckenridge went underwater, twice. Homes became islands surrounded by sandbag walls, pumps running to keep the seepage out. In Fargo and Moorhead, heavy equipment moved earth into new dikes. The permanent dikes were raised. Sandbags arrived everywhere. The cities and colleges opened stations where sandbags were filled fast, by hand and by machine. Almost, but not quite, fast enough to keep up with the cars, trucks, eighteen-wheel flatbed semis lined up to receive them. Everyone discovered the height of their own property.

In Fargo, Denise and Kim's house looked doomed. Rose Creek, another coolie, was backfilling from the river fast. One long wall made of sandbags and plastic had started behind the houses and needed to grow. Lines of people, people from everywhere, passed sandbags from the street, where they were dumped by the truckload, through the yard to the wall. On top of the wall, Richard placed bags and made sure the structure would hold. Forty thousand sandbags to protect just five houses.

Out of their basement came Denise's looms. Door frames were ripped out to remove the sixty-four-inch ten-harness jack loom with the eight-box fly shuttle, the forty-five-inch twelve-harness loom, the fifty-four-inch eight-harness countermarche, and more. From the first floor, the books and furniture and dishes and whatever wasn't bolted down were taken upstairs.

Outside, men in waders walked the wet side of the wall, looking for places to reinforce. The line passing sandbags went from one house to the other, good humor passed with each bag against the weight of the river, and the certainty of loss. Very few people in the lines could tell you whose house they were trying to save. It didn't matter. These were homes. These were the places that mattered.

Weird things happened. A town called Dillworth, farther away from the river on the east side of Moorhead, flooded. But not from the river. Overland flooding. Too much snow turning to water on the flat prairie land too fast. Then several sections of land southwest of Fargo turned into a moving square of water heading for town. Looking at the size of the water still to come, Fargo city officials decided to split the town—to build a new earth dike through south Fargo, to try and save downtown. Several thousand homes, including Denise and Kim's, were on the wrong side.

Companies let their employees off to work the sandbag lines. Some places closed altogether. Not out of business, yet. They simply knew where they were more useful. And in the middle of the rising water, an ice storm large and strong enough to wipe out telephone and power for thousands, then another blizzard, and downstream in Grand Forks, a fire in the already flooded downtown.

If the dike in Woodlawn Park in Moorhead failed, and for a long while many people were sure it would, then the river would surge toward the college—and probably do so through our old house. Our neighbors ringed their homes with sandbag walls. Our house slightly higher then the predicted crest, Maureen and I decided to put some bags at the back door just in case; but, if the water got any higher than that, we all knew we'd be on the evening news riding cables up to helicopters.

We moved everything out of the basement of the old house, except the washing machine and dryer. Those, I said, we could get upstairs fast if we had to. We plugged the basement drains against the advent of sewer backup. And then we watched the water begin to come through the walls. Every newscast on radio and television told us the ground was saturated, that the earth here could hold no more, and the pressure was increasing. The old house did not have a sump pump, so there was no place for the water to go once the drains were plugged. Hardware stores imported thousands of utility pumps. After a night with a five-gallon wet vacuum, emptying it every three minutes (sitting on buckets, Maureen and I timed it), one of those pumps sat in our basement too.

When the radio announced an evacuation order for our neighborhood—the dike, they said, was about to fail—there were people banging on our back door. Friends and colleagues wanted to know how they could help. What did we need to get out, they asked. The National Guard moved door to door, fast, helping to spread the word. The washer and dryer got moved to the kitchen. Maureen made it home from work, on the other side of the river, and for just a moment we stood and wondered if we could do what we'd been told. Could we simply walk away from this house, even before the river reached it?

Then the evacuation order was rescinded. Premature, the mayor said. The dike would hold for at least some time more.

⌇

"That's what you love about your children," Richard said.

I had asked him which of his own projects he liked the best, and he'd said he liked them all.

"You love this subtlety of why they're different, and you can't love one more than another or less than another. But you love them because of what they are. And so that's what makes it difficult to say, 'I like this more.' I have such fond admiration for the North High School project. It's a fairly ugly building when you sit down and look at it, but I mean, to me, it has so much poetry in terms of the process that I went through in getting it to that. I learned so much. I probably still today know that building more or better than any building I've ever built, and that's thirty some years ago. That's a very special building. Cass County Courthouse is one that's really very high on my list."

"Why? It is very unlike the high school."

"Oh, very much. And that's the difference between before Washington and after Washington. So now, I can't say North High School is one I like from a design point of view. It has, like your children, very emotional reasons for being a favorite. Cass County Courthouse is very special to me because it does what I said I was doing in many instances. That's using my residential projects as learning laboratories for what I really do, and that's commercial work and bigger projects. The ones that have a broader range.

"I think you can go back to that time, which is now a few years, and it would have been almost heresy for Fargo architects to not put a flat roof on a courthouse addition. It would have almost been heresy. I think you expect to see it today, but, that building was done very much parallel with another one we did, which is another favorite. The Commons Townhouses. They were, I daresay, the first apartment houses in Fargo that had anything other than a flat roof—except there were some mansard roofs which maybe broke the way, if you will. Those terrible, terrible, fake, applied, mansard roofs. But those projects started to say the traditional values have something that can be used today. Those were new concepts for Fargo, North Dakota, at that time. They did come from the work we were doing in residential, which really are projects that are most fun and most enjoyable."

⁓

The floodwaters fell. Denise and Kim's house did not move downriver. The Woodlawn dike held, and our old house survived. The river water came nowhere near the new house.

We found buyers for the old house, and then they backed out. We found another buyer, a friend who knew our house well, and the deal held firm. It was time to make a capped foundation into a house. It was time to build the new home.

Richard went into the hospital, an emergency visit that turned into a gallbladder operation. Then, when he was out and we were all at the conference table again, he held his side because a bandage was leaking. "Richard," we said, "it's your heart and soul we want in this project. But, really, *only* your heart and soul."

Rod and Hal showed up with lumber. The plumbers showed up with pipe. The electrician showed up with wire. We weren't talking about a napkin anymore. We had plans.

൭

What can you say about watching a house go up, except that it's wonderful? The stud walls go up, and suddenly there are spaces for doors and windows. Real spaces. Not just the fuzzy-edged space of the imagination. There are rooms now—rooms in the places we thought they'd be, but now rooms we can move in, and through. Living room. Dining room. Kitchen. Bathroom. Closet.

Floor and roof trusses get placed, the stud walls for the second floor go up. And now there are bedrooms, a space for the laundry, bathrooms, a linen closet, and a library.

Every day we drive to the house. Kate and Andrew explain where their beds will be, where they will keep their clothes, where they will do their homework, and where they will play. Maureen and I stand in every room, looking out the window spaces or trying to get the feel of the place. We walk from room to room a thousand times, learning the routes, to see if they feel to our feet and our hearts the way they promised they would on paper.

Plywood goes up. The roof goes on. The doors and windows are set, and the siding arrives. We pick out plumbing, and lighting, and carpet, and somehow it all shows up and goes in. Sheetrock gets taped and then painted. The inside doors are hung and trim boards placed. We pick out the stone to surround the fireplace. The first floor is hardwood oak, and we peer through windows as men in socks sand it and apply the stain.

Even though the house isn't finished, we know we've already moved the important things. We've moved the desire, and the hope, and what we

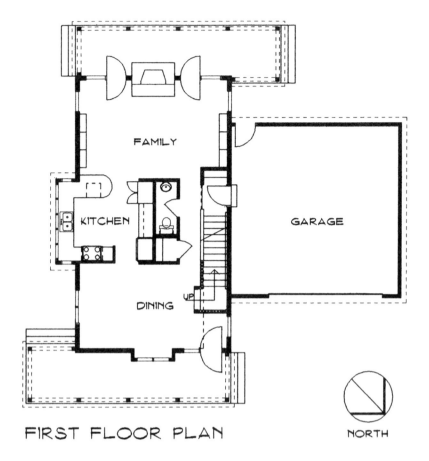

FIRST FLOOR PLAN

NORTH

imagine for our futures. *This,* now, is the place we mean when we speak the word *home.* This is *our* home. *Our* desire.

⟡

"So here's a question for you, Richard. And I don't know if there's a way to answer it. But what do you own in the projects you do? If you look at the courthouse, or the Commons, or the hospital you're doing now, they're all very different. And none of them look like Denise's house, or ours. Where's your own stamp in all this?"

The light coming into the conference room is beginning to fade. Winter daylight in northwestern Minnesota leaves early. And there are things to be done still.

"I've told you before," he says, "about the photographer who was com-

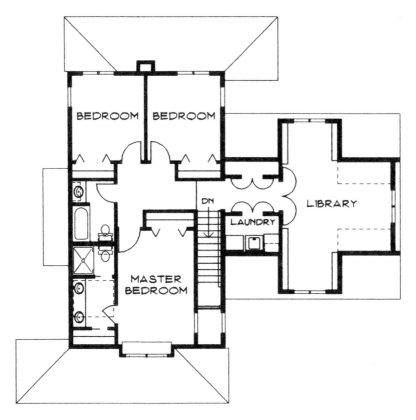

SECOND FLOOR PLAN

ing across the country and stood out front of the Koons' house, the one on Elm Circle, and started taking pictures of it. The owner, Koons, came out and said, 'What are you doing?' He said, 'I'm traveling across the country taking pictures of houses that I find interesting to me. I found one other one in North Dakota. It was on a hilltop out in Bismarck.' And lo and behold, it was a house I did out in Bismarck. That photographer's eye takes two very different styles of houses and saw a, I think, a commonality. The commonality is present in the courthouse and, to some degree, is even present in the hospital."

"What is that?"

"That is being very distinctive design-wise without trying to be different, and it's taking very ordinary elements and assembling them in a way that's extraordinary. That's the commonality between your house and Denise's

NORTHWEST SIDE ELEVATION

SOUTHEAST SIDE ELEVATION

FRONT ELEVATION

BACK ELEVATION

house and the Koons' house and the courthouse and the Commons. They use builders' windows; they use stock wood trusses; they use commodity siding and shingles. It's the way they're crafted and put together."

"Is that what makes good space? Is that what makes a good house?"

"I don't know that, again, I would single it out to a house. I think every good design has to have a concept. So it's not just what makes a good space. It's what makes a good design. A good design has to have a strong concept, and a concept is a statement. The intention has to be clear."

"The intention of the space?"

"The intention of the whole, and the whole includes spaces, finishes, function—all those things together. You can't separate or single out or divorce the whole, the whole picture, the whole breadth, the very essence of what is it being, what does it want to be. It's the whole. Is that too obtuse?"

"I'm wondering," I say, "how much of it you actually have in mind when the backhoe shows up and the hole is dug."

"If it's a good design," he says, "and your house is, that's crystallized long before."

"But there were a lot of things we hadn't talked about."

"Oh, but we knew what they were going to be. We knew what the appetite was. We knew what the budget limitations were. We knew the clients and the limits that they would work within. And there's no right or wrong. I mean, it's not that it has to be this finish in order to be perfect, you know. We talked endlessly about the siding. It didn't materially change the house. It wasn't the siding we thought we were going to start with, and, in fact, it maybe has some strength from the color we would have been too timid to put into paint on wood. There is no right or wrong. It's the carefulness with which those ordinary things are put together.

"So the use of the metal siding doesn't make a design bad or good. It's how you use those ordinary things getting back to those common denominators. It's how we make ordinary things extraordinary, and by building them into a part of a concept. You cannot have a successful design if you don't have an important idea, if you don't have a challenging idea, if you don't have a meaningful idea that you're trying to communicate. If you're just trying to put four walls around a function, it's not going to be successful.

"That leads back to a question I didn't answer some time ago then: what makes a good space? It has to do with what are you trying to achieve.

What's the idea that's bigger than the wood or the plaster or the Sheetrock?"

"Is that idea an aesthetic, or is it function?"

"It's all that. For your house, that idea is what's going to be a neat place to live in? What's a neat way of assembling spaces together if it's going to meet the appetite of this family to make them better enjoy being a family through the house and what is it able to do to them, with them, for them? How can we shape space spaces? So we don't begin by saying, 'Let's make a tall ceiling or let's make a square space or a round space.' We talk about 'Let's make a space thick,' and I think, the adjectives you brought to the picture were 'slow, open, tie together, move.' So that shapes the idea of my concept, you're buying into it. It's giving me the keys that the space can form from it."

"That would be a way to talk about the similarities then between Denise's house and ours, which, except for the prairie look from the outside, are very different on the inside."

"And yet I would still categorize both of them signature pieces. I think at least the professionals in the community can look at them and say, "Ah, that's Moorhead." A layman might not catch it, but people who are familiar with the choices—yeah, that's Moorhead. Those are true signature pieces.

"The signature pieces, in what I hope is a much deeper dimension, respond to the site, to the context, and the desires and needs of the people who live there. One of my favorite houses is perhaps the Scheels' house. And to appreciate that, you have to know Bob and Joan Scheel because you can almost look at them and say, 'You live in that house.' That house mirrors them so perfectly, absolutely perfectly. That to me is a wonderful, wonderful comment."

⁊

We moved in August. Not gracefully, of course. One large rented truck, the cars and vans and smaller trucks of our friends. We had a lot of stuff already in boxes, and a lot of stuff still loose. Find an empty box, we said, fill it with whatever you see. We'll sort it out later, at the new house. Our friends laughed when they opened drawers, unemptied, and found our socks, or worse.

Still, it was a wonderful time. Maureen went to the new house, to receive whatever came. Kate and Andrew loaded boxes and played with the friends who stopped over. I tried to offer some form to the leaving of the old house, and drove the rented truck from one to the other. Our friends, from first light to well after dark, told home stories. Stories of moving. Stories of staying in one place. Stories that tried nothing less than to explain the nature of desire.

The elm trees in front of the old house never looked fuller, or more green, I thought. And the squirrels—we should have named them. As I carried boxes to the truck, cracks in the sidewalk I'd long since memorized and forgotten came fresh to my feet again. I can't say I felt bad leaving the old house, the nearly perfect house set among the homes of friends. I felt, instead, thanks. And hope.

There were no trees at the new house that day, and there aren't any still. But they're coming. The grass was only a promise. Our friends carried furniture and boxes in the door, up or down stairs, into the rooms that seemed most accurate. Maureen and I took every chance we could to explain the house, what we wanted from it, what we hoped we would find. In the old house, we said, we behaved and lived together only in the ways that house allowed. In *this* house, we said, we have asked the walls to follow our hearts. Every corner, every knob and faucet, says something particular about what we want from a house, about the ways we want to be near each other, about the ways we want to be near to ourselves. And our friends, holding our old stuff in our new house, listened to these dreams, looked at this space, and smiled.

Home Stories
4.

This one belongs to my wife, Maureen.

When we were moving to Moorhead, Minnesota, to the house we rented before we bought the house we owned, before we built the one we're in now, we were still able to put completely everything we owned in one rental truck and drive cross-country. She drove our car while I drove the truck. She would pull up next to me to signal a question about an exit, or just to wave, and two or three days were spent quite nicely watching the counties and states and rivers and trees go by.

We left South Carolina, where we'd been living for two years, drove to Missouri, where we had family, then drove north. We arrived in Fargo and Moorhead at the same time as a windshield-slamming, tree-tearing, heart-thumping, old-fashioned whopper of a thunderstorm. We'd been watching the clouds build all afternoon, and the storm that came from them was no brief interlude.

"Well," we said to each other in a grocery store parking lot, "that's some welcome."

A double rainbow, a first for both of us, trailed from the back edge of the storm cloud.

We pulled up to the house we were renting, already knowing the owners had not left. We were a few days early for move-in. But they had said we could pile most of our stuff in the living room until they were out.

So that's what we did. The couches. The beds. The drawers and even the refrigerator. All of it hoisted off the truck and into the house. Then, with only a few clothes and our dog, a then one-year-old Shetland sheepdog whose name is Story, we went over to one of the college dorms, nearly empty for the summer, to settle in until we could have the house.

Or, to be exact, we settled in as a couple for only one night. The next day, I caught a plane for a two-week conference in the mountains of Vermont. Maureen and Story stayed in the dorm for three or four more nights, then walked the half block to the house and were given the keys.

So far, so good. Right?

The first afternoon and then night in the house, Maureen decided to get things in order. She hauled box springs and mattresses up the staircase, accomplishing the impossible twist at the landing. Drawers and dressers as well—all of them pushed and pulled and cursed over as the corners of the house began to fill with our belongings.

Maureen had the radio on, background noise as she worked to make this new place a home. When the sky darkened again, then turned a familiar shade of green, she listened more carefully. Thunderstorm watch. Tornado watch. Thunderstorm warning. Tornado warning. The city sirens blew. The sky lowered, and the wind shook the sixty-year-old elms on the boulevard like crazy. The rain hit the windows hard enough to make looking out that side of the house impossible. Somewhere close: a tornado.

On a cordless phone with her parents, in the basement with the dog, covered with blankets, not knowing yet which way was north, or remembering exactly which corner of the basement you're supposed to be in if a tornado looms, not knowing any of the county place-names offered by the radio announcer yet, Maureen waited, and listened.

First night in the new house, she thought. First night in the new house, Scott's off playing in Vermont, and I'm sitting in a cold, dark, damp basement, in a town where I don't know anyone, wondering if I'm about to die.

I'll remember this, she thought.

5.

And then there is the time a man came into our house.

Technically, we cannot say he broke in. The back door was unlocked. We were all awake, and at home. He simply was not invited, did not tell us he was there, and was looking for stuff he could carry.

But, as is usual with the stories that stay, these are not the important facts.

This happened at the first house, the one we rented. Our first summer had turned into our first fall in town. The elms that line Sixth Street had turned fiery and sharp, and we imagined we could smell the Minnesota winter we'd so far only heard stories about.

On this particular evening, we had been resting in the living room, watching television. At some point, Maureen said she was going upstairs to bed. I said I'd watch television a while longer, but that I'd be up soon. I was lying on the floor, our dog's head draped over one of my legs, my hands behind my head.

A doorbell rang on the television show, and Story jumped up. I quickly grabbed her by the collar and told her to be quiet. She looked at me—and if a dog can accuse a human of being an idiot, that's the look I got. She barked once, low and quick. Then she did it again. I explained, rationally I thought, that it was only the television. I told her to sit down, and she refused. Instead, she barked again, low and quick. I still had hold of her collar, and I was not polite in my urging her to sit and be quiet. She barked again.

Our dog is a good dog, if high-strung the way Shelties are. And the fact that she was insisting on her bad behavior was a first. Maureen, who had been in the bathroom, came down the stairs in a flimsy robe and sat next to us in the blue light of the television.

"I hear something too," she said.

Suddenly, our dog was Lassie and I was Timmy. "What is it girl?" I asked. "What's the problem?"

I let go of her collar, and she ran through the dining room and kitchen, to the stairs that led to the back door. She barked loudly, and mean. I turned the landing to look into the basement, and I saw the man who had come into our house. A large man, who outweighed me by at least fifty pounds, was walking around in our basement, turning on lights, opening doors, looking for whatever he was looking for.

The fact that he'd been drinking was probably not unusual for him. The drinking made him slow, however. One hand again on the dog's collar, I asked Maureen to call the police, and for some reason I got it in my head that I could keep this man in our house until the police arrived. He lurched up the basement stairs, and I pushed him back down a few. Maureen, stretching the phone cord as far as possible, appeared again at the top of the landing. The dog was barking loud enough to bother everyone.

The man came up the stairs again. "I'm sorry," he said. "I'm sorry." And in a truly false moment of bravery, I looked at him and said, "I don't want to have to hurt you." He looked up at me, realizing I'm sure how impossible it would be *for* me to hurt him anyway, even moving as slow as he was. We pushed each other on the stairs. Despite the dog I had in one hand (I was worried she'd be hurt if let loose), I had the advantage of higher ground, of leverage. He had the advantage of weight. I knew the police were coming; a stalemate was as good as a win. But I could not hold him long enough. He ran to the end of our backyard and disappeared into the darkness.

The police came—flashing lights in our driveway, a story for our new neighbors. The man got away.

But there's one detail we didn't tell the police. One small piece of how the struggle on the stairs really ended. And it's this fact that keeps the story going.

Maureen, police in her ear on the phone, robe falling open, her husband wrestling with an intruder on the back stairs, decided I needed some help. So, in the midst of the shoving match, she handed me a knife.

Not just any knife, mind you. Not a dinner knife. Not a steak knife. Not a carving knife. Not even a Swiss Army Knife. Instead, when her hand reached into the drawer to find the right weapon to aid her husband, she chose—a butter knife.

The man and I stopped pushing each other. I looked at the knife. He looked at the knife. When he made to get by me again, I let him pass.

I looked up the few stairs at Maureen. "A *butter* knife?" I asked.

"Well," she said, "I didn't want anyone to get hurt."

Gravity

. . . one of the fundamental forces of nature, the force of attraction existing between all matter. It is much weaker than the nuclear or electromagnetic forces and plays no part in the internal structure of matter. Its importance lies in its long range and in its involving all masses. It plays a vital role in the behavior of the universe. . . .
—WEBSTER'S ENCYCLOPEDIA

Six o'clock on a Friday morning in Moorhead, Minnesota, and the thunderstorms quite literally roll over town. Squall lines and gust fronts sneak up over the houses I can see to the west, tumble and bounce over rooftops toward my own home. The top of the bell tower at the Lutheran church on the other side of my backyard disappears into the mist, as if being eaten. Then the mist fades, and I can see daybreak sunshine lighting the tops of roiling thunderheads.

This is a dramatic morning. Standing in the western window of our library at home, what I see could humble a physicist or a theologian. And there are few things I love more than heavy weather, blizzards and windstorms and lightning and hard rain all. The simple motion of it over or against the earth.

But, as luck would have it, I'm about to leave. Driving west once again through North Dakota, the Badlands, into Montana, I'll spend the night, perhaps in Billings, perhaps in Red Lodge, then travel south through the Bear Tooth Pass into Yellowstone, down into Jackson, the Grand Tetons, and finally, into Park City, Utah, just outside of Salt Lake City. I'm expected to talk to some writers about what happens when their work gets off the page, but I'm not thinking very much about writing this morning. I'm thinking about thunderstorms, rain, and hail. I'm thinking of the way the wind moves over the flatland of the prairie, what that can do in storm-time, and I'm thinking of lightning. I'm thinking about how large weather will call me out of bed in the middle of the night, just to watch. I'm thinking about how very pretty the prairie is, how much at home I feel here, and the simultaneous desire I feel each day for a mountain, or an ocean shore. I'm thinking about landscapes and what we want from them.

I hear on the radio news this morning that baseball-sized hail fell in western North Dakota, and rainwater runs a foot deep through the city streets of Medora. "Those poor cowboys," the disk jockey says.

Listening to another station, I learn that a plane traveling over south-western North Dakota on its way to New York was forced to divert to Denver because of turbulence.

In the sky northeast from my window, where I stand with one last cup of coffee before the land around me moves just a little bit faster than the interstate speed limit, crimson and red—a patch of clear to allow the sun-rise through. To the northwest, the gunmetal gray of storm clouds. And to the southwest, a little bit of clearing, some brightness—a kind of promise for early-morning travelers.

I'm taking this trip in no small part because it will take me somewhere I've never been, to the Bear Tooth Pass, to the northern Wyoming and southern Montana mountains. I've been in mountains before. In the Swiss Alps. In New Zealand's Southern Alps. In the Tombstone Mountains of the Canadian arctic. In the Blue Ridge Mountains, and the Berkshires, and yes, in the Rockies before, too. And each visit has filled my head and heart with a very real thrill. Yet, and this much is curious, I've always been very happy to rediscover the flatlands. Each descent from switchback roads and mountain views has lifted my heart. It's good to be home. And then, stand-ing in any one of the many windows of my house, looking at the flatness, my eye has tried to push the visible just a little more than possible. Looking over the wheat fields, I know there are hills in the invisible distance.

So here's another question for you. What do we want from the viewed surface of the earth, from the way the earth rises and falls away, or doesn't? What do our hearts tell us we need from the shape of the land?

If our calendar pictures and postcards are any indication, if the art we frame and hang over our fireplaces and on our bedroom and office walls are any help at all, then it's clear that we are drawn to the dramatic, and from there to the mysterious. Ocean views are dramatic, not only because of their size, but because of their implication. We don't know what's over that horizon, and so our mind is drawn to that wondering. We don't know what's under the surface, the beauty of coral or the simplicity of teeth, and when we find ourselves standing on the beach our mind stares at the po-tential. Add a whale's spout, however, or sunlight filtering to a school of fish, or the rusting hull of a shipwreck on a sandy floor, or the clear eyes of a leopard seal off the coast of Antarctica—anything, really, to provide a contrasting element, and that contrast, that mystery, captures us. Two tex-tures in seeming opposition.

Likewise, hills and valleys and peaks get matted and framed because their vaulting nature leaves so many edges exposed, so many places to wander or hide. Perhaps I'm wrong about all this, but I suspect that what we find beautiful in nature we find beautiful not only because of its surface, the blue-green of water or the brown-green of rock, but also because that surface is a strong hint of some other possibility, some finer detail sure to come.

People who live in the mountains or visit them say, "You can see so far!" Yet, living on the prairie, I know I can see farther. The difference is one I believe of a framed and unframed landscape. In the mountains, you see more surface. You see more dirt, more rock; but you see less far. On the prairie you can't see nearly as much surface. The surface falls away with the curvature of the earth, but you can see forever.

If the mountain promises a million specificities, then the prairie promises infinity.

❧

6:30 A.M.

It's funny how you can turn a corner in a town or a village, even one you know very well, and it appears as if the world has changed. As I turn the car westward on the entrance ramp that will take me to I-94 and then through North Dakota and into Montana, the sky becomes the overpowering prospect of the prairie.

There is no sky anywhere on the planet like there is on the prairie. A little bit north of me, the sky is dark black—clear evidence of rain falling. To the south and to the east, clearing skies and scattered clouds. But as I cross the border into North Dakota what I see to the west is nothing less than thrilling. The clouds look like mountains. Not just *a* mountain, not just one or two or perhaps even three—but a kind of rolling and massing together. Foothills. Valleys. Ranges. Summits. As I look at the mountains this morning, the cloud mountains over the Dakotas, there are pinks and blues and whites and grays—and it's easy to imagine exploring here. It's easy to imagine a kind of dreamtime hiking. The promise of some new way to arrange the limits of what is possible is, I believe, for each of us, alluring. As I turn a small corner in the highway though, the top of the sky disappears as I'm thrown into another downpour cell.

Just west of Fargo and Moorhead this morning, the farmland is green. Green pastures of wheat. Green pastures of sugar beets. Green pastures of soybeans. We're too early in the season for the wheat or the barley to adopt their golden hues, too early for the heads of sunflowers to take over the stage. Everything here is young, still leaping upward from the earth. And it's clear this is a healthy place.

I remember a story told to me by two friends, a professor and a student. Standing thigh-deep in a field of young soybeans, the professor was suddenly transfixed by the sky over her farmland, while the student, who had parted the tops of the plants and stuck her head below that canopy, was equally amazed. Each of them called to the other, to share their discovery.

Who can say what we want from our landscapes? What kind of gravity calls to our souls? The green flatlands, the rain-soaked streets, the dark sky to the north and still to the west, these mountains of sky and sunlight. For me, at least, each of them is thrilling, dramatic, exciting—choose your own word.

Of course, it makes sense to point out the obvious. No single part of the land we see, the land we find hateful or magic, exists by itself. There is always a context that allows the other to be perceived. If the ground here were not so level, I wouldn't see these cloud mountains. I wouldn't see the tops turning now from a rosy pink to a brilliant white. I wouldn't see, slightly to the south, the dark gray of what looks like fire smoke but I know is only rain.

We are drawn to the mysterious, but the mysterious needs the mundane.

By the time I'm forty-seven miles west of Fargo—a quick stop for coffee in Tower City, once again an entrance ramp to a westbound highway—the cloud mountains are gone, the torn clouds are gone, the sunshine full as the highway steams and the water evaporates. In the far distance though, a kind of grayness and haze; I don't know if I'm seeing the lingering darkness of last night, or storms still in the way. And the ground has changed from the absolute flatness of the Red River Valley. Small rises now, small valleys. My eyes try to catch what's behind each contour or promise.

⤥

7:40 A.M.

Just west of Valley City—jet-black sky and lightning to the north—the road narrows to one lane, maximum of fourteen feet wide. There is water from a lake on the interstate highway here, earthen dikes on both the north and the south sides of the pavement. The highway is below lake level at the moment. The ground gently rises and gently falls. If I didn't know better, I'd swear the mourning doves try to ride the bow waves of trucks and cars. Red-winged blackbirds scoot across the highway in front of every car. And I find myself wondering if this isn't it, this combination of storm and bird flight and pressing water, isn't what we want—simply proof that the planet still spins.

The morning-show disk jockeys on the radio talk about beer from Belgium.

The cloud mountains have become a thunderstorm. Repeated lightning strikes from sky to earth. As my car and I dip through a small valley, I read a warning sign: "Watch for Water on Roadway." Yet another lake threatens the interstate. On the eastbound side of the highway, a young woman in a sedan has pulled over and cleans her front windshield with a beach towel. I think this is a bit odd, and laugh until I wonder how much water might actually be on the pavement, then suddenly discover the reason she stopped. A cloud of insects—several hundred flattened against the safety glass in seconds. There aren't enough of them to darken the sky, but certainly enough so I can see, in my rearview mirror, the thousands of them swarming. Mayflies.

In Jamestown I pull off for gas and yet another cup of coffee at the McDonald's, and I watch a crane lift a large red billboard to the top of a steel post. The sign urges me to visit White Cloud, the albino buffalo, an animal considered sacred by the plains tribes of Native Americans now become a cuddly, sentimental curiosity to lure road-weary people into town, perhaps long enough to buy more than a cup of coffee and a tankful of gasoline. I ask the lady at McDonald's if she's seen White Cloud yet, and I get a kind of sardonic, half-apologetic/half-embarrassed grin. She says no, she hasn't.

"I wouldn't know what to say," she tells me.

In Jamestown, a fiberglass replica of an American bison—one of the many oversized roadside icons we've come to somehow admire—is locally famous. It shares the same highway as the fiberglass prairie chicken in Rothsay, and the world's largest Holstein in New Salem. Any one of us could pull off at these places, have our pictures taken, then show the pictures to people we might know in Sacramento, or Tallahassee. We could say we'd been on the prairie, and have visual proof. And, frankly, I'm happy people stop to have their pictures taken with the Jamestown buffalo, which probably won't toss them into the air before sticking a horn up through an esophagus.

But the sign urging me to visit White Cloud is something different. White Cloud looks more like a misshapen lamb than a buffalo. And its appeal, at least on the billboard, is cuteness, which is a lie.

࿉

107 miles west of Fargo.

There is a point in every trip when the car and the driver seem to settle into each other and, as a pair, settle into the road. Where the driving itself almost becomes transparent and you watch the landscape roll by at faster than a mile a minute.

There is a point in every trip when the driving becomes fun. Bright-silver grain elevators, red barns, cattails in the marshes, red-winged blackbirds, motorcycles, and eighteen-wheel trucks all blend into a kind of moving diorama. From my point of view, I'm sitting still and the world is racing toward and then away from me, and I've got the Rolling Stones on the radio. Clear blue sky in front of me now. I've seen a dozen mountain ranges erupt and then dissipate in the clouds this morning. Lightning strikes, strong wind, mass annihilation of mayflies, and an invitation to see an albino buffalo—and this trip is just beginning.

A little bit more than one hundred miles west of Fargo, and the landscape here rolls . . . what? To say the landscape rolls "gently" would imply too much action. Hayricks and hay bales are stacked in some fields. The grains and the beans are still green. Harvest is a good ways off. It's a midsummer on the prairie—full of promise and grace and a little bit of danger, too. And in front of me, still, the gravity of those mountains. Those real mountains of stone and wood and ice and fluid need.

࿉

9:45 A.M.

193 miles west of Fargo.

I cross the Missouri River at Bismarck.

One of the great many things I do not know is where most people believe the Midwest ends and the West begins. Perhaps no one has come up with a border that means anything. Political boundaries have nothing to do with the edges of a bioregion. Cultural psychology has oftentimes nothing to do with fact. As far as I'm concerned, however, on the northern plains the change from Midwest to West is the brown Missouri River. West of the Missouri River the land changes quickly. Hills rise into buttes. Rock piles dot farmland. The dominant color of the earth is brown now, not green. Every rise in the highway affords a view of miles and miles of buttes and arroyos, valleys, hills. The horses in the pastures this morning don't stand still here. They gallop and cantor.

On the east side of the river, the stories are farm stories, weather stories, stories of large-scale immigration, community stories of harvest, famine, hope. On the west side of the river, the stories take on the names of leading characters. Custer. Sitting Bull. Lewis and Clark. Theodore Roosevelt.

ᑲ

10:10 A.M.

220 miles west of Fargo.

Approaching the town of New Salem, I'm sure the topic of conversation in every car, the only thing in the minds of those traveling alone, is one of the few things on this planet I wish would simply blow up. The cow.

The world's largest Holstein cow the billboards say, a fiberglass monstrosity perched on a hillside. These kinds of icons have been celebrated all over the world, yet the New Salem cow stands to me as perhaps the worst of them all. Not so much because it's a cow, but because it's huge and the land here has its own magic. Despite the change into a western light, the land here is still more flat than not, and you can see the cow from a very long distance. Almost like an auto accident that is grotesquely fascinating—no one can turn away from the hints of what might be possible in our own lives—as you're driving to or away from New Salem, you really can't look at anything other than the cow.

I've told many people many times that, if I were to ever go cow-tipping, this is the cow I'd go after. Take a chain saw, take off its two left legs, and watch the thing topple over. It worries me that I've said this so often, because if anybody ever does it, the police are going to come looking for me. I don't know why we want to put something like that in places like this.

The clouds this morning cast shadows on the hills that seem to race up one side and down the other, as if the shadows are enjoying their own kind of topographical roller-coaster ride. The Jeep rises and falls, sways left and right. The act of forward motion is an act of joy on the western side of

North Dakota; and, as I look forward to the Painted Canyon, to the Badlands, what I can't turn away from in my rearview mirror is the world's largest fiberglass Holstein cow.

There are times when you can pray for an appropriate lightning strike.

~

12:00 P.M.

314 miles west of Fargo.

If we can judge what we want by where we stop, by where we linger, by those places that afford, somehow, a moment of wonder, or peace, or a hint toward some larger definition of home and our own place in it, then the Painted Canyon is an essential place. For many people, *this* is what the Badlands look like: the canyon suddenly falling away from the prairie flatland, the reds and the greens and the browns, the coppers and the golds, all shining in the earth from the exposed hillsides, colored in layers like the walls of the Grand Canyon. Little bits of river down in the bottom meander around puddles left by last night's rain. It's the kind of sight that easily finds its way onto calendars and onto postcards. There is an awful lot of surface here. Acres and acres going up and down for every acre that goes left or right. What is it about seeing so much surface, so much topography, that always seems to capture our imagination? The buttes and the rises of the last couple hundred miles seem like mere hints as to what *this* can mean in terms of a physical beauty.

At the rest-stop interpretive center, senior citizens, children, a group of bicyclists riding from Seattle to Washington, D.C., all stop, walk to the stone retaining wall and gawk at the scenery. Everybody at the retaining wall is looking down as if the hole in the earth here—as if the canyon somehow pulled their eyesight. Nobody looks up. Nobody looks at the clouds or the sun breaking between them. Nobody comments about the wind or the sound of the birds—the crows, the killdeers, the sparrows. Everybody's captivated by what isn't, the earth that's missing, the hole that's created the Painted Canyon.

Cameras click right and left. People will remember this, I think. Perhaps they will put their pictures of the Painted Canyon next to their pictures of White Cloud.

The parking lot here is filled with campers strapped into the beds of pickup trucks or towed. And it's a wonder that the people who leave them are going to walk the complete distance from their car to the wooden fence or the rock retaining wall. Bermuda shorts, polyester jackets, office shoes or heels. Most of these people need a good diet plan.

This is the snob in me, I know. And it is entirely unfair, I know. Watching these people, however, I grow angry when it's clear no one actually wants to touch the Painted Canyon. No one wants to go hiking here. No one wants to feel the heat of their own body as they crest a hill and discover some grazing bison.

To get into the rest stop, you have to cross a cattle guard and pass a sign that says: "Buffalo are Dangerous—View from a Distance." And I wonder if these people believe it.

What is it we want from our landscapes? Is there a gravity to the sight of the earth? The cynic in me wants to shake the film out of the cameras here, to defeat the pin-in-the-map, slide-show mentality. But I'm also glad these people aren't down in the canyon, getting hurt, hurting what they see or fear. And when the cameras have caught enough, I notice a change in the people at the retaining wall. They affect a posture very much like one would have in church—quiet, slow-moving, staring for long times off into the distance the way one would consider statuary, an alter, a stained-glass window, or an idea. I doubt they are aware of this change themselves, even though I believe they are being spoken to.

And perhaps what draws people is, in fact, that openness, the fact that between here and the next rise in the Painted Canyon there is not so much dirt but so much perceivable space.

Unlike the others at the wall, the cyclists who have stopped here are without exception strong. Their fine muscles would be the envy of most Olympians. They stop at a support truck, change to or from riding shoes. All of them smiling at the sight.

The cyclists are part of an organization called Bike Aid, working toward sustainable transportation. They do this every year. They ride from the West Coast, from several starting points, to Washington, D.C. One of the men I stopped and talked with is from Australia. This is his first time to the States.

"What a lovely way to see the States," he said.

Every single one of them is smiling, even as they tease one young woman about the proper way to fall off a bicycle. I will admit I envy them—the slowness of a bike ride across the country, the ability to taste and touch and feel every bit of it, weather included.

A couple nights ago, up in the Bear Tooth Pass, they tell me, it snowed. And I can feel the gravity of that sight and those mountains pull.

⌒

3:20 P.M.
480 west of Fargo.

At a rest stop west of Miles City, Montana, I take a few minutes to stretch my legs and watch the clouds dance. For the last few hours I've been parallel to the Yellowstone River, the highway on a rise in the southern end of a valley. On the north side, a range of buttes, bluffs, cliffs. Very pleasant driving—the browns and golds of the hillsides, the greens and golds of the fields. The topography here, the way the land is shaped, calls attention from the highway. What's over there, I wonder? What's in that valley? What's around that bend? I think one of the attractions of this kind of landscape is that an answer seems so easily possible. You can't look at the sky and say, "What's over there?" because what's over there is just more changing sky—no body, no address, no place.

When you look at a range of hills, it's inevitable and natural to wonder what's on the other side. More dangerously, it's also possible to believe that where you are is somehow yours. This is my valley. That's your valley. But, for me at least, something there is that doesn't love a wall.

Gravity.

Gravity may be the weakest of the elemental forces, but there's no escaping it. Gravity is what will finally stop the outward rush of everything from the last big bang, and start the rush back home. Gravity holds us to the planet, holds the oceans into their place and the atmosphere to the globe.

And gravity, remember, plays a vital, that is, life-filled, role in the *behavior* of the universe. Gravity pulls us into valleys, over hilltops, around bends and rivers. Gravity is for humans pretty much the same thing as curiosity, or desire, or hope, or love. We want to know what we don't know. A mystery always needs to be solved. The mysterious, even if it's the face of God, always needs to be chased. Standing at the Painted Canyon overlook and looking down into it, it's inevitable that we would wonder what it's like down there. I should go visit down there. Watching the names of places go by on signs—Crown Butte, Grassy Butte, Sentinel Butte, Home on the Range—it's natural to wonder what stories rest behind the names. I should pull off at these places, get to know someone well enough to ask honest questions. Here at the rest stop overlooking the Yellowstone River, a stand of trees, green farmland, and then the browns of the buttes, it's impossible not to want to simply leave the car, walk down the hill, hike toward water.

Of course, there are also other reasons to want to leave the car and hike into the bush. As I leave the rest stop, local radio out of Miles City is having a brainteaser contest. The question: Which of the following is both a princess and a slave? Ada, Ophelia, or a few others. The answer: Ada, daughter of the king of Ethiopia enslaved by the Egyptians. The prize: a copy of the *Stepford Wives* video.

✍

5:51 P.M.
600 miles west of Fargo.

In Billings earlier than scheduled, after a change from brown earth and buttes to forests of pine, aspen, spruce, and others I can't name, a landscape of green trees and bushes and grasses, then back to the same broad valley holding the highway and the Yellowstone River, I'm anxious for mountains. I'm anxious for that change, that *other* thing, the rise in the earth that, from my windows at home, I can imagine and need but not quite see. This land around Billings looks nothing, really, like the Red River Valley. But the change is not enough yet.

I stop at a hotel for a moment, check reservations farther on. A nice desk clerk brings me a phone and a phone book and gives me a map and helps me with directions.

The sky is once again a deep blue—clouds my field guide call *cirrus radiatus* and *altocumulus duplicatus*. The man on the radio says there may be more storms this evening. And all I can think about is how close I am to the mountains, and how invisible they still are.

A short while later, I turn off the interstate and join Route 212, heading toward Red Lodge. I'm told I'm less than an hour away. The signs here already read "Yellowstone Park," yet I still can't see the mountains here.

✍

6:33 P.M.
636 miles away from Fargo.

Just south and west of the town of Boyd, I turn a bend in Highway 212 and a dark shape in the distance reveals itself slowly. There they are—the mountains rising in blue-gray from the green fields, the small hills, the rock outcrops I'm following now. Almost as if there is a border. And, at seeing them, I'll admit one thing. I am thrilled. I can't wait anymore. The mountains! My foot presses harder on the accelerator now. I find it difficult to look at anything other than the huge earth rising in front of me. And whatever desire for the earth I have in me says it's time to go meet it.

DAY TWO

Red Lodge—elevation 5,555 feet.
Saturday morning.
10:00 A.M.
673 miles away from Fargo.
Checked into the Best Western last night. A friendly place with a desk clerk who is also a professional photographer, who has his pictures and slides with him at the desk, to show if you linger and chat. Pictures of mountains in sunshine, in rain, and in snow. Pictures of the sun over mountains. Pictures of the moon over mountains. And good advice about where to eat.

Finding the legs to walk on again after a day in the car, I went over to Rock Creek, the narrow, rocky river that runs through town, got out my fly line, my rod, and discovered a place to wade in. I'd been told the creek was two or three times its normal size right then, fast and rolling with runoff from the mountains. It seemed to be one continuous rapid from top to bottom. I waded in, in two or three places, tried my luck and it didn't happen. No trout.

But that *other* thing was there last night. The size of the earth had changed, and my own proportion to it. It doesn't matter how many miles measure the distance, the mountains are the opposite of the prairie. Standing in the river, or walking in town, I could feel the simple weight of the earth around me in my breathing. Perhaps, I thought, with so much rock and dirt now above me as well, I actually weighed less here. Perhaps gravity pulled me ever so slightly in a new direction, sideways toward the cliff face, or up toward a summit. Not enough to be measured on any scale, but certainly enough to be noticed. And this change felt good.

A little while later in the evening, still looking for trout, I came upon another lodge with a bridge across the creek where I was told I could wade in. But the river was cascading over itself in whitecaps and boils here too. Beautiful to watch. Lethal to enter.

The lodge has a little stocked pond outside the front desk, and the clerk said I could try my luck there, which I did. Immediately after getting out my fly line, a small crowd gathered. Other men and women brought out their fly lines, and pretty soon there were two and then three and then four of us casting into this small pond. None of us caught anything, despite the trout rising and leaping, boiling the water on their own. These are educated fish—cast at daily, caught and released a hundred times by guests of the lodge. We all stood there, practicing our technique, embarrassed by bad casts, and not one of us caught a fish. Still wearing shorts even though the temperature was falling through the thirties, I finally left when my knees were shaking from the cold.

And as I was leaving, as I was talking with one of the men about what fly he was using, and bemoaning the fact that these were experienced fish, he said something fly fishers often say to each other. "Yes," he said, "presentation is everything." And what he means by that is the way the fly lands on the water, the way the fly line floats or doesn't, the way the fly moves if it sinks. If it doesn't look exactly like the bug it's trying to imitate, a trout will not go for it. But the phrase stuck with me for a different reason.

Presentation is everything. Isn't *that* what we want from our landscapes, for them to be *present?* To rise up and hit us hard? To not disappear into the mindless repetition of suburban lawns? To somehow force us into psychological reaction? To wake us from our sleep? To be that kind of gift?

Especially now, the morning of the second day of my trip, as the gray clouds have come back full and thick and steady rain falls on the town of Red Lodge, I'm wondering about presentation. I'm told the pass is probably open, but almost certainly it's snowing up there—and icy.

Presentation. What do we want from our landscapes? And what do we do when what we want is not what's delivered? The mountains are not supposed to be foreclosed by low clouds and rain. The mountains are not supposed to be cold in July. Instead, the stereotype says sunshine, dappled meadows of alpine flowers, waterfalls of brilliant-white airy foam, and not a single bug beyond the butterfly.

Frankly, I'm rather glad when the world works against what I can easily imagine or expect. But in the back of my head I heard the stories told by friends, prairie people like me, who have made this trip before me.

"You know," Cathy said, cups of coffee between us in her office, "I really wasn't sure if we were going to make it. And I don't mean just over the pass. I really wasn't sure if we were going to get out of there at all." She was telling me about driving over the pass in an unexpected snowstorm, her father at the wheel, when she was a little girl. She was telling me about the first time she realized her father couldn't really do everything, that he was human, and mortal, and what it felt like when the car began to slide and she saw that he, too, was scared.

"I'll never make that trip again." This comes another time, from another friend, Duane.

"Bad weather?" I ask.

"No. But I was driving this old boat of a Ford LTD. I couldn't see over the hood. All I saw was air, and valley. I couldn't see the edge of the road, and there were no guardrails. I remember looking out the window at the switchbacks still going up, and thinking about how easily I could drive off the road. I was white-knuckled the whole time."

"Really?" asks Linda, the three of us standing in a corner of the college bookstore. "I've made that trip. And it was wonderful, really very beautiful. No problems at all."

"I'm looking forward to it," I offer.

"Never again," says Duane.

Sitting here in the foothills of the Bear Tooth Mountains looking south and west out of town, I can see snow in the mountains. I can see the green hills rising up into the rocks, and even on this low morning I am drawn to that weight. I am sure there is something physical about the attraction of granite to flesh.

Had breakfast at a place called P. D. McKinney's, waiting for a promised clearing in the clouds, wanting to see, at least partially, the rise of the land and the space of the valleys. Sat at the counter and had German sausage, two eggs over medium, toast, hash browns. The hash browns probably weighed three-quarters of a pound by themselves. The eggs were perfect, the sausage was spicy, and the humor of the waitresses made a very pleasant morning.

⚉

11:04 A.M.

675 miles away.

I begin the Bear Tooth Pass. Leaving Red Lodge, the most immediate sensation, oddly, is one of driving down. A broad valley opens up into the Bear Tooth Mountains, misted this morning, shrouded in grays and blues of smoke and haze. The hills are forested in evergreen. Vertical rock is red and brown and almost white. People are out jogging this morning, walking even in the rain. A line of cars comes out of the valley—perhaps those that have come over the pass. A short line of cars is in front of me as we head into the mountains.

At the Exxon station, I asked the attendants if they've heard anything about the pass. "I'm sure it's snowing up there," one of them said, "but you might break through the clouds. It'd be pretty nice up on top."

"Nobody's come down and complained too much," the other one said, smiling.

The highway is open. I'm driving down into a deep valley. This is fun.

⌇

11:15 A.M.
682 miles away.

The Custer National Forest. As far as I can tell, I've been driving downhill ever since leaving Red Lodge, which doesn't make sense. The mountains are getting taller and taller on both sides. The rock faces, each of them, and every corner I can't quite see around pull the eye, go up, and sideways and around corners. A streambed appears and then disappears. The trees get close, then provide a vista. The clouds lower, then open.

I wonder if the change in scale and perspective doesn't lead to a trick of the eye. I have felt that I have been driving downhill, but I pass Rock Creek every now and then, which is flowing back toward Red Lodge, and I know water has to run downhill.

My eyes tell me my car should be coasting, that I should be worried about the brakes, but my car won't accelerate. A small group of mule deer off in the jack pine watch me go by. I believe I'm driving uphill, and the way the mountains rise, it's just a trick of the eye to make me think otherwise. Rock Creek tumbles white against the green backdrop. It roars fast, the sound of it filling the air. The highway climbs into the mountains, the mountains climbing faster than the highway. Even in the clouds, what a drive!

I can see snow on the mountaintops. A quick look to my left, and I can see several layers of switchbacks going up the hillside, and my own laughter fills the car. To the right, the valley and then sharp peaks, rounded domes, a full rising of the earth. Oh, what scenery! My God, Charles Kuralt was right! This is, without a doubt, the prettiest drive in America!

෨

Noon.

694 miles out.

I'm stopped at a scenic overlook—a short hike takes me away from the parking lot and up to an observation point. There are mountain goats here. And bighorn sheep. And pika, and rock squirrels, and marmots, and chipmunks. A sign tells me one bit of earth I'm seeing is named Line Creek Plateau, and another is named Hellroaring Plateau. I know there are stories, probably good stories, behind these names, but somehow I'm also sure the names will diminish the place. I don't have language for the way the mountains fall into valleys, for the way the rock becomes dirt becomes trees becomes water. I don't know how to explain the new rhythm of my heart in my chest when I sit and wonder about how much there is to imagine about what I see.

I've been playing leapfrog, stopping at pullouts to look, to make small hikes and then drive on, with an older couple driving a Land Cruiser, Texas license plates. Here at the overlook, the woman gets out and turns to me— we're friends already, having smiled and waved at each other as we motor over the rising mountain—and says, her voice thick with the music of her accent, "Isn't this *something!*"

I agree with her. This is certainly something.

The rainfall turns to snow. I dig my raincoat out of my pack, hike around in shorts and a raincoat in the snow of the Bear Tooth Mountains.

෨

12:30 P.M.

Above the tree line, where rain has turned completely over to snow—a fresh dusting covering the rocks and grasses—the road levels out a little bit. The more permanent snowfields, tinged with pink from an algae, are now as much below me in valleys and gullies as surrounding the roadside or resting thick on the edges of small lakes. As I reach a plateau, the snow is falling in wet, heavy flakes.

12:45 P.M. I am now in Wyoming. The snow has become a snowstorm.

12:50 P.M., the snowstorm is worsening. The haze and the fog are closer and thicker. Visibility is much reduced. Guardrails disappear from the highway. Tall posts, deep enough for mountain snows, mark each side. A sign tells me that the gates may be locked and the highway may be closed suddenly and without warning in storms.

1:00 P.M. I'm tempted to put the car in four-wheel drive just for my own peace of mind. Still going up. Once or twice I stop at small roadside pull-outs and take pictures. This is near the top, I'm sure. A high, windy plateau. Small lakes in every depression. Snowfields. At one pullout, a father and son standing by their truck eat cold chicken and tell me they've just hiked up from a lower lake where they'd been camping. Both of them are tired, though smiling. They tell me they wanted to get out before the snow made them stay. I feel the pull of my own obligations, as well as the fact that I'm not prepared for much of a stay, and get back in the car.

1:18 P.M. A wall of snow to my left on the uphill side is about ten feet deep. Clearly, this road has been plowed recently.

1:20 P.M. A chairlift? A goddamned chairlift! On the downhill side of the road, the steel pillar supporting the cables. No one is here for sport today, but the thing is still there. Here. At the top of the Bear Tooth Pass, some-one once stood here and wondered how the place could be *used*. As if the thrill of simply being here wasn't, isn't, enough.

Just beyond the lift, a snow cat with a snow blade parked on the side of the road.

1:21 P.M. That snow cat may have been up at the summit. I am now def-initely going downhill. The snow continues. Visibility increases and de-creases as the mist and the haze get thicker and lighter. Snow still covers the fields on both sides of the car. When the haze lightens, though, I can see that there are tremendous valleys off to the left—large mountains there somewhere.

1:24 P.M. Heading back uphill again. More snow walls border the high-way. The one I'm passing now is probably eighteen feet tall. Names and dates are carved into the face of the wall. *Mark loves Jennifer. The Anderson's. Hi. Wow! June. July.*

1:26 P.M. At a little pullout, I pass a sign that says, "The Bear's Tooth" with the sign pointing off, and all I see are mist and snow. Visibility is two-tenths of a mile. Cars on my downhill side appear suddenly, headlights shining. The drivers are not smiling.

~

2:35 P.M.

714 miles out.

I am at the place where Bear Tooth Creek runs into Bear Tooth Lake and where I've just spent an hour or so in drizzle as well as downpour rain, chasing rainbow trout—and winning. Coming down out of the height of the pass, nearly eleven thousand feet above sea level, the snow made me wonder if I'd be trapped for a very long time, and then it disappeared into rain. At a log cabin store, the "Top of the World Store," I bought fresh hot coffee and a fishing license for Wyoming—asked directions for a place, anyplace, I could find water and mountains and strong fish. Directions to this campsite, this small marsh where river becomes lake, were given happily. A beautiful setting of a green mountain with patches of snow at the slopes, thick forests of evergreen.

What is it we want from our landscapes? What is it that pulls us to them? Standing at the end of the Bear Tooth Creek flowing fast into the lake, rolling over boulders under willows and pines, what do I get here that's different from the prairie? It can't be just the change in scenery that's important. Why is the peace I feel here, the fundamental relaxation of my spirit, so much different from the peace I feel in my own home with my family?

There is a great deal I don't know. But I suspect something about all this. I suspect what we desire from the shape of the earth is a hint that we still don't know the whole story. Casting for these trout, I find myself glad for the snowstorm in the pass. I have a new story to tell now, a story no one will expect. And, casting for these trout, in the shadow of these beautiful mountains, I suspect I'll have these stories with me when I get back home. Each walk on the flat prairie, itself wonderful and large, now holding mountain storms just over the visible horizon.

~

2:55 P.M.

The sign says, "Cattle on highway" and, indeed, there are.

~

3:21 P.M.

741 miles out.

Yellowstone National Park. Northeast entrance, elevation 7,325 feet.

I've been passing through a burned area, part of the big Yellowstone fires of a few years ago. Lodgepole pines on both sides of the road, little more than vertical charcoal, though the brush underneath them is deep living green. Still going downhill. I'm not sure where they've all come from, but the road is now filled with motorcycles, sedans, every type of car you can imagine—the going made slow because of pickup trucks pulling campers.

A bison on the side of the road. The animal is just lying in the grass, quietly chewing on something, facing the road—almost as if the Park Service said, "Sit here for awhile—we need a scenic opportunity." The cars all slow down so everybody can take a picture, and then, after fifteen or twenty seconds, off they go. In each car, a camera holds another slide, another trophy. And I wonder if anyone knows, or remembers, last winter, when the bison were shot by the hundreds when they left the park to find food by ranchers as well as Montana state officials, because some people were afraid the bison would infect beef cattle?

What is it we want from our landscape? Can "Saw a buffalo" be enough of a story?

⌇

4:07 P.M.

769 miles away from Fargo.

Tower Junction, 6,278 feet above sea level.

It's a long drive through the north end of Yellowstone. Every turnout is filled with eight to ten cars. Every possible pulling-off place filled with two or three. Everybody taking pictures. As I sit at the Tower Junction, in front of Roosevelt Lodge, I see twenty or more people on a trail ride. They're all on horses, but none of them are really riding. Most of them look petrified. Still, the horses have been doing this for a long, long time. What are these people looking for?

⌇

4:53 P.M.

788 miles out.

I pull off the road, the perpetual parking lot at Yellowstone, to visit the brink of the upper falls in the canyon, and I don't even get out of my car. The lines going up and down the walkway are tremendous. There is something to be said for viewing nature, and there is something to be said about viewing it alone. There's an old phrase: if you love wilderness, stay out of it. It's selfish of me to wish everybody else was gone. I'm sure they wish I was gone, but it doesn't deny the fact that there are too many people here. License plates from Ohio, Georgia, Tennessee, Idaho, Montana, Wyoming, Minnesota, North Dakota, Texas, Utah, British Columbia, Virginia, Colorado, Turtle Mountain.

What do we want from our landscapes? At the Artist's Point overlooking the Grand Canyon of Yellowstone, people are smiling, happy, laughing, patting each other on the back, almost saying, "Wasn't that something?" And yet that something is available because of a manicured, paved trail to a point overlooking the canyon. Nobody's hiking here; nobody's getting off into the canyon itself. Is it enough to see it, enough to have only the visual? Is it enough to get to a place like this so easily? To not get out and hike, to not get out and touch the mountain?

I'm tired, I know. And ill-tempered by the press of people, the ease of being here, the consumerism of a photo-op visit to a national park. And yes, I *know* I'm trying to get through the park as fast as I can. I know I'm no noble guide here. I have a long way to go before I sleep tonight. Other mountains. But if this was where I was stopping, then by golly I'd want to get my boots dirty. What stories do these people tell each other when the day has faded into starlight? How close the coyote came to the car? How they could smell the sulfur-cauldron area even with the air-conditioning on?

Gravity. What do we want from the shape, the rise and fall of the earth to our feet? What calls to us, any of us? In the mountains I thought I'd had a beginning of an answer. Here, it's all a mess again.

∽

6:10 P.M.
829 miles from Fargo.
The Continental Divide, elevation 7,988 feet.

∽

6:48 P.M.
857 miles out.
Jackson Lake to my west, and beyond it the Grand Teton Mountains—really very pretty even though they're shrouded and gray in mist. Finally

making some speed on the road. Through the rain, it's tough to look over my shoulder at the mountains. With the rain, the forests look more like a tropical rain forest than anything else. It's lush and green and water spills from narrows in the hills at every turn.

The clouds close in again. Valleys in the clouds reveal valleys in the mountains, however. The steel gray of the clouds giving way to the reflected steel-gray snowfields, the lake reflecting it all. The greens and dark blues of the forest and grasses on the mountains. Twilight is coming on—even this early. I pass nearly twenty cars, all pulled over to the side of the road to watch a moose frolic in a marsh.

What do we want from our landscapes? What kind of gravity calls us away from the places we collect our mail—and what are we really looking for? For me, at least, I'm wondering if this valley might be one possible answer. Broad and flat, filled with sage and willows, its aspect is very much like the prairie I love at home. There's open ground, good space to move, or run, or dance. But, and here's the change, the scene is framed. All four sides of this valley reveal visible mountains.

At home, I can see forever. But a foot is as perceivable as a light-year if there's no border. Here, in this valley, I can see less far—but I can know what I see. So you tell me: What do we want from the shape of the planet? Do we feel the tight closure of a steep canyon more intimately than the breadth of a summit view? Or is shape finally not the issue at all? What kind of gravity pulls us from home to home? Could it be we're just looking for the Other, for hints toward awe, toward a better articulation of the mysterious? I'll admit I really don't know.

Yet, south of Jackson, tight by a new river and heading once again into the mountains, I'm already wishing for unframed sky.

Home Stories
6.

I am in third grade. It is 1965, and I am playing Little League baseball, though I don't remember asking to play. My father is the coach of the team. I am the oldest son.

I am playing catcher. And I am good at this, perhaps because I am brave enough not to flinch when a bat swings over my head, perhaps because I am not old enough yet to recognize it is another third grader who is swinging that bat. I am very good at being a catcher. Other teams wish I would play for them, too. A coach from an older boys' team has asked my father if I could play for his team, seeing how we have different schedules. All of this makes my father proud.

What bothers my father, and me, is the fact I am not a good baseball player. I cannot hit the ball. If the bat were the wing of an airplane, I could not hit the ball. If the pitcher throws a ball that sails forty feet from the plate, I run thirty-five feet to make my swing. I am an easy out. My father gets this look on his face when I walk up to the plate, bat in hand. I think he half thinks I will hit a soaring home run. I think he half thinks my turn will not be over quickly enough.

Sunday afternoon. We are at home. Aunt Mary Lee, Uncle Gerry, my cousins Michael, David, and Michelle are coming over for Sunday dinner. My mother has made a roast. There are mashed potatoes, carrots, onions, wine, iced water, and pie for dessert, with ice cream. Dinner is ready, and the kitchen smells wonderful. My mother has left the kitchen and placed my younger sister, Joi, in charge. Joi holds her wooden spoon like a scepter. My father says, "Let's go outside." He is holding ball gloves and a bat. I know he wants to practice my hitting. My mother walks to the door. "Can I come, too?" she asks.

The three of us walk to the front yard. My father decides to play catcher, so he can guide me through my swing, and my mother has to pitch. The two of them practice a bit first, and I look at the road in front of our house. Aunt Mary Lee and Uncle Gerry's car will come into sight just past the next house, near a small slope where I've been learning to jump with my bicycle. My father calls to me. I walk over and he hands me the bat.
    "Steady, now," he says.
    My mother throws and I swing. I hear nothing but air. She throws again. My father yells for me to swing. I cannot hit the ball. If the bat were four times its width, I could not hit the ball. My mother throws again.

The day is not hot, but I am beginning to sweat. My father is beginning to be frustrated. My mother is wondering when our company will arrive. She wonders how long it will take for our dinner to be ruined.

"Try it the other way," my father says.

I don't understand, so he turns me around, shows me how to swing left-handed. My mother thinks it's a good idea. Both she and my sister are left-handed. My father, who is right-handed, golfs left-handed. I don't think it feels right, but I'm willing to try.

I lift the bat, then see Aunt Mary Lee and Uncle Gerry's car.

"They're here," I say, thinking we are finished. I don't want to strike out in front of my cousins.

"Just one more pitch," my father says.

My mother winds up and throws the ball. I do what my father says and watch it all the way to the plate. As it approaches, I swing as fast and as hard as I can, and I hear a sound I have not heard before. My bat and the ball have met. Aunt Mary Lee and Uncle Gerry, and Michael and David and Michelle are pulling into the driveway and I have hit the ball!

However. My first hit is a foul ball. Not a long, graceful arc into the bleachers down the first or third baseline. Not a pop-up for a good catcher to follow, throwing off his mask as if he were storming a beach. This is a short foul tip. Into my mouth.

Aunt Mary Lee, Uncle Gerry, Michael, David, and Michelle are getting out of their car, and I am swishing broken teeth around in my mouth. I am not yet sure what's happened. My mouth hurts, and I can feel blood filling my gums. I can see it spreading down my white, starched Sunday shirt. I look down, and a long, red, sinewy stream leaves my mouth and falls, slowly and thickly, toward the grass. My mother runs to me and looks in my mouth. I have picked out what teeth I can find, thinking perhaps I've swallowed one or two, and looking at the ground to see if any have fallen out.

Michelle looks at me and says, "Gross."

My father walks over to the car, talking about how tough I am. I'll make a good catcher, he says. My mother bends down in front of me. I understand now that I am hurt. I see her looking at my shirt as much as she is looking at my mouth. I understand that I've ruined this Sunday afternoon. My injury will take time to correct. Someone will have to drive me to the emergency room while others pay little attention to her roast. I feel the blood still running.

My mother looks me full in the face. She looks upset, and I am waiting for her to say mother things. I am waiting for her to say she loves me, that it will be all right, that it was a noble swing. And she tells me each of these things, more than once, as I am hustled toward the car and medical attention. But looking at my cousins, I also know this is a story that will never go away. I know, in third grade, that my baseball career is over.

At Home So Far from Home
1. QUEENSTOWN

Is it possible to come home to a place you've never been? How many new ways is it possible to fall in love?

Because I have the good fortune to escort some college students on an overseas adventure, I am sitting this morning on a large rock in the shadow of a row of poplar trees, on the shore of a lake named Wakatipu, just outside a small town called Queenstown, in a region called Otago, on the South Island of country named New Zealand. It's a cold morning and I'm fairly bundled up. I've brought some coffee from the youth hostel, where I'm staying, and its steam rises to my face. The dawn is almost complete. The clear-blue crystal water breaks in small waves over the gravel beach.

I'm about as far away from the place at least the mailman thinks he'll find me as I can be, yet—let's say it honestly—I'm suddenly more at home here, at the shore of this lake, at the foot of these mountains, than I've been in a very long time. And I don't know why.

Wakatipu is a mountain lake, not so very far across but very long and winding, the only flat surface in otherwise rugged country. In the short distance to the east from my rock perch, a range of mountains called the Remarkables drop their sheer faces into the lake. Angular and jagged, unforested, cut and broken with a thousand small valleys and rifts, these peaks this morning are snow covered and cloud capped, dirt brown and slate blue and snow white all. In places the sun comes in and illuminates a wall or valley, turning a field of snow and ice into a beacon, a rock face into a mural of colors, the morning into theater.

When you think of the Definition, the Thing itself, the picture in the dictionary, you think of mountains like the Remarkables. It's got everything to do with size and weight, with comparing a less than six-foot-tall human body with huge earth, with placing human time next to earth time, with feeling quite small, with feeling like you're going to fall into the abyss and love every minute of it.

To my right, much closer but across the lake, the more rounded Mount Cecil and then Walter's Peak catch what sunlight can break though the cloudy sky. Snow comes about halfway down Mount Cecil. Grasslands go about halfway up. Sheep graze Walter's Peak.

How can I talk about Queenstown? If you're standing at the waterfront, looking right, left, straight ahead, or around to the back, you look into mountains. You look at hard rock and begin to get a sense that this place wasn't easy to get to. But once you do manage to get here, once the passage has been found, once the trails have been made, you also see this is a place you must get to. There's something—I don't want to say spiritual—*personal* about Queenstown.

Perhaps my reaction is just one of contexts, the prairie kid suddenly in the hills. But I don't think so. I've been in lots of mountains before. Something about Queenstown is different.

ᔕ

"You're going where?"
"Queenstown, next."
"Ack, that's a place for tourists."

ᔕ

Queenstown *is* a tourist town. When I break myself away from the shore and walk the waterfront, I pass the ticket and information center for the TSS *Earnslaw,* an old coal-fired steamer, built in 1910, that takes people over for a day at Walter's Peak, for a day at a sheep station and a meal on the water. I pass signs for air trips around Milford Sound, a fjord on the South Island's west coast. I pass docks where half a dozen companies promote their jet-boat rides.

In town itself, shops promote horseback riding, mountain-bike rentals, and bungee jumping. There's Eichardt's Tavern, the Queenstown Bay Center, art galleries, the ANZ Bank, the Park Royal Hotel, *Te Aotearoa* New Zealand Souvenir Shop, antiques, wool shops, Queenstown Bay Trading

Company, the Hide Shop. Above and behind them all, of course, there are the mountains.

Helicopters buzz overhead, taking tourists on sight-seeing excursions, or off to jet boats on a particularly wild part on the Shotover River. Jet boats buzz in and out of the harbor, making a grand, explosive, tight circle as they come in. Fishing excursions get ready to go. Water taxis roam about. There are autumn colors in the trees that line the inlet and go up the mountainside, the dark green of the conifers often in brilliant contrast. There's snow on every peak.

Queenstown is not the American version of a tourist town. There is a McDonald's, there's a Kentucky Fried Chicken and a Pizza Hut, but they're discreet, not loud. There are no billboards in the hills, and there aren't any go-cart tracks; there aren't a hundred thousand cheap little ways to spend your money that have nothing to do with where you are. New Zealanders are not the type of people who want to ride a go-cart around a small oval track that could be as easily in Peoria as Katmandu. What they do, they do honestly—and I don't mean in terms of cheating. When you get on the water, damn it, you're going to get on the water. When you go up in the mountains, you *go up* in the mountains.

Most New Zealanders I believe are pacifists, but there's very little about their energies that's pacific.

It's very much a doing city, and it's very much the type of city, if I could choose the place to spend the rest of my life, I would choose.

I spend my day getting bearings, looking in windows, finding my way about. I ride the skyline gondola up one of the mountains behind the city, 450 meters to the top, and I have lunch in the coffee shop there, looking out over Queenstown and Lake Wakatipu toward the Remarkables. What can I say about this? I'm as impressed as I can be with just the geography.

I call home to my wife, Maureen.

"So *tell* me about it," she says.

I do my best to describe what the town looks like, how the mountains shape the shoreline, and what I feel about it all, but I do a lousy job.

"It's heaven," I say toward the end of my description. "I can't tell you how happy I am to be here."

"You miss me that much, huh?"

Another silly mistake.

"What's going on there?" I ask.

"Nothing. *Nothing* is happening here."

I suspect she's wrong. I suspect there's a great deal going on at home. But I suspect there's little new. She's living in our routine while I am happily outside it. Every step I take puts my foot in a place it's never been before, brings me to things I've never seen, adds something fresh to my own history. Her steps are replays.

I tell her I love her, that I miss her terribly, that what I really want is for her to be here with me, for our children, to be here with both of us, but it's almost lame. When we hang up, I exit the phone booth and walk around a corner so I can see the lake again and Mount Cecil rising from the far shore. It's twilight now, and the water has turned purple. Mount Cecil is a dusky brown. The Remarkables, however, catch the setting sun long after it's set in town, and they explode that light. I take the deepest breath I can, let it out as slowly as possible.

⁂

It's evening now, almost dark. There is a black-and-white cocker spaniel running around, a golden retriever sitting on the back of a jet boat. Kiwi children run about the harbor shore, playing.

The entrance to the Queenstown Harbor is split by a long sandbar. There's a post at the end of it with an aqua-green light on top marking the limit of safe travel. The jet boats have come in, making their turns close enough to the light post that passengers could touch it. The *Earnslaw* has come in. Ducks have congregated at the shoreline. Some are feeding, some are bathing themselves. The carts that sell coffee, cappuccino, stuffed baked potatoes, are closing up. The crowds are clearing. The sun has set behind the mountains. But through the clouds, a patch of sun moves slowly up Mount Cecil, then the Remarkables. Wood smoke rises from people's chimneys and from autumn leaf fires burning. In the distance I can hear the sound of a single chain saw.

People walking the waterfront are most often couples. Two women, a man and a woman, a woman with several children. Two German shepherds play at chasing ducks in the shallows.

There is a wishing well at the waterfront, a stone well with a little roof over the opening. The sign on it says, "Wish for your return to Queenstown."

The lights are coming on—the cabin lights, the pub lights, the balcony lights at the Park Royal Hotel. On the pedestrian shopping street there's a little less traffic. It's time to move in for the meal.

At night in Queenstown, amber and white house lights, streetlights, dot the hillside looking out over the lake. Only the green sandbar light casts a reflection. Waves come up on the shore, the wind rustles in the trees, traffic moves occasionally on the streets. The Southern Cross is almost directly overhead.

Behind Mount Cecil the Southern Lights begin a display. They begin gently as just a faint glow, a brightening, as if the moon were trying to rise from the west, causing the mountains to become a silhouette. As the evening grows deeper they get brighter, more dynamic. A small group of men and women walking the waterside stop near me to watch. They *ooh* and *aah* when the curtains and sheets of color are brightest. One of them starts to applaud, then they all join in. Even me, quietly.

ᔑ

A bright, sunshiny, warm day after a cold night. The Remarkables are brilliant! The surrounding hills seem electric in autumn colors. Branches from a giant willow tree near the waterfront swing in the breeze, brush themselves into the poplars. Tandem parapenters—a type of tandem skydiving where you strap yourself to an "instructor" then jump off a cliff with a parachute open behind you for a ten-minute glide over and through the landscape toward a landing on a rugby field—float off the mountain behind the gondolas rising from the city to the Skyline restaurant and observation deck.

I want to see the parapenters land so I take a taxi from the town center back to the hostel, really not that much of a distance, to get my camera and then get back to the rugby field in time to see them finish their descent. The driver hears my voice, asks me where I'm from, asks me what I think about Queenstown so far. I tell him I like this area, this country, very much. He says that's good to hear. He thinks people around here are different than the rest of the New Zealanders. People around here aren't so caught up in every little thing that bothers other Kiwis, he says. I tell him I understand why, that it makes sense to me.

Just off the rugby field where I'm standing there's a horse in someone's yard, grazing. Above me the yellow parachutes spin in lazy circles over the green pine-forest hills. There are three of them now. When they finally approach the field I see the clients are three college-age women. As they near the ground their faces are tight lipped, wide eyed, filled with determination, remembering I'm sure whatever instructions they were given about how to land and not tangle their legs with the man behind them. Once they land, however, it's all smiles and hugs and cries of "We did it! Wow! What a sight! Did you . . . ?"

Their reactions are important to me. While I have no desire to leap off a cliff strapped to someone else and a parachute, I have bought a ticket that will take me out of town, through some mountains to a fairly remote part of the Shotover River, out to Skipper's Canyon where people hurl themselves off a bridge with a glorified rubber band attached to their legs, where the world's highest bungee jumping that's not from a helicopter or balloon takes place. Bungee jumping started in New Zealand. I don't know if I'm going to jump yet. But I know I want to see it.

&

It's sometime just after noon, and after an aimless walk around town I'm standing in the shop where you sign up for bungee jumping. A. J. Hackett Bungy, it's called, after the man who supposedly started it all. If I wanted to, I could sign up for white-water rafting, jet boating, helicopter trips through canyons, parapenting and tandem skydiving, all sorts of dangerous thrills here. Videos play from monitors in the two main rooms showing happy people doing crazy things to themselves.

Everyone in here has either just come back from some adventure or is waiting to go. The differences between the two groups are clear and immediate. The survivors are relaxed, talk loudly, watch the videos of their own leaps of faith made just an hour before, point out the smallest details to those who were with them. Those who are waiting to go are wound tighter than clocks. Their smiles are quick and nervous. They too watch the monitors, more closely than those who've gone before, but the details are lost in the act of imagining their body in the place of the one flailing about in midair on the screen.

A beige Land Rover pulls up to the curb and a man gets out to collect us. There are nine of us, it seems. Three women and six men. We all get in, and the truck pulls away from the shop, away from Queenstown, off onto a dirt road leading through the mountains.

Quickly, I discover I can't spend time creating an imaginary fear of leaping off a bridge—I am more worried about this road! One-lane wide, almost, this road is cut into the hillsides, sometimes muddy, sometimes covered with a thin sheet of frost or ice. There are no guardrails to keep us from the drop-offs, which often fall away from the road down several hundred feet. The brown and green and then snowcapped hills we're driving through are dramatic and sharp, but I'm not spending very much time looking at them. Our driver, he's told us his name but I can't remember it, is very casual with his driving. I can't get used to his being on the right side of the car. Every corner is a blind corner.

I'm sitting sideways on a bench in the back of the Land Rover, and all I can think about is what would happen if we were to slide off the road, the tumbling and flipping and certain death from multiple fractures.

We stop three times on our way to the bridge. Two of the stops are to enjoy the scenery, rock formations with improbable names like the Upside Down Elephant (really, it does look like that!), and mountain valleys cut deeply into tussock. At the first of these, a few of the men run behind a large rock to relieve themselves. The other stop is to deliver mail at a remote sheep station. As we drive, the driver asks us all if we have questions, but the only question that gets asked is about height. Is this cliff or this drop-off as high as the bridge, we ask? No, he says, the bridge is much higher. Each of us in the Land Rover laughs, but it's not from good humor.

Finally, the bridge. Skipper's Canyon is deep and narrow, sheer rock faces cut into the hills. At the bottom, the Shotover River looks only inches deep. The rocks are clearly visible, which is not a comforting thought. The bridge itself is one lane, a brown steel suspension bridge. Its roadway is wooden. As we drive across it, initial exclamations of "wow!" or "shit!" give way to silence inside the Land Rover. It's 229 feet from the bridge to the water.

We turn around just beyond the bridge and walk back to its center where four or five instructors are waiting for us. There's a scale for weighing us (we got weighed at the shop in town, and our weight is marked with blue felt pen on the backs of our hands), and there are several very long bungee cords. More immediately, however, there is this distance from the bridge to the bottom.

Intellectually, I know things look higher from the top than they do from the bottom. Standing at the top of a swimming pool high dive gives a much different perception than standing at the bottom. But knowing this does not help the feeling of endless space below this bridge. Knowing this does not make the fear go away.

An American woman named Tana is the first to go. She and some of her friends played rock-paper-scissors to see who went first. She gets a towel around her ankles, some nylon wrapped around the towel, the bungee cord attached with a metal hook to the nylon. Feet bound, she shuffles to the end of a small platform built onto the bridge. One of the instructors lets go of the cord, which gives a small tug at her feet and the both of us a nearly coronary seizure.

"You want to jump out as far as you can," an instructor says. "You want to get a type of pendulum effect. If you jump straight down you'll go like a yo-yo, just down and then boing right back up."

"You want me to jump out?" Tana asks.

"As far as you can."

The instructors start a countdown, and we all join in. Five, four, three, two, one, Bungee!

Off she goes. No hesitation at all. A five-foot-tall woman with short dark hair has just leaped from a bridge, and everyone around me is smiling. There's no sound from the canyon, either. No screams, no terror. Just this woman falling and falling and falling.

When she gets near the bottom, when the cord begins to stretch and pull her away from a bloody death on the riverbed rocks, she starts to yell. I can't tell if she's speaking words or pronouncing something more urgent and physical, but I can tell her cries are happy ones. She must have jumped out away from the bridge as the instructor told her because when the cord extends its full length she swings under the bridge on her first rebound. Then she appears under us again, falling again, screaming again, having the time of her life. A jet boat appears and answers a question I hadn't thought to ask; how to get down? When Tana stops bouncing, the bungee cord is slowly lowered until the men in the boat can collect her. When she's disconnected, she waves bravely to those of us still above her. The jet boat deposits her on a beach fifty yards downriver.

"Who's next?" one instructor asks.

And it all starts over. The fear, the certainty of death. The same fear that makes me back away from the platform makes a man named Steve step up. He gets the same routine of towel and nylon and cord, the same instructions to jump away from the bridge. In the Land Rover Steve told us he'd jumped before, several times in fact. But it takes three countdowns before he leaves the platform and falls away from us, getting smaller with each second. Then the others go, one by one, no jump any easier for having watched the others. Finally, there's only me and the instructors on the bridge.

"Have you decided if you want to jump?" one of them asks me.

Suddenly the bridge is a very crowded place. Every student I've ever had, those who've hated me as well as those who've liked me, my two brothers and sister and various colleagues and friends are screaming, "Jump! Jump!" My parents and Maureen are screaming just as loudly, "Don't! Don't!" My daughter, Kate, is saying what she always says whenever we get in the car, "Go Daddy." It's a moment for courage and will and inner strength.

"No," I say. "I don't think I will."

I don't get any argument from the instructors, but there's this chorus inside me now whispering "coward, wimp." When we drive down to the river to pick up the others, they all look at me and say they can't believe I didn't go.

The ride back to town isn't nearly as scary as the ride out; the sheer drops don't look so far down. Everyone talks about what they felt, what they saw, what it was like to fly.

2. DUNEDIN

Noon. Walking about downtown Dunedin this morning has been the same experience as walking in Manhattan, or Chicago, or any metropolitan area. The buildings are smaller and the air is exponentially cleaner, but the mass of people filling and crowding the sidewalks then storefronts, the pace of their business, is just the same.

The center of Dunedin is the Octagon, a variation of the town square or circle. The center of it is a small grassy and many-treed park with striped canopy shelters built for catching a bus or taxi. The street that circles the Octagon is itself rimmed by shops and markets. There's the Mackenzie Country Clothing Company, the Civic Center, Canterbury of New Zealand, the Visitor's Center, St. Paul's Cathedral, the Warehouse for New Zealand, the Baker's Oven, the Senior Citizen's Club, several others.

The Octagon is built on a hill with St. Paul's toward the top. It slopes downhill from the cathedral toward the Baker's Oven and the Ski Barn. Just to the side of the church, on the inside of the roadway, a statue of Robert Burns shows the poet seated on what appears to be a rock. The plaque gives his life span. "Robert Burns, 25 January 1759–21 July 1796." He's a good-looking man, looking out into the distance toward the harbor. Behind him the cathedral and the hills—around him the sites of a bustling city.

According to *A History of New Zealand,* one of the founders of Dunedin was Rev. Thomas Burns, "a censorious old bigot who was a nephew of the poet. Supported by the Association of the Lay Members of the Free Church, these two [Capt. William Cargill was the other] decided to plant a Free Church settlement where 'piety, rectitude and industry' would feel at home, and where the inhabitants as a body would form 'a vigilant moral police.'"

Looking at Robert Burns, sitting in the wake of his nephew, I find myself wondering how a man who dreamed of a moral police would meet the man who penned, "Lord, hear my earnest cry an' pray'r, Against that presbytery o' Ayr." Despite the rain and lowering clouds, Dunedin is made brighter, I think, having placed Robert and not Thomas in its heart.

Things are hopping this noon. The McDonald's (I just poked my head in) is filled with a number of birthday parties for children. This is a town with a hundred coffee shops, most of them single storefronts that head deep back into the buildings, some of them a little more artsy than others, all of them busy. People have lunch outside as well and throw bread to pigeons. The traffic is constant and loud. People park where they're not supposed to. Despite the overcast sky and the occasional rain, it's warmer today than it has been.

Dunedin is not a big city, but it moves like one. Perhaps it's only that I find myself walking about at noontime and happen to have an urgent hunger. Perhaps it's just my own need to see as much as possible of this city in a single day. But I have this feeling that I'm missing everything important.

༄

Two o'clock. I come up to the Otago Early Settlers Museum on Cumberland Street. On the outside a Romanesque brick building, the portcullis painted orange and purple and blue, on one side there's a train in a room with glass walls. On the inside, the Otago Early Settlers Museum is filled with the things one would expect—the Victorian clothing, the tea services, the diaries, the glassware, the furniture, the uniforms, a few swords and cannons. The train in the glass room is the Josephine. According to the museum literature, the Josephine is New Zealand's oldest preserved steam locomotive, one of only four Double Fairlie patent models in the world. The others are in Ffestiniog, in Wales.

Other rooms hold the Albion Press, a lighter than previously known letter press, some old penny-farthing bicycles, stagecoaches and train things, a horse whip, an exhibit of contemporary photography.

There are exhibits of pioneer life: the homes, the utensils, the furnishings, the farm equipment, the flour mills, the shovels. Then there are the whaling try-pots, whaling boats, an exhibit of the shore-whaling stations, and a small monument to the laying out of the town by Charles Henry Kettle, the surveyor.

Certainly these things should be a connection back to the things I know, to the history of America. These things are well outside my own history but part of the development of my country, a part of our history and folklore. Whaling, frontier life, forestry, each of these things is very much like our own history. Even down to establishing a new religious colony and the later gold rush, this history should give me a sense of home. Yet, for some reason, I feel farther away from home in this museum than I've felt so far. I'm mostly alone in here, the heels of my boots echoing loudly in each room, and each display reminds me I'm half the planet away from Minnesota.

ॐ

This morning began with breakfast and politics.

The breakfast was several bowls of flakes, muesli, granola, dried and regular fruit, all for the mixing. Milk and cream. Strong black coffee and very hot tea.

The politics begin with sports, mainly the New Zealand national rugby team, the All Blacks (named for their uniforms), and how some years ago they broke the old sports ban regarding South Africa. They made a tour of that country, and the South African team made a tour of New Zealand.

"Didn't that bother you?" I ask.

There are several of us at the long head table in the dining room.

Andrew Howe, a medical student, is doing most of the talking, explaining what he can.

"It bothered a lot of people," he said. "Riot police were called in when the South African team was here to handle the crowds and demonstrations."

"So why in the world did New Zealand go there, why did they invite that team to come here?"

"Mostly because they have a great team, a real contest."

This isn't a debate, I see, it's a history lesson. Some of us go for toast or more coffee. Somehow the conversation shifts to a more general style of warfare. Andrew explains that New Zealand has historically gone to war with the English, signing on to the time and date of whatever declarations are made. But this creates a bit of an oddity, he says. When England declared war on Argentina over the Falkland Islands, by virtue of geographic placement and time zones, New Zealand did so first. England declared war sometime in the morning. New Zealanders, who were just finishing their suppers, discovered they'd been at war all day.

"And then there's the nuclear problem," he says.

"I thought New Zealand was nuclear free," I say.

"We are. But at least as far as America is concerned, that's the problem."

It seems the States pulled out of a mutual-defense treaty between Australia, New Zealand, and the United States when New Zealand declared itself nuclear free and signed the South Pacific Nuclear Free Zone Treaty. Or, more exactly, we dropped New Zealand from that alliance. The United States and Australia still cooperate, as does Australia and New Zealand. It's just the Kiwis and the Yanks who don't agree. When New Zealand became nuclear free, the United States sent a warship to make a call at a New Zealand port. New Zealand asked if the ship carried nuclear weapons or ran on nuclear power. The United States has a "neither confirm nor deny" policy when it comes to what may be aboard ships. New Zealand refused entry to the ship, and the treaty was torn.

"Your country decided to push that issue," Andrew says.

My country. People come and go from the table, plans are announced for the day, advice is given and received, fruit and coffee fill plates and cups and then the stomachs of the people who retrieve them. The company is warm and friendly. Outside a steady rain falls, the sound of it occasionally loud through open windows. I feel very far away from my country.

I can imagine the argument for excluding New Zealand. New Zealand happens to sit at a place where not very much happens. Our national military interest is lower here. In one way, it's a sound military and economic policy.

However. However! My own politics are antinuclear. My own politics are always confused by tangential things like ethics and what I see as our inherent responsibility as a world economic and military power. Sitting at this long table this morning, I remember something said to me at Le Café in Christchurch by a man sitting next to me while we both warmed ourselves with coffee by the fire.

"We don't want to be led by the Japanese. It's not that we don't like them, it's just that their understanding of democracy is young and fairly shallow. We want to be led by the United States."

Democracies depend on dissenting voices. It's a part of the definition. If we're going to be honest about establishing a world democracy, and if we're going to be honest about leading the world in that direction, we're going to have to admit to partnership with those who don't agree. It will cost us money. But it very well could save our souls.

∽

What I find most remarkable in this museum are the portraits. In the portrait gallery they are everywhere, seven or more rows of them from floor to ceiling. As the sign says on an immaculate eight-station bank table, "The museum has a nationally important collection of original portrait photographs which date from 1860. They include many of Otago's early settler families. The photographs themselves are examples of almost all the known photographic techniques since the invention of photography. Part of the collection is on display in this Edwardian-style presentation, dating from 1908, and many more are in storage. There's an index. Please ask if you want to."

On one wall there are Mr. Hugh Frasier Ayson, Mr. and Mrs. Alex Ayson Milton, Alex Johnston, Mr. and Mrs. James Freeman, Mr. and Mrs. John Wilson, Mr. and Mrs. W. Brash, George Hutchison and Mrs. George Hutchison, Thomas and Mrs. Moodie, Mr. and Mrs. Richard Sandilands. The dates here are 1852, 1858, 1848, 1865, 1856.

The people in these pictures look hard. Few of them smile, though in general the women look happier than the men. I realize these steely poses were a photographic convention, but it makes me wonder about the lives of these men and women. It makes me wonder about what it was like to leave ordered England in the days of Victoria and enter the frontier, to leave a country well established in its contexts and habits and move half the planet away to a country of harder weather, harder homes, harder fields to plow. These are not the smiling pictures of friends. These are pictures of people setting themselves to the task of enlarging the world.

It is impossible to glean a personality from these faces. It is impossible to tell who told jokes, who drank too much, who maintained the moral order. I stare at them for a long time, wishing they would speak louder. I have lots of questions for them today, because I feel so far away myself.

In the same room as the portraits there is something called a polython. A wooden cabinet about six feet tall then three feet wide, the top half of it an arched glass window revealing a large silver disk set on its side. A small boy and his father walk up to it, plunk a coin in a slot, and I discover the polython is really a large music box. Ethereal, fantasy, wind chime–like music fills the room, and I can almost imagine the faces in the portraits relaxing to the pleasant memory.

൭

Five o'clock. I'm in a van that's traveling the shore of Otago Harbor, winding its way the length of the Otago Peninsula toward seals and penguins. The day is still gray and gloomy. The rains are occasional but definite when they come.

I didn't think I'd be able to do this. I'd been told the best time to see the penguins is at sunset, when they come back to shore after a day of feeding at sea, but the regular twilight tour has been canceled for unknown reasons. At the tourist information center, a group of us stood about solemnly, depressed about not getting out to what's called the Penguin Place. Then Nikki, one of the women at the counter, said she knew a tour bus that could take us, if we were willing. Most of us said we were, a phone call was made, and shortly thereafter a van pulled up and we all got in.

Not too far out of Dunedin we discover our van driver is Nikki's mother. This brings a few laughs about calling Mum when you need something done.

"Ah, but she's a good girl," our driver (none of us ever think to ask her name) says. "Did she tell you that she's off to Africa in a wee bit?"

"No."

"She is indeed. She's going to live in tents with some nomads. Next year she wants to go to Antarctica."

The van is quiet now, trying I'm sure to imagine Nikki, a young woman who looks like any freshly scrubbed and well-dressed college student in the States, in the wilds of Africa or on the ice of Antarctica. I find myself thinking about Kate, what I would say if she popped into the house one day and said she wanted to spend some time living in a tent or a superinsulated ice station. Would I meet her request with enthusiasm, or would my parental concern make me hesitate, derail her hopes?

Both trips are ones *I* would like to make. However. Nikki's mother says she encourages these trips, thinks they're absolutely marvelous. I admire Nikki's mum.

Nikki's mother is obviously proud of the daughter, yet quite game for an adventure herself. After an hour winding the coast of Otago Harbor at low tide, we pull off the shore road and up to a small white house. This is where we can get a key that will let us pass the fence that surrounds the Penguin Place. The keys aren't so much for security as to gauge how many people are on-site at one time.

Nikki's mum gathers the key and a set of binoculars for each of us in the van while we take the chance to stretch our legs and look at two penguins held in pens here while they recover from some illness or accident. These are yellow-eyed penguins, the rarest in the world. One of them looks fine. The other has an enlarged eye that looks like it could quite simply fall away from its head.

When Nikki's mum has the key and the glasses we're all quickly back in the van and on our way. After five more minutes or so, we turn off the paved road and drive for ten minutes on a single-lane path through the hills. Once again, the simple shape of the landscape captures my breath and imagination. The way one hill sweeps down under brown grass to a hollow or small valley then lifts itself into another hill seems almost magical here. Sheep graze the landscape up to the roadside. One other car passes us, heading back toward town, then all too quickly we find ourselves parked at the top of a bluff. In front of us, the far south Pacific Ocean.

"I didn't think it would be, but this is definitely worth the money!"

This comes from Miles, one of the men who rode with us in the van. We haven't seen a single penguin yet, but he stands near the bluff's edge, looking out to sea. The day's drizzle has lightened, though we can see storm cells move slowly east.

"You're looking toward Antarctica there," says Mum.

"Wow," says Miles.

We follow a narrow walk path to our left. Fifty steps from the parking area we come to the top of another bluff that looks down on a broad, protected sand beach. Two hundred yards or more from the bluff and we're on the one on the far side, maybe a hundred yards from the water to the bluff in back, and even with the rain and the strong wind coming off the ocean now, it strikes each of us as a perfect beach, another example of the definition itself.

"Look at that!"

I'm not sure who says this, but we all find what she's seeing in an instant. A small black shape in the water. It rides a wave to its crest and then jumps, explodes really, or rockets, like the wave gathered it up and shot it, down into the trough between the wave and the one in front of it. These are not small waves. The day is coming just to darkness—and without delay the penguins are coming in.

All I've ever really seen of penguins before are those on television and in zoos, where they waddle awkwardly and look cute. This one penguin, however, is a sleek and very fast animal. It hurls itself from one wave to another, each time taking large leaps between them, looking much more like a fast-flying fish than a bird. When it gets to the water's edge, it transforms itself into what we've seen before. It stands, begins the slow waddle, gets knocked down by a larger incoming wave, stands and waddles some more.

Each of us standing on the bluff has our binoculars glued to our eyes. Another penguin appears in the water and we forget the one on the beach immediately.

We can't get any closer. Although this is a tourist venue in so much that tourists are taken here, this is an honest rookery. The penguins are not accustomed to humans. Their nests are in the bluffs surrounding and protecting the cove and beach. There are no gift shops, no place to buy film or postcards. Just the wind and water and the site of rare and endangered penguins coming back to land. The two penguins wind their ways to the bluffs and we all stand quiet, too far away for the penguins to hear us even if we hollered, waiting for more.

Over the bluffs from the Penguin Place, at Taiaroa Head, the very end of the Otago Peninsula, is the Royal Albatross Colony, the only mainland albatross colony on the planet. We can't see the rookery from here, but every now and then one of the large birds comes gliding down the shoreline. Binoculars scan the skies, then the waves, then the skies.

After some time we move back to the parking area and then beyond it to more bluffs on the other side. New Zealand fur seals rest in kelp beds just below us, their grunting loud in the darkening air. The simple pathway does not separate us. It's not uncommon to see them both below us to our left, and above us to our right—every now and then grumbling when someone's flash camera disturbs their slumber. There's nothing to prevent one of us from coming up against the other, except the polite advice of Nikki's mum. Focusing my camera on a pup below me, I get scared into an Olympic sprint by a menacing bellow right behind me. A large bull seal I hadn't noticed, hidden in a small overhang, chases me from my spot.

Gray shapes rise and dive in the far distance, and at first we think it might be whales. In this part of the world that would be blue whales or sperm whales. It turns out to be another series of seals heading toward shore.

Farther down this shore there is a colony of spotted shags, acrobatic birds darting along the bluffs and nesting on sheer faces.

Nikki's mum is as interested and as engaged and awed by seeing the penguins dart through the waves, by seeing the albatrosses, by coming within inches of fur seals that are not domesticated or presented for tourist fondling, as we are. It's a bleak scene off the coast—gray, hard weather moving in from the southeast, clearly visible miles out to sea—but there is also that sense of the new, of the wonder-full, of the way even the taste of an intaken breath can be a surprise.

Nikki's mum lets us stay as long as we desire, which is until full darkness has made it impossible to see. We return the key and binoculars at Mc-Grouthers Farm. We ride back to Dunedin much quieter than we rode out. I get dropped off at Knox College too late for supper. In room 14, I rest on one of the couches, light my pipe, watch the blue smoke curl around the posters of rock stars on its way to the ceiling, look over some of the material Nikki handed me at the Tourist Center.

"Yellow-eyed Penguin. *Megadyptes Antipodes.* Height: 32 inches. Weight: 12 lbs. Age: 22 years maximum. Eggs: 1–2. September–November.

"Southern Fur Seal. *Asrctocephalus Forster.* Weight: 300 lbs. Age: 30 years maximum. Length: 7' maximum. Pups: December–February.

"Spotted Shag. *Stictocarbo Punctatus.* Height: 29 inches. Weight: 6–7 lbs approximately. Age: unknown. Eggs: 3–4. September–December."

How far can a person be from home? What are the honest connections we have with a place, with a history or community? This has been an odd day for me. Too much, really, to make sense of. Politics, religion, poetry, commerce, the history of frontier life, the future of seals and penguins and birds. What kind of place can I find for myself? What are my responsibilities to these things? I can imagine spending a lifetime engaged with only a fraction of any single issue.

Or am I looking at it backward? In just this one day it's been possible to come up against all these issues, to meet them and attempt to make some sort of personal sense with them. Where is the border between breadth and depth?

I envy New Zealanders. The size of their country, the closeness of it all, the very-far-away-from-everyone-elseness of it all, lets them see the planet in ways I had not imagined.

Is it possible to come home to a place you've never been?

Without a doubt.

A Home Story

7.

It's January now. A new-moon night. A mug of coffee still very hot. Time to say thank-you.

Well after midnight, the new house has grown quiet, Kate and Andrew asleep in their own beds. Tomorrow is a school day, and even though we've spent just less than half a year in this house, in this new home for us, there are routines already. Early bath. Lots of time for homework and book reading. Lots of time to settle, to rest, to unfold toward the evening. The bus comes early. Both parents head off toward work.

If somehow, however, they would turn themselves oddly enough to wake for a moment, and look out their windows, they might wonder what's happened. Kate's windows look southeast, over the large field toward a county highway—car lights at night far enough away to be reduced to a single moving point as pretty against the darkness as airplane lights against the sky. Andrew's windows look southwest, toward the church parking lot and into a neighborhood on the other side—house lights and streetlights illuminating snowbanks, garage doors, other windows where sometimes we can see the shapes of people moving.

Tonight, however, neither child would see what they already expect. The air has been getting warmer the past few days, temperatures in the upper twenties, and nighttime has brought blue-dark fog.

Maureen is asleep in our bed, but if she were to look out the bedroom window she would see under the street lamp what I see from a window in the library. A glowing in our front yard. In town, where there are trees, hoarfrost is gathering on elms and maples and birches and spruce. Standing at my window, looking at the fog thick enough to make the far side of our close street difficult, my first impression is the usual one. Quiet. Layered. A kind of blanket settled down over this new house. To be in a house when the fog comes in is to feel, somehow, more at home. To feel more safe. To feel more in place than on those days or nights when sunshine, or starlight, or the simple promise of someplace else, makes you want to find the car keys, or the snowshoes, or the old and trusted pair of hiking boots.

But this first impression is wrong. The more I stare at the lighted fog under the city street lamp the more I see it's racing. The prairie wind, the one real constant here, has not closed down. Not even tonight. Not even enough to allow the illusion of a calm. Dense billows of evaporated snow light up as they pass, shoved northward, wisps and then more billows following. It looks quiet out there at first, but a better description would be to say the wind's just too thick to be noisy now.

We put a library in this new house, a place to work and read and let sunshine fall on open storybooks, and there are windows on three sides of it. Windows look northeast, northwest, and southwest. Windows, I think. We got lots of windows. And from each of them, I have watched the way the land and sky here move.

Jackrabbits at full sprint across the snowfield.

A red-tailed hawk gliding up and then down the larger ditch, no more than two feet above the grasses, silent, not even flapping once as it pointed into the wind and arched its wings, looking for mice.

A thunder-and-lightning storm so large one night it called me away from the desk just to pull a chair to the window and watch. Two hours watching it coming. Thirty minutes of window-pounding, roof-thumping hail and rain and wind. Two hours of watching it head southeast. Try as I might to return to the desk, to the work I knew I should be doing, something about this storm demanded attention. Something in me demanded, too.

From these windows I've seen the sugar-beet harvest. The waiting game with the weather, everyone needing enough cold the beets can be stored aboveground outside, and needing to pull them when they hold maximum sugar.

On Wednesday nights, Saturday nights, Sunday mornings, I've watched the parking lot at the church fill with cars, vans, pickup trucks, and then watched well-dressed men and women and children hurry to the church through the cold. I've seen weddings gather there. And I'm sure I'll see funerals, if I pay enough attention.

Standing in these windows with Andrew, we've seen airplane lights in the distance descending toward the airport in north Fargo. And when Andrew's asked me if those lights are Santa's, I've assured him they are.

Standing at this window, watching the fog do a fast dance around our porch and driveway, a dip under the street lamp and then a leap to the roadway, I can turn my ear inward to this quiet house, to the echoes of the stories already collected. Slumber parties. Stomach flu. Thanksgiving with family from out of town. Christmas morning, the kids nearly leaping the full length of the stairs in anticipation. Christmas dinner with friends come over. Bowls of popcorn in the basement watching rented movies. Bowls of cereal before dawn on school mornings. Sudden moments, too many to make any one of them more special than the rest, when we've discovered ourselves upstairs, or down, without remembering having moved. All the ways in which the house works the way we wished it would.

Standing here, listening to the house, looking at the fog, I know there is a world beyond what I can hear or see this night. I've not told the story about the Morley River yet, or the one about Wright Pass, where the Yukon meets the Northwest Territories. I've not told the story about Wyoming trout, or the one about deer on the Bluestem Prairie. And then there are all the stories I still hope to learn. Maureen has stories, Kate and Andrew have stories, too. We make a new one each day. We hold on to the ones that make us smile and the ones that break our hearts. We can learn to love from them all.

Motel Mind

❊ ❊ ❊ ❊ ❊ ❊ ❊ ❊ ❊ ❊

DAWN MARANO

And I realized the impossibility which love comes up against. We imagine that it has as its object a being that can be laid down in front of us, enclosed within a body. Alas, it is the extension of that being to all the points in space and time that it has occupied and will occupy. If we do not possess its contact with this or that place, this or that hour, we do not possess that being. But we cannot touch all these points. If only they were indicated to us, we might perhaps contrive to reach out to them. But we grope for them without finding them. . . . We waste precious time on absurd clues and pass by the truth without suspecting it.

—MARCEL PROUST

THIS MORNING when I woke I was still a traveler in a dream that begins as a door clicks shut. I was leaving a room hundreds had checked into and out of; a room appointed with a combination of banal colors, patterns, and textures that invite ambivalence, gradual dismissal, and eventual amnesia; the kind of room that permits travelers to arrive with a sense of relief and leave with a minimum of regret.

But as the door in this dream clicks shut, I do feel a regret that is oddly familiar. Once again I'm loaded down with my belongings, fearful I've forgotten something—an earring, a shoe—but I'm anxious, too, about the attachments to people and to places these things I carry represent. Something about living in this rented room has released me from history, from connectivity and obligation. I know that what I'll regret is losing the delusion of perpetual possibility, that stubborn young hope in me that at midlife still refuses to surrender. In this rented room I have been anonymous for a time. In a rented room, I think, I could always be anyone, anywhere at all.

I am at the airport when I realize I've lost track of my baggage. I can already feel a dread certainty that my suitcases will not be among those tumbling from the carousel at my destination. And someone has relieved me of my carry-ons, too; sent them, I'm sure, to the belly of the wrong plane. In this detail is a subtle reproof my waking self will find amusing; probably I smile in my sleep: I routinely travel with a ridiculous burden of carry-ons, technically within FAA regulation, to be sure, but in weight and bulk, far beyond my capacity to manage. Airline attendants smirk, watching me carom down narrow aisles; passengers stare or scowl; sometimes kindly older men help me heave parcels into overhead bins or sacrifice the unused space under the seats in front of them. When I finally sit down, I'm always spent. Chagrined. Humbled. I resolve to reform, every trip—and I never do.

In this dream, though, I don't even make my flight. When it ends I am standing alone in the airport concourse while strangers surge and eddy purposefully around me. My suitcases, my hefty carry-ons—all gone. So, too, I've just discovered, is my ticket. Where in the world was I going?

Home, I wake thinking, *but where in the world is that?*

I lie in bed for several minutes feeling restless. I do not care for this dream, do not welcome its memory. Days will pass before I can appreciate its intricacies.

I've come to understand my dreams as a borderland, not only between consciousness and sleep, but between what I know and what I don't yet know that I know. Characteristic of everyone's dreams, this one teases with what it promises to reveal and then withholds. They know us so well, our dreams: encrypting their messages, creating enigmas. They know how we tend to value the quest over the prize and the question over the answer. They mean to keep us wondering.

I do recognize the vanity in this, that I've determined my dreams have something significant to relate, that I've recruited myself as my most faithful disciple. But how can I resist a teacher so canny as to offer me revelation disguised as a word game? It seduces me, this dream, first with the pun, then with the riddle.

I think of that moment at the motel door, all of that troubling luggage with which I felt myself again burdened, the baggage of my life I'd rather jettison than carry; my belongings, then, that I was tempted to disown, transformed there at the airport into the reassuring and indispensable—and suddenly missing—evidence of my *belonging*.

And then the riddle: If a woman can show you her baggage, can describe where she lives but can't tell you where she belongs, does she have a home?

⌒

I begin nearly every day looking to the west toward the expanse of the Great Basin, stretching to a false horizon a few miles away and then beyond to other horizons I cannot see. I know that on one of those horizons, on what could be thought of as the opposite rim of the basin, a friend is beginning her day on a ranch. Linda pulls on a jacket and lets the screen door clap shut in the jamb behind her. Halfway to the barn she hears John's voice above the calves bawling; it is branding time. Maybe—as often happens when she's mending a fence or helping her husband turn a stubborn cow in a tight draw—a line of poetry is occurring to her. The trip wire of words stops her midstride; she turns back for the house where there is paper and a pencil. But a gust of wind off the playa tips the idea over in her mind. Linda moves on across the yard, on to the hard work her hands know.

Between Linda's homeplace near the Warner Mountains in California and my home lodged against the Wasatch Front in Utah is a succession of other mountain ranges and valleys: a landmass like shirred cloth. But there are few places in the Great Basin like this busy Eden the Mormon settlers insistently wrested from the sagebrush and then claimed with greedier plants. Most of the Great Basin is desert still: the landscape of revelation, of the necessary deficiencies and hardships that prophets and pilgrims once favored, making their way to heaven.

A mug of coffee is the only company I share most mornings, standing on this deck overlooking the valley. In the distance is Great Salt Lake, that shallow saline pool evincing a permanently plugged drain in the geography. A few miles beyond the liquid lake is a dry lake and what was left behind as water receded and evaporated: the stark, white Bonneville Salt Flats. Once a feature inspiring awe and desperation among nineteenth-century pioneers traversing it in wagons, the flats can now be crossed in under an hour—less, if you're driving the kind of vehicles that break land-speed records at the Bonneville Speedway near the border of Nevada; or more, if you stop to read the dozens of messages that travelers before you have left. Chunks of black basalt are arranged and rearranged constantly along the roadside, spelling out professions of immutable love on the white crust of salt.

My coffee is nearly tepid by the time the scrub jays notice me and begin a squawking clamor for their daily dole of peanuts. The sun to my back has not yet cleared Grandeur Peak. When it does the shadows of the Wasatch still shrouding the valley floor will withdraw like long skirts trailing a widow in her weeds, and light made a million years ago will finally shine on this pocket of earth.

Geologists say this basin landscape is very young and actively remaking itself: faults opening and closing, gaping awry like cheap zippers; ranges lifting, valleys between them flexing wider. Reno and Salt Lake City, where I live, are moving steadily apart. But the geological definition of *young*—twenty million years or so—as it pertains to the regional topography I've come to know is scarcely useful, brevity and lack of perspective being the defining qualities of my humanity. For testimony concerning resilience and long life we Westerners look to other beings, organic like us. In southern Utah is a stand of quaking aspens, forty-seven thousand clones from a single plant, covering 106 acres—reputedly the world's largest living organism. In the White Mountains of California are bristlecone pines that were seedlings when Cheops was building his pyramid, and in a national forest not far away are the sequoia, some with circumferences greater than the Sixth Wonder of the World, the Colossus of Rhodes, was tall. In Arizona, there are saguaro cacti growing a mere inch per year on parched, rocky *bajadas* yet managing to outlive that most venerable and prolific of Old Testament patriarchs, Abraham, by several decades.

All of the sciences, though, however dense and incomprehensible they may seem, offer a language seductive to the mortal mind: centuries locked in tree rings, the plasticity of land, the speed of light. In the face of such spans, such powers and magnitudes, we are relieved of culpability for our own frailty, our impotence and inertia. These are forces we can barely imagine: the life force sustaining a bristlecone for another millennium; the momentum propelling the comet Hale Bopp through our solar system; the erosions and uplifts altering the geography we see every day, albeit imperceptibly. These are forces that make time and distance irrelevant, and absolutes, like truth, relative. I was raised in Los Angeles, and though I lived for many years almost completely ignorant of the natural world and its rhythms, the might of restless land rocked me from that oblivion—and my bed—on February 9, 1971: the San Fernando earthquake. Now, little more than twenty-five years later, I live on the very edge of yet another fault, with a potential for destruction at least as great as that of the San Andreas. I could tell you I know where I am, but somewhere deep underneath us the incremental truth of plate tectonics is making me a liar.

As for what I do believe is true? Less than ever before, it seems, but still more than my parents who are sure of nothing in our world but grave portents of our world's end: earthquakes, floods, tornadoes. Poisoned soils. A hole in the sky a continent could slip through like a button. Babies in Dumpsters. Anti-Christ candidates. The phone lines hiss with their fears. I tell them they watch too much television. I tell them about the broad-tailed hummingbird I came upon trapped in our garage last summer, battering itself senseless against a window; about the heave of its minute heart and lungs against my fingertips; about how much I wanted to possess its perfection forever; how hard it was to open the palm of my hand. Forget Nostradamus. Life, I tell them, let's talk about that.

Yet one afternoon, a few dozen miles from my parents' home in Tucson, I watch researchers at the Biosphere II facility factoring our odds in the race to save our atmosphere. Once the subject of bad press and some ridicule, Biosphere II is now an extension campus of Columbia University's environmental studies program. I sit through the orientation, but I skip the tour, preferring to explore on my own, preferring not to hear the canned lecture from the elderly docent. There are five biomes at the biosphere: desert, thornscrub, savanna, rain forest, and ocean, plus a separate agricultural sector where experiments on cultivated plants related to the greenhouse effect, for example, are being conducted.

I stand outside the savanna biome, the landscape that, according to E. O. Wilson's biophilia theory, is the one *Homo sapiens* if given a choice has always called home. Inside the windows, on a small promontory of earth, an intermittent breeze is teasing dry grasses sealed away from true seasons; strange how my ears yearn for a sound to accompany what my eyes see. Here, outside the biosphere, time seems suspended by the afternoon fermata of cicada song.

Nearby I see scientists gathering data in a multimillion-dollar greenhouse and hovering over computer screens in a futuristic command center. From my side of the glass observation stations, none of them looks particularly optimistic. I buy a copy of the Biosphere II souvenir video in the gift store for my parents. Over iced tea and ham sandwiches, I tell them about my favorite part: Alan Alda is interviewing a technician in Biosphere's tropical rain forest. She radios the command center for a rainstorm, and Alda quickly raises an umbrella. He beams. It's pouring, for gosh sakes, *inside a building.*

The new educational mission of Biosphere II is at least defensible. Outright offensive is the new venture from the Ogden Corporation I read about in the *Wall Street Journal:* indoor, ersatz "wildernesses" that are being constructed inside shopping malls. The first of these artificial nature preserves has opened in Ontario, California, and features five biomes representing that state's deserts, forests, and seashores. Fake giant Joshua trees. Fake redwoods. Fake tide pools. Full-spectrum lighting simulates dawn and dusk, and hidden scent canisters emit a forest fragrance—but the animals are real enough, the king snakes and boas, the bobcat, the yellow-bellied marmot, the roadrunners and eels and crabs, all of them living in approximations of their natural habitats. "We're trying to put a state of mind in the animals," says F. William Zeigler, Ogden's vice president of conservation and science, "to provide the furniture, the rocks and trees and water pools for them to utilize. Whether they think they are outside or not, I don't know if they have that capability. Certainly they'll learn that this is their home." And so, too, the visitors to the exhibit? I wonder. But for the sake of the human species and the fate of the natural world, we can hope not.

I do not tell my parents about the Ogden Corporation's boondocks-in-a-box. I do not tell them that estimates of the number of species on our planet range from four to ten million—that the best of minds and intentions couldn't keep a thousand of them functioning properly inside Biosphere II for even two years. I do not point out the obvious: they can make it rain, but they'll never make a cloud inside that marvelous structure—and I would miss clouds too much. When I hand the video to my mother I say, "Watch this. You'll see. Everything is going to be just fine."

Back in Utah after my visit to Arizona I go on much as before, following the approach of each morning—maybe wondering a bit more seriously how long before we'll all be indoors, under glass full-time, using walkie-talkies to call in rainstorms over the wheat fields in the Midwest dome, replacing canisters of forest scent in Woodlands sector. On the east-side deck of the house, I drink my morning coffee. In the spring and early summer I watch nests of robins hatch and fledge; in the winter I watch does and yearlings, which feed at night on the ornamental shrubs now supplanting their historic winter forage in our neighborhood, saunter back up into the foothills at dawn. After the deer pass, the motion-sensitive security light mounted on the neighbor's garage blinks out again.

Most often though I just wait to watch morning on Great Salt Lake, the lees of a much greater lake gone now for tens of thousands of years. The house I live in is built on the edge of a memory of old waters, and each morning I keep my appointment, waiting for daylight to awaken that flat sheet metal–blue body dreaming of itself, of its mighty past, there on the horizon.

The Oquirrh Mountains, blue also, rise to the south of the blue-lake memory, marred by a decaying socket at Kennecott's open-pit copper mine where an entire mountain has been pried out of the landscape. On a denuded slope to the north a thin trail of smoke rises from a smelter stack.

Antelope and Stansbury Islands are a bruised blue, unlike the sky that at dawn is moving away from indigo. By the end of summer, the sun is setting over the lake itself, and most every evening I watch this, too: the sinking light dancing a sheen across the water. I watch the molten reaches of the lake-light cool: White gold. Rose gold. Steel blue again.

To the south, at Point of the Mountain near the state prison, hills that should slope gradually to the valley floor are beaten flat as hammertoes. There, gigantic wind-driven standing waves slammed to shore up until about fifteen thousand years ago. The deck on which I stand overlooks Lakeline Drive, only a half-mile run of paved road. But looking northwest I can follow the old lip of lake along the bench of these foothills to Ensign Peak. Every July we drive north to fly fish on the Snake River, and I find myself staring out the window all the way to Idaho at this ghostly shoreline several hundred feet above the floor of the basin. Farms and ranches and orchards are washed up against the rim where high tide has come and gone on the ancient lake.

Some mornings before I hear the water begin running through pipes to feed my husband's shower; before I hear joggers approaching, sneakers slapping the asphalt; before I hear the snuffling of neighborhood dogs, the clinking riff of their collar tags telling the progress of their rounds; before I hear the neighbors calling instructions as their children head off to school; before I hear the children's voices and laughter, fleet and clear as wind instruments in this improvised orchestration—sometimes before I hear any of these sounds, I can imagine what was. In my mind's eye I see the remnant waters of Great Salt Lake rising to inundate this valley floor once again. I can see Lake Bonneville, a thousand feet of deep dream, roiling across suburbs and trees, buildings and thoroughfares and three county lines all the way to the Idaho border. I can imagine the rhythm of old waters, lapping below me. I can feel the old story moving again.

I must have stood in front of that mural at the Utah Museum of Natural History for a very long time, so long that the group of college students I'd joined had moved off with their professor to another display. The mural depicted the east bench above our valley in the Pleistocene epoch of the Cenozoic era. The time of glaciers in retreat, carving Yosemite Valley, leaving behind the bed of Lake Agassiz in the upper Midwest and here, the ancestor of Great Salt Lake. If the mural hadn't been roped off, I could have stepped forward and pointed to the exact location of my house. A camel was grazing there on a grassy slope, the shoreline of Lake Bonneville a few yards away from the four-hundred-gallon hot tub in my backyard.

The past is close to the surface of life here. The dead seduce the living, murmuring secrets, whispering mysteries. The tracks of a *Tenontosaurus* lead to a vanished riverbank; Anasazi cliff ruins stand watch for an ancient enemy. In the Ibapah cemetery tin markers, bearing names tooled with a hammer and a nail, weather not far from the pony-express trail where a few stagecoach passengers and riders stopped for the last time.

We drive the mountain road to Oatman, Arizona, one Christmas Eve on the way to visit my parents, and we understand then—in the way our bodies sway and in the way our eyes dart—why this was one of the first sections of historic Route 66 to be bypassed. Even the engine of a four-wheel drive protests on the steepest inclines. The overturned hulk of a late-forties Oldsmobile rusts into oblivion at the bottom of a ravine. The narrow strip of pavement rises and plummets, intestinal in its writhing, and we understand something about the terror of dirt-poor Dust Bowl migrants who had to pay locals to tow their cars to the top of Sitgreaves Pass.

Clark Gable and Carole Lombard took these curves at a dangerous speed on their wedding night in 1939—somehow we understand that, too. It's nothing we can prove; just a story we tell ourselves in the car about lovers and a road and a March night: Clark finally gets a day off from acting like Rhett Butler. After the wedding in Kingman, Carole, the impetuous one, says, "Clark, honey, let's scram." So they speed back for the border of California, and get as far as room 15 in the Oatman Hotel before ardor catches up with them.

Room 15 is locked this morning. So we feed overpriced carrots and alfalfa pellets to the herd of wild burros wandering through town, descendants of the pack animals gold miners turned loose or lost.

But the past does not always speak to me and invite my engagement. Last summer not five minutes from my house, a train of sixty wagons re-enacting the Mormon arrival in Utah in 1847 rolled down Emigration Canyon after a four-month, thirteen-hundred-mile journey. The event had everything going for it: a company of common people transformed by uncommon circumstance; faces of faith and resilience and joy. But I was left feeling strangely disappointed. What role did I have to play in this celebration after all—as a gentile, as the Other somewhat grudgingly tolerated here—welcoming Mormon pioneers home to their Zion? So I watched the earnest progress of the wagons and horses and handcarts that afternoon, nursing the petty resentments of a persona non grata, thinking, *Not my people. Not my history.*

It was months later before I revisited this thought and felt ready to revise it: I live in the West. Of course they are and of course it is.

✍

There is a light chop this morning. Small waves slap at the narrow beach. When a man jogs by I am imagining his legs churning the water, stirring up silt and a wake of small shells. Instead, he stirs a covey of California quail, loitering in my yard under a stand of scrub oak. The covey flushes, quitting the ground cover with an explosion of wings, anxious chitters and clicks, and the man, who is as startled as the birds are, smiles to himself. His heart is racing with surprise and pleasure. I like him immediately. But there are too many of us here now. Too many houses, too much asphalt. When it rains, I know immediately if a new foundation is being dug in our subdivision: the streets and gutters run red with sediment.

A cop once told me our neighborhood was nicknamed CB Heaven: high enough on the bench above the valley, he explained, to clear the usual radio interference. But all is not peaceful in heaven. When the teenagers cruise by on summer evenings, when I can feel the bass beat from their car stereos in the soles of my feet, I find myself thinking about the camel grazing at the edge of another time.

I wonder if I'm alone in a paradox: I am most at what I might call home in a place where I don't see myself belonging. The way I felt staring through the mural at the museum. The way I feel always in the desert, in the mountains, in the ocean, where the elements and inhabitants of the natural world do absolutely nothing to make me feel welcome; instead these respond to my presence with an utter, though sometimes wary, indifference. I feel opposite of this downtown in any city, where everything I see has been erected or supplied or packaged for my convenience and comfort, entertainment and diversion; where I see myself constantly, the insatiability of my human desire and selfishness, mirrored in everything, everywhere I look.

In ways I don't quite understand, this paradox is related to my motel mind, to that departure and regret when, outside a rented room, the door clicks shut on a dream space where anything is possible, where I don't recognize myself, and I go back to being what I am, go back to where I live.

If we meet I will tell you that I was born in Saint Louis, grew up in Los

Angeles, and live in Salt Lake City. But home to me is only an idea, one that has occurred to me elsewhere, in places that sometimes had no names, and only for a moment at a time. Standing in the bottom of an Idaho river gorge while a summer thunderstorm blew through, I watched a scrim of rain approach with sun behind it, felt the drape of it brush through me, and turned in time to watch it sweep on. A matter of seconds. Hiking in the red-rock landscape of southern Utah, I once picked up a flat chunk of sandstone and licked it. On my tongue, in my hand in an instant: rain come to the desert country. The taste and smell of blessing.

It is only in these moments I come close to knowing what I might mean if I spoke the word *home*. Remembering these moments and learning the stories that go with them is the closest I can come to dwelling there.

The air pulses before a dozen pairs of wings moving toward flight. The planet turns, the sun clears Grandeur Peak, and when I look again, the jogger is gone. I have belonged elsewhere, but today the quail and the story now suspended between two strangers will suffice. Memory is home of a kind, and there is no sadness or regret on these mornings at dawn. There is only this: the lake memory recedes and the neighborhood wakes up.

⁓

My father is the one carrying the briefcase. Dark brown, leather, but not a style that holds its own over time, acquiring character with age. Every unyielding corner is skinned, and dull metal shows through where the brass plating has worn off hinges and latches. The briefcase is an accessory I have not seen in the many years since he retired, but I could tell, walking beside him a few minutes ago, he felt rectified, having its weight, like a pendulum, moving him forward again. In the briefcase are notebooks and papers: the sum of my father's research to date. He is working to find our home.

The traffic behind us is a wavering eddy in the plate-glass doors of the library. People on foot and in cars nudge one another with a resigned impatience. It's the weekend of General Conference, the biannual meeting of the Church of Jesus Christ of Latter-day Saints. The perimeter curbs of the walled compound known as Temple Square are bumper-to-bumper with dust- and bug-encrusted motor homes, bearing license plates from dozens of states. Out-of-towners may park free at the meters; my father and I, in my car with Utah tags, gave up after twenty minutes of hunting and settled on a lot charging exorbitant rates a block away.

We'd taken the freeway into town, a gamble on any weekday, but especially today with so many tourists drifting from lane to lane, balking at the off-ramps, confused by Brigham Young's master plan: a city built and streets numbered according to a Cartesian coordinate system with the Mormon temple grounds at zero—north, south, east, and west—forming the intersection of the x and y axes. Inspired as the mathematical foundation of Brigham's city is, it has been undermined over the decades in the outlying suburbs where streets with names are predominant. Some people, it seems, still want to raise families on Elm and Roosevelt and Yale, not at 3246 South 2233 East. But ask anyone who lives on Elm Street to give you their coordinates—here or anywhere in Utah, and many places in Arizona and Idaho, places settled by Mormon pioneers—and chances are, they'll be able to do it. In the fiefdoms of the kingdom of Zion, having a map has always been optional when it comes to knowing where you are in relation to everyone else in the community—and the church.

Inside the high blank walls enclosing it, Temple Square is swarming, I know, with people taking the tours, snapping pictures, and recording miles of videotape. Friends usually ask to be taken here when they visit Salt Lake City. I'd much rather drive them to Great Salt Lake or Antelope Island to watch shorebirds, but we usually end up at Temple Square instead, standing in the acoustically splendid Tabernacle or outside by a memorial statue, listening to an inspired young guide tell us about the miracle of the seagulls: 1847. The first harvest is under way, eked from the desert of this strange, new, and inhospitable homeland; the grateful Mormon pioneers are in their fields; the sky goes black; the locusts descend; the grain, all that's between the pioneers and a harsh winter to come, is being devoured before their eyes. And then.

And then, the seagulls arrive by the thousands to devour the devourers. The harvest is spared. God's mercy is visited upon the devout and righteous. Amen. It's a wonderful story. But it's not my story, and miracle enough for me in this landlocked land with its ancient landlocked sea is to hear, waiting in the drive-thru at the dry cleaners, that broken and astonished cry of a gull, wheeling overhead.

The walls and spires of Temple Square. Crowds. Traffic. Morning sun. My father and I occupy the foreground of the reflected scene, a distinct, unmoving cipher in this composition. I am wearing a pair of shorts cut high enough on my thighs to telegraph that, no, I am not wearing temple garments; no, I am not one of you. I was not aware of dressing with conscious intent for this errand, but now I wonder. I've lived in Utah as a minority, as a non-Mormon, for many years, and though I carry the identity of an outsider in a deep recess, I know a part of me is constantly registering and reacting to the largely homogenous makeup of this community and its dominant faith.

But it's also true that I've grown into an adult woman here, and that the signifiers I chose pointedly when I was much younger and insecure and obnoxious—my sophisticated (or raunchy) clothing, my expletives, my cigarettes—are no longer consciously charged with meaning. I imagine those wooden platform shoes I cast from my closet in 1979 holding in colloidal suspension for a while along with the rest of the flotsam from those early years in this state. Then they, along with the Nik-Nik shirts and the Baggies of used press-on fingernails, and the Captain and Tenille albums, and the crushed butts settled into the silt together, trapped by the hardening strata of sedimentation in this formation I call my life.

"Well," my father says.

"Yes," I say.

He's anxious to get inside the library, the nerve center of the LDS Church's vast genealogical record holdings. My father has lost a few inches to age, some of his imposing height, a good bit of girth around his waist. The changes in his legs and arms still startle me the most. His limbs have thinned; the muscle tone is gone. The flesh gathers around the knobs of joints like a bad job of papier-mâché. He is wearing trousers and one of his nicer shirts, but I had to suggest the ensemble. He was an artist by profession and is still by avocation, but in his later years especially, any sense of color and pattern involving his own clothing is no longer apparent. Or maybe it's just that seventy-three years of living have provided him more interesting and important things to think about than his wardrobe.

He has shaved this morning—sometimes he doesn't for days now—and his hair is clean. He's wearing Old Spice aftershave, which my mother reports he does only when he sets out for the Mormon library back in Tucson. She suspects he flirts with the women working there. I've seen him flirt; it made me smile, actually, this glimpse at what my father may have been as a younger man—and I've seen these women, too, who made me think, *Dowdy. Unimaginative. My mother has nothing to worry about.*

This morning my father has even polished the smudges of oil and flakes of dandruff from the lenses of his glasses, and this particular proof of his meticulous grooming is the reason I keep my sunglasses on, not the hot golden glare of sun just now cresting the peaks of the east bench. I keep my sunglasses on because I've been told enough times now to believe it true that whatever I'm thinking or feeling shows in my eyes, clear as the price of dime-store goods rung up on an old-fashioned cash register. I keep my sunglasses on because I am silly and sentimental and I am crying a little. I do not want my father to know that I know he is old.

He doesn't seem nervous, which surprises me: this imposing building we're about to enter; the staggering amount of information inside it; the fact that we may be the only two people entering who don't belong to the Church of Jesus Christ of Latter-day Saints. Genealogical research is an important pursuit for faithful Mormons, believing as they do that departed family members who didn't have the opportunity to accept the LDS faith in life may do so in the afterlife through a ritual called Baptism for the Dead. I'm not privy to the specifics, of course, but when I explained the general concept to my mother, she was horrified. There she'd be, all settled nicely in Paradise—until, that is, the day a diligent Mormon temple worker came along to effect her compulsory relocation.

My father and I both know, of course, that the church doesn't require researchers using the Family History Library to believe its theology—or any theology for that matter. Between us, my father and I have been counted at one time or another in the congregations of a half-dozen Christian denominations. But maybe what matters is that we share a belief with everyone here that we deserve to know where we came from, who we came from. My father believes this, anyway. Until just recently I haven't had a reason to think much about it.

Dad's preoccupation with genealogy came late, after his retirement and long after most of the relatives who might have helped his investigations were already dead: both sets of grandparents and great-grandparents, of course, his parents, his only sister. My father and mother left Missouri in 1956 and moved west with millions of other families following postwar jobs. New Mexico, then California. One of my favorite pictures of my family was taken in Albuquerque in 1959. My father is wearing a bolo tie and cowboy boots—gone native, you might say. I wonder what his father, the stern Saint Louis banker, might have had to say about his son's getup. But my father's smile in this photograph is radioactive. Here in this dusty desert town he's escaped his father's censure at last, and looking at my father's smile I understand something about how quickly and gladly my parents drifted away from our Midwest relations; about how many things a thousand miles can change; about why I never had occasion to meet any of my father's people.

I never met any of them, but here I sit at a workstation in the Family History Library with my father ready to spend hours scouring books for clues about family members even more distant and obscure than the dead and buried in Illinois and Missouri; following the faint traces of a 150-year-old paper trail. Before now, I've just listened to my father talk about his research on the telephone. He has to repeat what he tells me two or three times before it sinks in. And what I've learned mostly is that genealogy makes little sense to someone like me, growing up in a reclusive nuclear family of five. That is to say, I can't keep relations straight beyond first cousins—a liability of some proportion, considering the two extended families I married into: my first husband was Mormon; the second is Catholic.

Whenever we get together at Christmas my mother repeats the story about her father, Edmund, who sired an illegitimate daughter, P., by his brother Oscar's girlfriend, G., making P. her sister *and* her cousin both. It's as good an occasion as any, I suppose, for discussing irregular nativities—and while my mother's account is not exactly inspiring, it's at least as fraught as the one in the New Testament.

My husband's grasp of kinship being considerably greater than my own—his extended Italian family, the offspring of seven hardy brothers and one enduring sister, is large enough now to fill a modest motel—I asked him one day to explain *my* relationship to P. He patiently sketched a diagram and announced that P. was my first cousin once removed—or would have been if my grandfather had married P.'s poor mother. Since he hadn't she was just a person, legally speaking. So much for family values. Needless to say, this complication helps explain my mother's scorn of nostalgia in general and genealogy in particular. The good old days? Spare me, she says.

In spite of my mother's disdain, my father has become a zealous genealogical researcher. From his briefcase he extracts a notebook, and in the notebook finds the page on which he's summarized the ties in his branch of the family that almost, but don't quite, bind. Names and dates are printed in pencil with that elegant precision I admired as a child, watching him work at his drafting table, and admire still on the packages he mails to me at Christmas. Names and dates shaping—not a tree so much as his family vine, creeping across the page and down, and down, grafting other names and other dates to it as it spreads. But on one portion, it seems a blight has struck, stripping woody stalks bare of leaves. This is where information belongs that my father believes he's closing in on; today, we'll search passenger manifests, trying to find a name we recognize among thousands of immigrants who sailed from Germany for America between 1850 and 1870.

Immigration officers employed in the nineteenth century were not particularly adept or conscientious, it seems, at transcribing foreign names into English, even when the country of origin happened to use an alphabet similar to that of the United States. Let's say you're a member of the Wochele family. You're German—well, where you're from isn't really Germany at the moment, just a loose confederation of states that have been repeatedly conquered and offered as a bargaining chip in the grand game of empire building for the past couple of centuries. None of that matters, of course, in this new country where you've been standing in line for a very long time carrying everything you own after a miserable voyage across the Atlantic that you and your family were lucky to survive. When it's your turn, somebody asks, What's your name? "Vocka-lay," you say, so the man to whom you're speaking writes down Fauklee—or some other phonetic variant he thinks looks right—and that's just the beginning of the mistakes that proliferate in document after document, year after year. Until, that is, you or your children learn English well enough to put a stop to them.

Something much worse happened to my father's grandfather Jacob, though, involving not the neglect of a stranger, but rather a neglect in which he and all his heirs since were complicit.

The first time I can remember expressing a whit of curiosity about our background was in the third grade; some thirty years passed before it happened again. Probably we were studying geography when the epiphany came: not everyone in the world looked liked me and my very WASPish private-school classmates. I asked my mother about our nationality. On my father's side, she said, I was German; on her side, I was English, Irish, and Scottish—something called a Duke's mixture; a lineage sounding much like that afflicting mongrel dogs. What was worse, as I came to understand thanks to sixth-grade science, was that genetic code was a story my body would tell, whether I liked it not: my skin would always be pale and prone to freckling; my hair, blond; my eyes, green. Like her, my mother said, my Scottish blood wouldn't permit me to discard a leftover unless it had been in the refrigerator for at least a week, but thanks to my father's DNA, the refrigerator itself would be a monument to organization and efficiency.

By the time I got around to asking questions about our family again, all my grandparents were dead, the Duke's mixture and the German sets, and buried with them was many a fascinating story—not the least of which, I'm sure, concerned the daughter P. and the unfortunate mother, G.

My mother chose to shield me for many years from the extent of her contempt for her father, for both of her parents, for the farce of their good Christian lives. Now I realize that in suppressing the truth of their ignorance, their small-town bigotry, and their sordid intrigues, my mother made secrets of family truths. I needed to know those truths as much as she needed to tell them. Instead I trusted the appearances I was shown— *Everything is A-OK with us*—and by the time I understood what interesting questions hadn't been asked, it was too late.

My father's past was also unexplored territory. I remember him as busy: busy during the week making a living, busy on weekends, too, landscaping a berm in the front yard, building a utility trailer in the garage. Maybe ruminations about his personal history were muted by worries about a thirty-year home mortgage. Maybe he just assumed that his young children wouldn't be interested in his boyhood memories.

Or maybe he just couldn't compete with the television.

My evidence is strictly anecdotal, of course, but I'm inclined to agree with sociologists who blame electronic interference for disturbances in familial bonding. If we hadn't been able to afford that RCA, would I be able to tell you more today about my grandfather and grandmother than their favorite TV shows—the Saturday-night fights and *As the World Turns?* I know one thing: I couldn't tell you the date either of them were born or died if you held a gun to my head.

Failings: mine and my family's and my culture's. I acknowledge them, yet I still hold more distant ancestors to some special standard of performance. I go right on romanticizing the past, nursing fond fantasies of immigrant families to America who sat on front stoops and parlor settees every evening telling stories about the Old Country. For whatever reason, though, my father's father, or his father, never spoke about origin or homeland.

Silences—or soaps and sitcoms—where stories should be. How easily a family comes apart.

One afternoon after the children have been raised, the mortgage satisfied, and the last of the neckties retired to a shoe box in the way-back of a closet, a question occurs to my father that he doesn't recall ever asking: where are we from? His search begins with my great-grandfather's death certificate: *Jacob Seesler. Date of birth: August 26, 1852. Birthplace of Deceased: Germany. Date of death: June 5, 1923. Birthplace of father: Germany. Birthplace of mother: Germany. Name of father: Unknown. Maiden name of mother: Unknown.* Signed by my grandfather John Henry.

⚘

Frances, wife of John Henry, preceded him in death by twenty-six years. She was, by all accounts, a sweet and loving woman who, thirty years into her marriage to John, was a sad and lonely one as well. I never knew either of them, but I've wondered about them often; wondered what in the world my grandmother would have thought about what my father discovered after my grandfather died.

Maybe John was still trying to prove that deprivation was a virtue. Maybe, just as he'd saved and totted the kisses and kind words he might have spent on his wife while she lived, he was still withholding things, things he could see mounting up every day. Respectable banker that he was, maybe John thought loneliness was something that could be remedied or managed, like an account, with this continued saving and good record-keeping.

Or maybe after enough years without Frances, John's stubbornness and grief had finally become madness.

Here is what my father found when he flew from Los Angeles to Saint Louis to close up John Henry's house:

newspapers, stacked to the ceiling in every room;

hundreds upon hundreds of Chiquita-banana seals plastering the kitchen counters;

dozens and dozens of empty Coca Cola bottles;

packages of used razor blades, back in their waxy envelopes and banded with elastics like little aluminum love letters, each blade's life cycle recorded: the date it was put into service and the date it grew too dull;

a flashlight that wouldn't work until my father unscrewed the end and removed the sales receipt for the batteries folded inside that was breaking the circuit;

markers for bad debts John Henry couldn't collect;

valentines from lady admirers he wouldn't marry;

a German hymnbook, embossed and gilded on the cover:

Johann Heinrich Seesler

1900

and in a drawer, a wooden box. And in the box, two dreidels. One brass. One clay.

⁓

We forget, those of us spinning our twenty-first-century web of global communication, how easy it once was, and still is really, to lose people. I might take a certain comfort in knowing that I reside for various purposes, most of them capitalist and some of them nefarious, in hundreds of data banks. But those bytes that are me, are not me, of course. They may tell you I bought Maytag appliances in 1983 and in all this time have replaced only a single drive belt in the washer. But they will tell you nothing about the pleasure I take, pressing my face into a load of sheets just pulled from the dryer, and the memory it elicits of helping my mother gather wash from a clothesline on the first spring day in the Rocky Mountains. In the end there were John Henry's bizarre collections and mysterious keepsakes, but no explanations to accompany them.

This is the difference, of course, between what data and metaphor, or fact and story, have to offer. I was startled in my adulthood to realize how little my family valued either. But of the two, story was what I missed most growing up.

For a long time I thought we were just a family of poor listeners. When we found ourselves together on the patio or in the living room there was a provisional feeling to the gathering. We assembled, but only until some other, more pressing activity occurred to us. It was not unusual, a few minutes into the start of a story one of us was telling, for someone to get up and leave the room. My mother, for a tissue; one of my sisters, for an emery board or a Q-tip; me, for a Popsicle; my father, to let a dog out or in. If the storyteller looked up suddenly or stopped speaking, the departing member would still leave, but would shout, very politely, from the bathroom or the kitchen or the porch, "Go on, go on! I'm listening!"

It was later, when I was older, that I began to suspect no one in my family really knew *how* to tell a story anymore, much less endure one poorly told. Certainly our wayward, prodigal habits didn't improve the situation. All those goings and comings necessitated backtracking and tedious digressions. Every story was consequently twice as long as it needed to be and nearly impossible to follow. We interrupted to contribute asides or off-color jokes. Before long someone would start paring toenails or flipping through the *TV Guide*. Or the phone might ring, and everyone would volunteer to answer it at once. Or my father might say, "For Pete's sake, could you *please* get to the point?"

What I've started to believe is that story has been missing from our family for some time. Its absence is patently manifest in those *Unknowns* on my great-grandfather's death certificate, in the half knowns of my mother's past, in my father's yearning for a narrative coherence to his life. I can feel it, too, the missing story, every time I sit down at the keyboard or lift a pen.

Somewhere along the way we lost story, and then lost it again and again, losing as well the pleasure of hearing our own voice or someone else's celebrate the natural rhythms and cadences of language; the confidence of telling well, of knowing how to winnow the details of a narrative until the chaff splits away and nothing but the mature, wholesome grain of scene and summary remains; the wonder of making meaning; the exquisite taste of our own native tongue.

I know a few things: As a child my mother lived through a devastating tornado, but the havoc that twister wrought was nothing permanent, unlike the havoc wrought upon her spirit, growing up with the kind of secrets a small-minded and cruel Illinois mining town wants to make and keep. My father was born with the soul of an artist to a soulless banker who hid paper sacks of newly minted silver dollars so cleverly about the house it took my father days to find them all after my grandfather was dead.

If my family's plight is any indication, story is an indispensable communal act of affirmation. But it is also an act critical to human individuation, story being that against which each of us gauges who we are and are not; where we belong and from what and whom we must depart.

There are too many stories that my family has forgotten and lost, that we never learned how—or refused—to tell. The few stories that we remember are not enough to hold us together, not enough to help us stand alone.

～

Lacking fact and missing story, we're nevertheless a family of champion theorists, ready to speculate on or to debate any topic at a moment's notice, *with authority*. Are paper or plastic grocery bags worse for the environment? (So you haven't heard, eh? The timber and chemical industries have conspired to drive liberal environmentalists crazy.) Did Jackie know John was fooling around with Marilyn? (Don't be ridiculous.) And, a perennial favorite, What *are* those UFOs up to anyway?

My father's operating theory about his family mystery, his grandfather's origin, is based on the slightest of clues, half-recollected conversations, and a good measure of guessing. He suspects that his father's grandfather, Herr Unknown, had traveled to the United States first, then sent for his wife, Frau Unknown, and their son, Jacob, back in Germany. Jacob, he thinks, was orphaned on board the ship from Europe, and this makes a certain sense. A very young child arrives in a strange country and, having no idea where his surviving parent might be waiting, is placed in an orphanage, an institution of the sort that just happened to exist in Saint Louis for children of German descent and that my father just happens to remember existing because his father would take him along when the orphanage held its annual Fourth of July picnic—visits that were never explained.

Also not explained is this: In the 1900 census taken in Saint Louis, Jacob's last name was reported as Sessler by the enumerator and his place of origin, Prussia. Ten years later the last name appears as Seesler, but shows his origin as Württemberg, a German state. Aside from the puzzling discrepancies, these documents suggest that my father's grandfather did have information more specific about his home than his father's vague answer "Germany" on Jacob's death certificate would indicate.

Prussia or Württemberg? It could very well have been the former and then, ten years later, the latter. A world-history text shows a series of maps of what was probably my great-grandfather's homeland, an amoebic expansion and contraction of Württemberg's boundaries reflecting decade upon decade of revolt, war, conquest, and reconciliation: now an independent kingdom, now Prussia, now France, now South Germany. Two hundred years of takings and leavings that some believe etched a destructive longing for national identity deep into the German psyche.

But none of this speculation does my father one bit of good. Without a hometown, a village, he cannot track down either the civil or church records in Germany that might tell him the names and vital statistics of his great-grandparents; how and when and on what ship Jacob and his family set off for America, what port of entry that ship might have taken: New York? Galveston? New Orleans? The trail and the graves are cold.

There is, though, this one small tantalizing detail: My mother has maintained for years that my father's mother, Frances, told her that Jacob had a brother. Every time she mentions it, my father is furious. Hearsay, he scoffs. And besides, why would Frances tell her daughter-in-law something this significant and refrain from sharing it with her own son?

I have my theories about that, about a currency women exchange only among themselves: stories of the strange and silent men they love. Imagine you're Jacob. Imagine you're Jacob on the day they tell you that a nice family has adopted your brother and that you'll never see him again. Now imagine you're Jacob on the day they tell you that they want to find a nice family for you, too. But a nice, *Christian* family—that would be much easier.

Though I can't endorse my mother's variation on my father's family mystery without causing an argument, I have resolved to remember it: You're a young boy. You and your even younger brother, Jacob, arrive in this country in straits more dire than most. Your mother died on board the ship from Bremen, and you do not know where your father is waiting. New York? But that place they tell you is too large for small boys and too far away. When the immigration officer asks, What is your name? all you can think about is your mother, how you tried to say Kaddish, the mourner's prayer, for her when they slid her into the ocean, but you couldn't remember the words. Now you can't remember your name. "Seize-ler," you say at last. Yes, that's it. The man writes Sessler or Cessler or Seizler or Seesler. Then he asks, Where did you come from? You look at your brother; your brother looks at you. It's been a long, long trip. You're both very young. And you've never felt this alone.

ᡈ

Seated in the Family History Library next to my father, I bend over the columns of names before my eyes: page after page, boatload after boatload of dead hopes, scanning for possibilities. My mind keeps snapping in and out of focus. I find myself tempted for once to side with my mother who finds this genealogical exercise of my father's futile at best, a waste of time, and boring in the extreme. Not long ago, just to annoy him I think, she responded to a magazine ad that promised, for $12.95 and a few vital statistics, to return a complete genealogical record of her family. We learned by mail a few weeks later that, thanks to her chromosomes, we were direct descendants of Sir Francis Drake.

Maybe today my father and I will get lucky. Maybe we'll find *Seesler, Gerta* (or Margita or Elsa), *mother, with son, Jacob 5, husband, Otto* (or Sigfried or Adolf) who traveled from village x to embark from port y on a certain day, bound for city z, U.S.A. But even if we are lucky, even if we do find this critical clue to our origins, neither my father nor I will be one step closer to understanding the lives that came before us. We will have facts, yes, but still lack the story that would speak our belonging to it. I wonder after all this work and in spite of his unassailable hope if a part of me will refuse that cure my father's seeking, and won't always be, in some resolute way, homeless.

ю

If the Pleistocene camel grazing on the hillside where my hot tub is now had strolled the bank of Lake Bonneville northward for about three miles, it would have found itself in a canyon we now call Red Butte. For the moment there are just fourteen of us listening; fourteen of us who have rushed through or skipped dinner to make the six o'clock orientation lecture at the Red Butte arboretum in which Dick Hildreth is explaining the world—or, at least, explaining his part of it.

Dick moved to Salt Lake City in 1977, and here met, almost immediately, a vision that would shape the next twenty years of his life. What he saw were 150 acres of property above old Fort Douglas: an arid, sloping tract of land that nobody much wanted anymore—half of it scrabble and weeds, a few dirt-bike tracks, and an abandoned quarry; the other half, nothing but rock and soil, striated and pocked with craters from years of munitions testing and marksmanship exercises. But all of it, in all of its unloveliness, looked like an opportunity to Dick. People probably thought he was nuts. The Western sociopolitical ethic of why-save-it-when-we-can-pave-it still had more proponents than opponents in Utah two decades ago. This, they undoubtedly told him, is what a place looks like *after* opportunity's been wrung out of it.

A quarter century later, fifty acres of Dick's original vision for this property have become the Red Butte Garden and Arboretum. But higher up Red Butte Canyon, Dick had discovered something even more exciting in '77. He points to the aerial photograph of the area. There is Fort Douglas, its boundaries and networks of paved roads still clear, but contained now (like an organism captured inside the cell wall of another, more aggressive organism) by the massive complex of University of Utah development. Above the old fort is a thin black line encircling a fifty-four-hundred-acre tract of U.S. Forest Service land, designated now as the Red Butte Research Natural Area. The reddish Navajo Wingate sandstone that characterizes this wedge of land and explains its name is bracketed, as Dick indicates, by lighter limestone formations to the north and south.

Unlike the other canyons close to the large population center of Salt Lake City, Red Butte Canyon had been closed to grazing since 1905, meaning, as Dick knew, that this foothill-woodland ecosystem and the riparian corridor running through it was as close as anyone was likely to get to seeing a Wasatch Front canyon—or any Great Basin watershed for that matter—in its undisturbed state.

Red Butte RNA isn't fenced in its entirety—something that Dick, among others, would very much like to change. Aside from the impact that hikers and mountain bikers have on the area, the worst fear for the RNA is fire. It's a well-grounded fear: two people roasting marshmallows here not long ago started a small brushfire, and a blaze four years ago destroyed several acres. Scientists, like Dick, have made the best of that larger fire, flocking to study how the processes of recovery proceed. Permits are required in the area, but this isn't preventing users from entering it via adjacent canyons and ridges. Direct road access to Red Butte is blocked, however, by a sturdy gate with an even sturdier-looking padlock.

I had been to the mouth of the canyon several years earlier with an environmental studies class; had stood outside this gate in this grove of mature big-tooth maples, survivors that had somehow escaped decades of chain saws and brushfires. It was fall then; the maples had already been stung by several early frosts, and the first of blood-red leaves had fallen to the ground. Now the late afternoon sun filtered through June-green leaves.

There: where I'd hung on the chain-link, wanting in, while Ty, my professor, told of wonders beyond, a place a few decades closer to the adjective *pristine* where there might be found an isolated and as yet undiscovered stand of scrub oak, a rare hybrid species that had survived some sixteen thousand years. Such a hybrid had in fact been found in the Oquirrh Mountains a few miles southwest of here. Back then Lake Bonneville dominated the basin, shaping its landscape in profound ways; back then the lake reached into this canyon to the 5,150-foot level. It would have lapped this very gate—if gates, that is, which had yet to be invented, had been necessary.

Dick opens the padlock and waves our small caravan of cars through. The beneficent smile on his face makes me think of Oz at the threshold of the Emerald City. I drive by and wave back. Dick hasn't missed many meals lately, but he's no slouch: his legs, like all of our legs, are still the winter-pale color of canned albacore tuna, but his calves have been sculpted by miles of walks through wild landscapes all over the world. His face is weathered, burnished, framed by bushy unkempt hair, more gray now than blond. In the rearview mirror I see Dick climb back in the van that Trinka, the Nature Conservancy coordinator, is driving. Trinka has brought her son, Evan, along. Evan is ten. Back at the arboretum during the orientation to our nature hike, he'd snuggled close against Trinka's side. She'd rubbed the back of his T-shirt. Evan's bright and a little shy, but eager enough to talk to me, I'd already learned, with a bit of prompting.

Not long after the hike up the canyon begins, Dick's two botanical passions become evident: weeds and scrub oak. He's been on every continent, it seems, studying species of the latter; the former is the excuse for most of our stops. But a half mile in Dick pauses to show us a specimen of scrub oak, and I'm probably to blame for Dick's ten-minute narrative that I can only hope everyone else finds as interesting as I do.

This scrub oak, though not the ancient hybrid I'd hoped for, *is* different in appearance from the stands of gambel oak in my yard: the leaves are a deeper green with a sharp waxy sheen, closer, as Dick points out, to what we think of when we think of holiday holly. He tells us about the years of work researchers (like his beloved mentor, "Doc" Walter Cottam) devoted to finding an answer to the mystery of the Oquirrh specimen, no doubt influencing the genetic history of the plant before us: dusting oaks for pollen samples every spring, shipping the samples to one another's laboratories; cross-hybridizing this oak and that oak; producing generation upon generation of acorns; documenting the specific characteristics of each hybrid of acorn at each stage of its growth; theorizing endlessly—the ad hoc team of researchers trying to explain how a plant, which is wind-pollinated under the best of circumstances in a 250-mile radius, exists near Great Salt Lake, four hundred miles from Washington County, Utah, the only other place in the state where it's found.

Dick tells us how the team finally arrived at the conclusion that this isolated specimen in the Oquirrhs was in fact vestigial—not a transplant at all, but a living fossil from the time thousands of years before when the climate of Salt Lake valley was the same as the climate of Washington County.

I'm thinking, as Dick's story ends, about my father, about the astounding power of our obsessions, about people working alone all over the world because something will not leave them alone—nor would they it, probably, given the chance. They work on, though the only reward for whatever their obsession may be is likely hours, weeks, sometimes years, of unrelieved loneliness and a good chance of ridicule—or absolute obscurity.

I'm thinking, too, about voyages: voyages of pollen and people; about wind-borne and seaborne voyages; and about voyages of time. I'm thinking how time carries us onward, changes us, and changes the places we once called home. I'm thinking how a memory of home, or Eden, can make us exiles forever—or how (as the expression on Evan's face suggests) we might set aside our memories and our obsessions long enough to recognize and honor our present Edens.

Dick pulls us off the trail to tell us about a plant every few hundred yards. Unfortunately many of them in Red Butte Canyon are invasive weeds—yellow clover, thistle, goat's beard, butter 'n' eggs, dyer's wode—and the weed stories Dick tells are chiefly about means and measures of controlling and eradicating them. Some of the plants are edible, though, and Dick passes around specimens of these for us to smell or to taste—a twig of Ludwig's sagebrush, a sprig of salsify, an umbel of wild parsley, a sorrel leaf, a long taper topped by the purple blossom of a wild onion.

A little farther on we pass a box-elder tree. Box elders, like all maples, have separate sexes, and the female gender of this tree, which exudes a pheromone irresistible to box-elder bugs, is nobody's favorite in Salt Lake City suburbs. But Dick has that exultant look on his face that tells us we're about to have our prejudices massaged. He plucks a twig from the box elder, laden with what he calls its fruit: the paired wings of seeds, called samara. Evan holds a single set of wings aloft and releases it. Even at this immature stage, the samara flies well, spinning in the warm canyon breeze, "like helicopter wings," says Evan.

We've climbed to about six thousand feet now and are starting to see old cottonwoods with thick gnarled trunks; with tap roots we cannot see sunk deep, perhaps a hundred feet into the earth along the streambed. Farther down the canyon, the cottonwoods are much smaller and all of the same age, representing the second growth that Dick surmises began after the lime kilns at the base of the canyon shut down, and the harvesting of logs needed to fire them stopped. There are small stands of western water birch with cinnamon-red bark; trees I've never seen for all the hiking and fishing I've done along Wasatch canyon streams. There are thick walls of willows, the thickets of female willows most obvious, swathed now in seed-bearing cotton.

And there is, at the place where our group reluctantly turns around for the return trip, a lone curl-leafed mountain mahogany. It is the closest we can get to one on this hike, but we can see others from where we stand, punctuating the ridge high above, trimmed into lollipop shapes by deer and elk over many winters of foraging. It is not an impressive tree, this particular mahogany, hugging a craggy, brittle cheek of sandstone. I ask Dick if this specimen is stressed—*stressed* being a word I choose purposely, thinking of it as a neutral term not likely to offend our guide: Dick has been promoting the advent of this barely-a-shrub tree since we started our hike, and now it's obvious just how attached he has become to it.

"Oh, no," he tells me, "I think it's grown at least four inches already this year. It's doing very well here as inhospitable as this spot looks."

Dick sends Evan up the slope for a leaf: "Just one, though, Evan. A big one." A big one as it turns out is a little more than an inch long. The leaf is covered with a fine down—"It's furry!" Evan says—and its edges have begun to curl. This mahogany, like other plants we've seen in this dry canyon, has sophisticated survival mechanisms. When the near-drought months of a Utah summer set in, the leaves of the mahogany roll under to reduce exposure to sun and, hence, surface evaporation.

On the way back to the cars, Evan and I end up walking together behind everyone else. I'm never sure how these things happen; when I find Evan beside me, I have no conscious memory of how, exactly, our pairing came to be. I do know that I love being around children, and that their company has never been something I had to seek, or something I had to earn, like a favor. Their presence in my life is always allowed somehow, especially when I need it most, and although I've never felt in church or in prayer what I've heard others call a state of grace, this being with children feels the way I've always thought simple grace must feel.

"What's the biggest animal you've even seen outside of a zoo?" I ask him.

"A cougar," Evan says.

"Wow," I say, "you're a lucky guy. They call cougars the Ghosts of the Rockies, you know, so few people ever see one."

Evan tells me then about that day in Arches National Park, how he and his cousin Scotty saw the cougar; how no one believed them; how later that day, walking with his mother, the cougar had crossed their paths again.

Another animal story follows, about another camping trip, about the day he'd been bitten by a rattlesnake.

"A rattlesnake? Were you sick?" I ask. "Did you have to take an anti-toxin?"

"Nah," Evan says, "we're Christian Scientist."

"So there were prayers then. Were you scared?"

"No. My dad was there. He was so, you know, calm. And he's not even a Christian Scientist. But the next morning after the healing, when I woke up, there was nothing but these two little scars on my shin." Evan looks up. "I don't really tell this story to people. They think it's weird. They say, 'No way. You're making it up.' "

"Well, what I think is there's plenty we don't understand. Miracles and mysteries all over the place. Sometimes we have a lot of trouble understanding other people's beliefs. Sometimes we're afraid of what we don't understand and fear makes us angry. I wouldn't worry about it too much. I'm really glad you told *me* this story, though."

Trinka drops back from the pack of hikers and falls into step with Evan and me. I tell the two of them about having spotted what may be a pair of peregrine falcons near our home, not far from here. Evan begins explaining raptors' wings, the differences between eagles and hawks and falcons; how some wings are perfect for soaring; how others are designed for steep plummets from the skies.

"Here," I say, handing him my notebook, "maybe you could draw them for me, so I'll have a reference next time." Evan takes my pen and begins to sketch. I smile up at Trinka who mouths the words "Thank you." At first I'm embarrassed, wanting to explain to Trinka that this is no indulgence of a tiresome child, that this is about the joy each of us deserves to feel when called in any given moment, to be either a good teacher or a good disciple. But Trinka looks down then, studying Evan's drawings with the same intensity and interest with which he is making them, and I know that there is no misunderstanding between us.

"I like animals," Evan says, handing my notebook over. "And I like to write stuff, too, like you, like those guys in *National Geographic*."

I smile at Evan. "Good," I say. "You're very articulate, you know. I bet you're a good writer."

Trinka smiles and throws her arm around her son's shoulder and I watch them walk, linked that way, back to the van. Dick, the Wizard of Red Butte, turns to watch the last of the day's light leave the ridge top and then follows.

⌇

"I've lived twenty-seven different places," my mother says. "Here, I made a list." When she passes the sheet of paper to me, her hand trembles a little. She doesn't sleep well anymore, not since she quit drinking highballs before bed. Often it's four or five in the morning, long after the all-night radio talk shows are over, before the insomnia releases its grip. She won't see a doctor, refuses to take medication. What she does do is work crossword puzzles and make lists. Menus and grocery lists. Lists of old songs she remembers and their lyrics: *Oh, the moon shines bright on Charlie Chaplin; his shoes are crackin', they need a blackin'. And his little green pants, they need a patchin' where he's been scratchin' mosquito bites.* Lists of peculiar words that had currency during her Midwestern upbringing: "loblolly," the gruel of mud you made between your toes after rain soaked the farmyard; "grimple," the family debris that collects at the bottoms of closets, on end tables, and in the kitchen junk drawer. Lists of things to do the next day: what to defrost for dinner, what errands she'll ask my father to run. Lists of questions and topics for our next telephone conversation. She's been at work on this list, places she's lived, for more than one sleepless night: the main entries are in pencil; the addenda are cramped above or below in blue ink or black.

At the bottom of the list is the house we're sitting in on Old Spanish

Trail in Tucson, the last house my parents will ever own together and for them one of the unhappiest. Here in this living room is where I learned the potency of my mother's hatred for her parents who themselves had come west, moved to Arizona from Illinois in the sixties. My grandfather Edmund had developed emphysema from too many years in the coal mines, and it was thought the dry desert air would do him some good. It didn't, much, but kept him alive a decade or two longer than might otherwise have been expected.

When my grandfather's health began its final decline, my father and mother moved their empty nest in California to Arizona to be near her parents—the worst decision possible from my mother's point of view, but inevitable all the same. In short order my grandparents bought a condominium less than a mile from them. And here on Old Spanish Trail, the resentments and miseries that my mother, like my father, had meant to escape when they left the Midwest were reanimated, reenacted on a daily basis until, after too many years for my mother's own good anyway, my grandparents passed away.

Now, it is my parents who have grown old—and like many elderly adults, grown ever more preoccupied with their losses and disappointments. Now it is their health, mental and physical, in slow, inexorable decline. My father walks the dog every morning and retrieves the mail when it comes. Every few weeks, the meals my mother has prepared ahead and frozen run out, and the two of them go shopping. Otherwise they sit in this living room with their memories of the dead.

About these last years in their last house my mother has developed a peculiar hypothesis, a sort of unification theory of their unhappiness. She believes that the historic trail under their street is somehow saturated with the suffering caused by cruelties perpetrated on and near it, and that these crimes against humankind create a miasma of despair that permeates contemporary dwellings and spirits like theirs.

Never mind that the trail wasn't one frequented by Catholic priests or U.S. Cavalry companies for the purpose of brutalizing and subjugating native peoples (as my mother's conflated version of Western history would imply), but was used predominantly by traveling clerics, explorers, settlers, and traders (granted, a few of them were Indian slave traders), and then for only twenty or so years—hardly a significant span given the millennia during which man practiced inhumanity to man. Never mind—as I explained to my mother recently—that the Old Spanish Trail from Santa Fe to Los Angeles didn't come anywhere *near* Tucson, Arizona.

Never mind, that is, the facts.

But if I look behind the absurd assertion that the past can punch a hole through time and ruin people's retirement years, there is metaphoric sense in what my mother is saying. She is saying that loss and grief can accrue over time, poisoning the land and its inhabitants; that places and people can suffer the toxic emanation of troubled history.

My mother probably still has a copy of *Ishi: In Two Worlds,* one of the first adult books she ever encouraged me to read. It is the story of a Yada Indian, the last survivor of his tribe, "the last wild Indian in North America," according to the cover, who wandered out of the hills in northern California in 1911.

The adjective *wild* in this blurb is something we notice immediately at the close of the twentieth century, revealing an insensitivity we profess to no longer tolerate, as well as the kind of binary opposition only an oppressor can create: what exactly is a tame Indian? One of the photographs in the book, the first taken of Ishi soon after he "surrendered," brings this question into high relief. Emaciated, hollow eyed, barefoot; dressed in a white man's overcoat, Ishi is slumped by a grief that at fourteen I couldn't begin to fathom—and know I never will. But I understood this much about Ishi, and this not until twenty-five years after I read the book: he was a man robbed of his context—family, tribe, lands. The emptiness his body evoked in that photograph, that carapace of what he was that day, is what human beings become when they are separated from their stories.

I have only to look at those blanks in my father's genealogy or at this list of my mother's two dozen homes to understand that history near and distant presses upon us all in ways we may barely apprehend. So does missing history, especially when the history that's missing is our own.

Here are some of those twenty-seven places my mother has lived: In West Frankfort, Illinois, on Oak Street, Fourth Street, and Fifth Street. On a farm outside of West Frankfort where the twister hit. From the farm, back to an apartment in town where she lived with the man she married in the aisle of a drugstore in Paducah, Kentucky. She was just sixteen. After the separation, to the Millers' in Saint Louis where she worked as a housekeeper and nanny; then to the Vizgards'; then to Pinkie's boardinghouse after the divorce where, my mother says, she finally "had a room with a door on it." (My grandmother never liked doors, the story goes, and took most of them down as her first act of occupation everywhere she lived.)

After their wedding, my mother and father moved to Winona, to Wyoming Street, to Cliff Drive. To Idlewilde Lane in Albuquerque where my mother was hospitalized with a nervous breakdown and didn't come home for weeks. In the meantime Dr. Langner, the shrink, put the doors back up, you could say, by inviting my grandmother *not* to move to New Mexico as she planned and to otherwise stay the hell out of my mother's life. To Plummer Street, to Swinton Avenue, to Odessa in California where a Big One found us. After the earthquake, to Denver, and finally to Tucson.

"Only one more move to make." My mother smiles. "R.I.P."

It has never occurred to me before this moment, how profound her sense of homelessness must be; why, given the ruptures and disruptions in her past, she might feel a kinship with those as displaced and abused as Ishi, and why she might appropriate a grief that is not her own. I think of my father, then, working with little more than sherds of his past, intent on reassembling the vessel of his family's history. And suddenly I see an irony in my parents' relationship I'd never noticed, in the opposing positions they hold: my father, whose home has been misplaced by history; my mother, whose history was cursed with too many homes.

In their individual histories of loss, though, is where my parents intersect with one another. It is also where, in the way my mother suggests, they intersect with the whole of human history that to a great extent is the history of the loss of home. Some loss is chosen; some is not, but either way, desire for home is aroused. And from this perspective, my motel mind can be viewed as a legacy of twenty millennia or more of human migration: movement driven by glaciers; movement driven by greed. Movement sanctioned or forbidden, imposed or voluntary. Immigrants, emigrants; expatriates and defectors; nomads and tourists. For every movement toward or away, whatever its motivation, something is inevitably left behind, something irrevocably altered, and something—a longing, a wanting—created.

In my parents' case, of course, the decision to leave all they'd known, everything familiar—streets, friends, the vernacular, the weather—was a loss chosen. But loss was not what my parents were thinking about when they took us from Saint Louis to Albuquerque to Los Angeles. They along with eight million others, left the East in the fifties for Another Chance, a New Start, a Big Break. Loss was not what my mother was thinking about the day she sat herself down at the dinette on Odessa Avenue in 1970 and deliberately severed the last of our ties with most everything east of the Mississippi.

On the dining room table in front of my mother this particular afternoon is a tin recipe-card box, yellow and pink fruit stenciled on the outside. Cherries. Bananas. Pineapples. In it are the index cards on which she keeps the names and addresses of people with which we'd continued to exchange Christmas cards over the years: relatives, old friends in the Midwest, neighbors from places our family once lived.

I've never met any but a handful of these people, and the box itself is nothing special, but taken together, the cards and the box have become for me a family artifact, a fetish. Not an heirloom; rather, an object with a significance far beyond its economic worth. An object with deep-seeded associations that only mental-health professionals can decipher. An object that children never mention until long after parents have disposed of it—at which point the fetish becomes a symbol of parental indifference and betrayal.

In short, I look forward to seeing this box every year because it means, simply, Christmas is coming. It means Christmas cards are coming from others to us, and what we'll do with them is what we've done with them for years: hang our favorites on ribbons in the living room and stash the tacky cards—with flocked designs or colored foil or goofy cartoons—in a wicker basket. The tin box, that is to say, is an object that speaks of connections and continuity.

But on this November afternoon, something is amiss. There is my mother. There is the tin box. There are the index cards. And there, a brown paper grocery bag at her feet. The top edge of the bag is neatly cuffed, like the legs on a freshly laundered pair of jeans, and as I watch, in horrified fascination, one index card follows another, cartwheeling into the trash bag. Just people in places we used to know. Just garbage.

When I bring up this memory my father, especially, wants to be sure I understand that it was not about callous negligence, not about (as my mother on the other phone extension terms it) throwing people away. Life in our family was increasingly complicated, stressful, he says. The fact was, he and my mother had lost touch with their past. Sending Christmas cards to people who no longer knew them, whom they no longer knew, was an empty gesture, a meaningless obligation. Best to be honest, he says; best to simplify.

All of us fall silent. My mind sets to work like a master tailor making the usual adjustments between what I know and what I'm being told; between reality and appearance. I once asked my parents to tell me in twenty-five words or less what their credos were. My father said: Take pride in your work. Take care of your own. My mother said: Nothing lasts forever.

When I speak again, when I assure my father that I'm not blaming him or my mother, I am telling the truth. When I assure him the Christmas-card incident is just another one of those memories of mine that's missing its context, like a nutmeat without the shell, I am flat-out lying.

The details of this scene—the box, the cuffed bag, the cards—and its context are perfectly congruent. This is as true as a memory gets. A sound bite even accompanies it, a word my mind is saying to itself as each proper name and place-name hits the bottom of the sack with a thwack: *gone gone gone gone.*

⌇

I have a theory that I have no way of testing. The theory is this: that the Christmas-card incident was nothing unusual, that it occurred in some version in millions of relocated families and that, moreover, it continues to occur today. Continues to occur in spite of dime-a-minute phone rates and Internet e-mail accounts. Continues to occur in spite of rock-bottom airfares and fast cars. Continues to occur because our bonds with people are inextricable from bonds with place, with home wherever home is. Sever or neglect relationship with too many people and the bond to place won't hold. Sever or neglect relationship with place and bonds to people won't hold. Mobility—the kind of mobility that became commonplace when my parents were young newlyweds—means that each of us forms more relationships with people and places in a lifetime than can possibly be deepened and maintained. The awareness of this is particularly hard on migrants like my mother and father whose primary relationships with the past, with home and with family, are fraught and fragile. And this wounded awareness of theirs, I think, has everything to do with those index cards in the garbage bag.

I stopped writing entries in my address book in pen twenty years ago. The pages now are blurred with the graphite residue of erasures, and I'm quite sure I've been rubbed out many times in many address books myself. It happens. You change jobs. You change addresses. You change spouses. It seems like work trying to reach out and touch so many, so far away, to explain how things are where you are, and it's easy, so easy to stop calling, to stop writing.

And if we're honest with ourselves, we also recognize that losing people can be a relief, strangely cleansing, even purifying. This is the allure of mobility; this is the seduction of the motel room, of rootlessness: the notion that we can always start over someplace else with someone else. It's nearly impossible to disappoint or to be disappointed by people you've only known a little while. Keep your life populated by a rotating roster of strangers and you never have to worry about accounting for the past to others. Without a past, without a future inhabited by people who knew us when, we are free to reinvent ourselves everyday.

And maybe it is this, the possibility for reinvention, that is the West's greatest appeal, now, just as it was when the frontier was still open, when the plains became a dust bowl, when the Cold War began. With each wave of migration, we had to reinvent the Western landscape as well: dam, irrigate, plow, and plant until the desert sustained us all, old-timers and late arrivals alike—and if it didn't, then pave a new road, pack up the car, and move somewhere else that might.

Reinvention as the West imagines it is dependent upon this unimpeded movement. Movement of this kind requires space. Lots of it. But the wide skies and open spaces that may still be found in the West are no longer, for a number of reasons—ecological, environmental, economic—ours for the taking. Though we've become by and large a region of "comers" and "goers" the land can support only a finite number of "stayers" in the manner to which most Americans are accustomed.

We seem unable in the New West, at least at this juncture, though, to believe in the finite. We continue to believe in perpetual possibility, in reinvention and in movement. And it is a belief we Westerners seem intent on proving to ourselves over and over: how free we are to pick up and go live someplace else. So we lose a few people along the way—ah, well.

In the early 1990s, the population growth rate in the Mountain West was more than double the national average. According to the U.S. Census Bureau, Los Angeles lost 36,944 residents between 1990 and 1994. IRS statistics show that 37,030 people moved to Utah during that same period. Where the eighty-six unaccounted for came from is anyone's guess.

Friends at parties would often comment, and not always pleasantly, on the number of California tags around. Soon I couldn't stop watching for them. I'd pass cars from California on the highway, then slow down to study their passengers in my rearview mirror. The drivers steered with the heels of their hands and talked with an uncommon animation while one index finger swiveled and bounced like the needle of a compass, left, then right: *Just look at it! No litter! No traffic! No graffiti! So much space!*

If my non-Mormon friends and I noticed the influx of emigrants, you can be sure it didn't escape the notice of the state's Mormon population. A depressed economy in California and a spreading disaffection among Westerners for urban living translated into a "boom" for Utah, bringing growth and prosperity—good things semantically speaking in conservative vernacular. But here, the rapidly shifting demographic also exacerbated fears of the Other unique to Utah that were nearly 150 years old; old, that is, as the settlement of the Salt Lake valley itself when Mormon pioneers, fleeing persecution in the East, crested that last hill and saw their Zion for the first time. "This is the place," proclaimed an ailing Brigham Young from the bed of a wagon that July day in 1847. There it was, indeed: Refuge. Freedom. Home.

The ratio of Mormon to non-Mormon representatives in our legislature, which varies little from one election to another, is usually around 85:15. We talk a lot about the issue of separation of church and state here, naturally enough. But you don't have to live in Utah long to notice that most of the more controversial legislation passed by that body is directly related to perceived threats to the values and ideals promulgated by the LDS Church. Certain legislative bills are like brake fluid, leaking out when that belief system is under pressure. And beginning in 1990 when the numbers of new residents from out of state began an exponential increase, there was suddenly a great deal of pressure.

In 1991, for example, the legislature banned advertising of alcoholic beverages on billboards and signs. You can still see the residual effect of the measure on taverns and convenience stores all over the state. Adhering to the letter of the law meant that "Cold Beer on Tap" became "Cold Bee" or "Cold Beer Nuts" or, as in the rural town of Salina, "Cold Beep."

It was a celebration of the subversive power of language and something that venerable transplants to Utah still chuckle about. But it was also the kind of episode that in Utah is taken as emblematic by those it affects of a larger, more hostile message: *This is our home, not yours. Here, you do things our way or you can move on down the road.*

How easy it is, too, to do just that, move on, find a No Vacancy sign at the next stop. For it isn't just in Utah that people arrive with certain high expectations and ideas about changing things, then come to feel discontent, discouraged, rejected, or defeated. Over the years, I've listened to so many newcomers and so many short-timers describe their reasons for moving to or from this or that place that I've begun to believe my mother might be right. We're all victims of a curse we've called down on our own heads. And if not, how ironic anyway that, having displaced and decimated the West's indigenous people to lay claim to their ancestral homelands, we've become a culture of displaced persons, more homeless than we dare imagine.

I am haunted by a voice that I believe haunts us all to some extent in the West now: *Keep the tank filled,* it whispers. *Keep the bags packed.*

෴

I saw Great Salt Lake up close for the first time fifteen years after I'd moved to Salt Lake City, and then only because my environmental science professor, Ty, loaded me and seventeen fellow students into a van and drove us there. On the way we stopped to collect samples of plants with a special tolerance to the salt eroded from the mountains and leaching into the soil for more than thirty million years. I have them still, these samples, under Scotch tape gone brittle in an old composition notebook: pickleweed, American three-square rush, salt brush, salt grass, greasewood. The tiny segmented bladders of iodine bush that burst between my teeth and made my tongue cringe with salt are collapsed and desiccated now.

They are not beautiful to behold, these plants that crab and scratch life into the salt playa. Toughs and outcasts, these. Thorn bearing, bitter tasting. Life, but stripped of pretension and pleasing extravagances like color and blossom, comely shape and scent. These plants excrete salt that forms crystals on their leaves, or they store it in their tissues until they whither from the accumulation. They are not burdened, that is to say, with graces and grand ambitions. What these plants are good at is surviving.

At the southern end of the lake, the van door slid open and over the breakwater we all went, picking our way along the beach toward the water with our notepads and Baggies. I hadn't gone more than a few hundred yards before I had to stop and then stoop. And then retch. The stench from the sand and the decaying matter that *was* the sand, as far I could tell, almost sent me back to the van. Ty patted me on the back, said something about organic decomposition being "a sure sign of a healthy ecosystem," and went on his way. After a few minutes I stood up and a few minutes after that, I followed.

At four o'clock that afternoon back on campus I was still in the lab looking at oolitic sand under a microscope: perfectly spherical grains, formed from the feces of brine shrimp coated with calcium sulfate. Shit to the core; sublimity all the same. It wasn't much, but it was something else, this perfect sand from the shores of Great Salt Lake.

I've been back to the lake once or twice since to hike on Antelope Island, to bird-watch. I still hope for another glimpse of Pink Floyd, the Chilean flamingo that escaped from Tracy Aviary in 1988 and took up residence at Great Salt Lake. Where he spends summers is a mystery, and so is his return every winter, when by subtropical standards the lake and the snowstorms that intensify over it are inhospitable at best. But the experts say that the high-mountain lakes in South America condition his kind well for inclement weather.

He's conspicuous enough: algae that the brine shrimp eat, that Floyd, in the next knot of the food chain, eats, keep him in the pink, and in his adopted community of birds of another feather, none is so statuesque as he. But Floyd is far from home, and if he migrates anywhere he migrates alone.

He wades among the flocks of shoveler ducks and eared grebes, the phalaropes and curlews and California gulls, and among these throngs, he is a paragon of several sorts: of resilience, of adaptability, of an abiding nature. But he keeps a low profile—as low as a flamingo can among more prosaic shorebirds. And no one seems to understand Floyd or what Floyd is anymore or where Floyd belongs—least of all, perhaps, Floyd.

Last fall a squadron of sandhill cranes and four whooping cranes, following an ultralight plane—the mother ship—stopped over near Heber, Utah, on its way from Idaho to the New Mexican sanctuary of Bosque del Apache National Wildlife Refuge. There are 371 whooping cranes left—total—in the world; only 230 still living in the wild, and of those only 165 belong to a migrating flock that breeds in Canada and winters in Texas.

An earlier experiment designed to save the whooping cranes failed. Whooping-crane eggs were planted in sandhill-crane nests. The chicks hatched, grew, and learned to migrate, but imprinted on their sandhill-crane foster parents and would not breed with their own species. The

Idaho flock, seven birds strong, imprinted on a human being instead: Kent Clegg, the rancher/pilot of the ultralight. If this flock and others like it can be taught how to migrate and still desire their own kind, it's hoped that extinction can be averted.

I wonder if what we're trying to teach the whooping cranes is some version of their lost story. I wonder if story, for birds like Pink Floyd and the cranes, looks like migration to us.

I wonder if, in imagining home, I have drawn the boundaries too small and in telling the story of home and destination, I have neglected the story of migration and journey. What if the experience of dislocation is a means of discovering ourselves? What if movement, in the sense that migration is movement, is a way of finding homes, not losing them?

Maybe motel mind isn't necessarily a state of loss and bereavement but a state of expectancy. Could it be the mind-set in which we're receptive to other possibilities of family and home?

Could it be that belonging is a story that only journey can create?

Part Two: To South Point

Treasure chamber was *heart*. *Word carrier* was *man*. *Whale's road* was *ocean*.
In Old English and Old Norse poetry, when a word was substituted with a metaphorical compound phrase in this way, it was called *kenning*, from the Old Norse for "naming" or symbol.

Maybe the birds had a road, too: *sky*. Today we'd call them flyways, the roads migrating birds take. Utah is in the central flyway, one of four birds' roads, identified in the 1930s by ornithologist Frederick C. Lincoln, that sweep between the North and South American continents from the tropics to the temperate and arctic zones.

Flyway, highway: we were falling in love in the thirties, after all, with gasoline and vulcanized rubber. While Lincoln was banding pintails and widgeons at Lake Merritt in Oakland, California, Cy Avery and a committee of federal and state highway officials were meeting in Pinehurst, North Carolina, to make the Mother Road, Route 66, a reality.

Path, trail, road, street, avenue, route, turnpike: passages we carve rather too readily in the earth, through mountains and rain forests; across oceans of grass and bodies of water; carve, grow dissatisfied with, then widen or abandon. Byway, causeway, highway, freeway: gravity bound and indelible all—as whales' roads and birds' roads are not.

This much is true: we do not travel lightly, we humans, as they. But our ways, like their ways, are the expression of a longing and approach-ment. Movement is the desire for Otherness made explicit. All ways are made from hope, but our ways, unfortunately, become the palimpsests of thoughtless human takings and irredeemable losses.

We do not understand precisely how birds migrate, but billions of them do, five billion in North America alone, by landmarks, like mountain ranges, perhaps; by the stars and the sun; by the pull of magnetic crystals in their heads. Imagine a journey this way: river road, moon road, pole road. The urge of subtle senses, mixing: synesthetic.

Memory can be synesthetic—a lullaby can be evergreen; mocha ice cream, the flavor of a sax riff. And memory of journey can be synesthetic, as well. Not electricity tripping synapses inside my skull, but a residual heat that is an idea of remembering, of waking.

～

And then I am awake the first time. It is night and strange, this motion: no stopping, just go and go. But there are my parents side by side in the front seat, and my heart-skip quiets in the soft tallow-white glow of music from the radio, rubbing their bodies.

Between their lightshadow shapes is the black roadsky and a dashdash-dash seam of white stitches pulling us along. And then I am awake the next time. It is morning. A door clicks open. Sucks once. Shuts. Cool dirt gaso-line air weeps into the backseat. Warm cedar chest air leaks from the quilt under my chin—the gone-house again. My mother says, singsong sad, Get your kicks on route sixty-six. One sister says, Is this California yet? When do we eat? The other one says, You have more room than me. Moooove.

SOUTH BY U.S. 89

I. 1982

I had a different husband then.

Sometimes I hear him when I'm driving around town: He still works at the same radio station, delivering news every hour during the morning commute. He always saves an amusing story for last; something with an ironic twist or a perverse slant that draws the morning disc jockey back on the air, that invites repartee. He tosses this last story to the drive-time d.j. the way you might toss a raw egg in a game at the church picnic, hoping the other guy will fumble—but not really. The only way *you* get to look clever and dexterous is if your opponent catches the egg and tosses it back. They've been bantering this way for years now, my ex-husband and the d.j.—and listening to them, you'd think they could go on forever, yucking it up about the human thumb that trophy fisherman found in the mackinaw's gut at Flaming Gorge last Sunday. I shouldn't be so hard on them. The station manager probably insists on this schtick to help listeners stuck in traffic jams ease back into the bright, twangy music after all those reports of terrorism and murders. The headlines haven't changed at all in fifteen years. I have, some.

I can't remember where we went on our honeymoon. Most people have memories that frighten them. What frightens me is what I've managed to forget. Was it a hotel room downtown? We couldn't afford much—that much I know. But I do remember a trip I took with this husband in 1982. I don't remember now where we were going.

But I do remember that it was winter.

౿

It takes no imagination whatsoever and involves negligible risk to drive straight through from one point to another. This is not an opinion my mother shares. What she calls imagination is a keen ability to envision and plan for the worst, and her past, sadly enough, has convinced her that the worst is an inevitability. *Living* is a risk she views as more or less intolerable.

Because it was winter, and because my then husband and I were undertaking a journey, and because she believed the death of loved ones was imminent at all times, but especially when any one of her children was traveling, my mother wrote out and mailed a list of items we should carry in the car with us:

1. Warm clothes including long underwear

2. A little water—You can eat snow

3. High carbohydrate food—roasted peanuts, non-salted—You shouldn't make yourself thirsty; raisins; graham crackers?; beef jerky; beans & a can opener

4. Three or four trouble flares
5. Flashlight and extra batteries
6. Army blanket
7. Galoshes, for both of you
8. Toilet tissue
9. Folding shovel and a scrap of carpet for tire traction

Beans? Snowbound in a closed car? Arrows meandered about the margins, directing me to other notations: "Don't run the motor and go to sleep. Carbon monoxide!" "Keep car gassed up so you can use the heater if you get stranded." "If you have to pull over in a snowstorm, park by a huge truck."

It was winter in the Great Basin.

We drove straight through.

The roads were bone dry. I wanted salted peanuts.

෨

I don't remember stopping even once to take a picture. I don't think we owned a camera. I don't remember thinking this was odd. I thought of us as sensible. We paid our bills. We drove the speed limit. We stayed on the pavement. We were settled in. I may have reasoned that only less sensible, unsettled couples took detours and unnecessary risks—and required cameras to prove it. I was young: desultory reasoning was nothing unusual for me. Or maybe, because I was young, now seemed more important than someday, and having no real affinity for my past, I wasn't concerned about recording the present.

We left Salt Lake City on a frigid November morning, headed south. By six A.M. we were rounding Point of the Mountain at Bluffdale. Nothing moved on the grounds of the Utah State Correctional Facility. Acres of concrete inside fenced compounds. Mercury vapor lights glowing a dull, desperate orange in the half night. The prison and, a few miles later, the Geneva steel works, belching rusty gray smoke, were the only landmarks I knew I'd recognize along the corridor of Interstate 15.

I studied the road map of Utah. Moab, Kanab, Kanosh, Panguitch, Ucolo, Tooele. Altonah, Kamas, Scipio, Neola, Uvada. Names I could imagine giving human organs, a gland maybe; not names I'd pick for a place where people raise their families, overflow park bleachers for Little League games, and sit on the crabgrass after, eating peanut butter and jelly sandwiches. I meant no disrespect. Writers, I knew, were just born this way, wondering about signs along the road, about the sounds behind the sounds of things. Pestering perfectly innocent words to death.

I'd never been on a road trip in the West. I'd never been camping. Or fishing. I thought hiking was something travelers did when their cars broke down in the middle of nowhere. After we passed the Geneva steel works, we *were* in the middle of nowhere, as far as I could tell. I started checking the gas gauge every twenty-five miles.

The passenger window was constantly fogging. I cleared it with my sleeve and watched the no-nonsense landscape of Utah's interior sweep by: farm country, cattle country, and farther on, to the southeast, coal and oil country. Unfamiliar territory. I was apprehensive, moving through it—all that remote rural strangeness: empty fields under a thin dust of snow—fields with soft, even furrows like the wales in a vast piece of white corduroy; junked pickup trucks, decrepit sheds and lean-tos slumped in the yard behind every house. At Spanish Fork, we bore east on Route 6, climbing into more arid grazing lands. The snow was spotty on hills spiked with pinyon and juniper—rolling hills, and mile upon mile of barbed-wire fences rolling with them. Stiff, lethal barriers wherever I looked, dividing up the spaces, separating the road from the land, arresting movement from one place to the next.

We came to the junction of U.S. 89 and turned toward Thistle. The highway swung through the narrow canyon in which the town nestled. I looked down on the roofs of a few modest houses, and the railroad track threading through the valley like a clumsily sutured wound.

I wondered how long I'd have to live in Utah before what I was seeing looked like home.

When I first moved to Utah people asked constantly where I was from. Certain characteristics made me conspicuous, a friend finally explained: my vocabulary for one thing; my wardrobe for another. "Have you ever even *owned* polyester?" she asked. Shortly before the wedding this same friend commented that my fiancé, the newscaster, wore a great deal of polyester clothing—not to mention shirts with pearlized snaps where the buttons should be. Did I know what I was getting into?

Of course, I told her. Of course I'd noticed our dissimilarities—and dismissed them. Insignificant. Irrelevant. He worked at a country and western radio station. He had an image to uphold. Besides, I said, this was love we were talking about. You know. Love?

"I know you can't sit through twenty minutes of *Hee Haw* without breaking out in hives," she said.

The summer before we were engaged, I accompanied my future fiancé to his family reunion. Everyone there came from somewhere in Utah. As usual, it was obvious I did not. I smoked; I drank coffee: these were habits that marked me as non-Mormon, as Other. Yet the dislocation I felt was somehow larger and more profound than our differing religious affiliations. I had imagined, I suppose, that I could find a story of home and family by simply marrying into it. But I was a stranger here in a way I hadn't expected, an alien in the midst of a ritual of recognition and of gathering in place I'd never before experienced.

The family from Randolph had driven the farthest and had to leave early to milk the cows. The father had huge sunburned hands with calloused palms; the right, hard and unyielding as a new baseball mitt when we shook good-bye. I was lonely, and my jaw was sore—the way it gets when I've been smiling too hard for too long. I wanted to go home with this family. I'd never milked a cow—I'd never *touched* a cow, except the parts that came shrink-wrapped at the grocery store—but I was ready to learn.

When the barbecue was over and it came time for the group picture, my prospective father-in-law handed me the camera with a wink. "You don't mind, do you?" he said.

To this day, I don't think he meant any harm, but the harm was done all the same.

⁂

When people asked me where I was from back then, I'd say Los Angeles. I'd say Los Angeles, knowing that it wasn't what I believed; knowing that I could never go home, that home was half a dozen different tract houses, knowing that *I'm from L.A.* had nothing to do anyway with the concept of home and hometown as native Utahns understood it—as the people at my ex-husband's family reunion understood it.

I said L.A., hoping that was the end of it. If pressed for details, I'd shrug and tell sardonic anecdotes about freeways and earthquakes and Valley girls; about a querulous talent agent who wanted me to sing like Petula Clark.

Petula Clark, I'd say. Who were they kidding? I was thirteen years old. But I think I sang "Downtown" in my bedroom about five thousand times that summer.

That, I'd tell people, is what growing up in Los Angeles was all about.

1982. I had a different husband then. I suppose it was lucky we lasted as long as we did. Five years. I don't remember much.

It was winter. Thistle came and went. We drove on.

11. 1996

Near the junction of State Route 6 and U.S. Highway 89, past Billie's Mountain, I drove by two cars pulled off to the side of the road, parked the way motorists park when someone needs a battery jumped. Beside the cars a couple was embracing.

At first I thought this was a morning tryst, rural-Utah style—but then I thought again. In the space framed by the noses of the two cars was a mailbox for a house, an address, that no longer existed. The community of Thistle, Utah, was a memory here.

On a spring morning in 1983, a massive tongue of rain-saturated earth had begun to move, heaving itself across the slim canyon through which I now traveled, until the mile-and-a-half-long landslide had shoved the highway and the Denver–Rio Grande rail line aside and piled up a natural dam across Spanish Fork Creek. In a matter of days the old town of Thistle was a new lake. Homes collapsed or floated away from their foundations; the railroad tracks came loose as the ties lifted under them. One by one the deluged cottonwood trees died. The residents, many of them elderly, most uninsured, were forced to relocate, abandoning their community. The November 1982 Mountain Bell telephone directory had been the last to include Thistle listings: fifty people; maybe the names of this couple, embracing in my rearview mirror, among them.

Can you still say, I wondered, when your hometown disappears under a relentless muddy flood, I'm from Thistle, Utah? I was thinking of my so-called hometown too. When the places you remember crumbled into earthquake rubble or disappeared under new office buildings and malls and acres of asphalt, or were in parts of town you'd be too frightened to visit now, could you still say, I'm from L.A.?

I turned the car around, drove past what I now suspected was a grief-stricken couple, back to the turnoff for the Thistle memorial, constructed to commemorate the losses here. There, a woman in sweatpants and a parka was circling the interpretive displays at the monument. Shelley was on her way to register a daughter at Snow College in Ephraim, Utah, that morning, she said, but had been drawn off the highway by a longing and a need. She had to see what was left of Thistle; relatives had been living here when the disaster struck. Hard to believe it had been thirteen years already. Shelley gazed off, matching the before picture on the display to the after landscape in the distance. She glanced at me then, shy suddenly; clearly, she hadn't expected to find anyone else at the memorial.

"There," Shelley pointed to one of the photographs mounted under the Plexiglass. "That was the little store. I remember walking with my grandmother after we'd finished shopping. I can still taste the candy she'd bought me."

She led me to another panel at the memorial where the town's last residents were listed. Shelley's finger slid down the column of names, a cursor, searching. "Here. These are my grandparents," she said. "The water rose fast. They didn't make it out with much. One of the houses lifted off its foundation whole, and they towed it away by boat, if you can believe it. See that roof up on the mountainside over there? No, higher. Way up. That's the roof of Grandma's house." Shelley saw the unasked question flicker behind my eyes. "They're okay," she said. "No insurance, of course. Impossible to start over in your seventies. But they're doing okay."

She had a carload of kids on this trip, Shelley did. The college-bound daughter, a son about seven, another son high-school age, a third boy, maybe his friend. The daughter circled Shelley and me like a red-tailed hawk. The little boy whined and interrupted our conversation. The high-school boys hadn't left the car to give the townsite or the interpretive signs so much as a glance.

I think Shelley wanted to stay a while longer, but the kids and their boredom were nudging at her attention, making her shy again. We said good-bye and moved toward our cars. I was rummaging in the backseat when I heard Shelley's older son say, "Well. Did you tell her the story of your life?" Snide. Dismissive. The loss here magnified suddenly: a hometown, a woman's memory, the story of that memory her son didn't care to hear. I winced. I don't know about Shelley; she'd already backed up and pulled away. Twin trails of dust lifted and dispersed.

Driving south again, I passed the couple by the side of the road a second time. Now they were sitting side by side next to the mailbox. His arm around her, her head tipped against him, their legs hanging over the shoulder of the road where muddy ground fell away to a shallow valley that was Thistle no more.

NORTH BY I-15

The first winter of our courtship my second husband, Don, bought me a pair of cross-country skis. Then we broke up. I'd never been cross-country skiing, and in the period of hazy reasoning that followed good-bye, I decided that taking a ski lesson would exact the appropriate revenge—and it might have if the instructor had asked me out. Instead he kept asking me for the time and after forty-five minutes of helping me stand up, he suggested I might give alpine skiing a try.

The next summer Don and I were back together, and Don surprised me with a backpack and a sleeping bag. I'd never in my life hiked more than the distance between the parking lot and the beach in Santa Monica, and the campsite in the Wind Rivers of Wyoming was a good ten miles in. That night I drank enough Jack Daniels to forget the last nine and a half of them and fell asleep swearing I'd never let anyone get me this far away from concrete again.

By fall, Don and I were history. But that spring we were feeling good enough about our relationship to go shopping for a canoe. We launched the new seventeen-foot Old Town on a river one perfect day in June. And even though I'd never paddled a canoe in my life, and even though we'd missed the take-out and had been floating for some eight hours downstream without seeing another soul, and even though Don had no idea where we'd be if and when we found another take-out, I didn't panic—until I heard the hiss of rapids around the next bend. By then I was kneeling in the bow paddling like a madwoman while Don shouted for me to stop!stop!stop! and let him guide us through.

"Just keep us pointed into the V!"

"What V?!" I yelled. "I don't see anything but frigging M's!"

We were off for a while, but on again by May, and that's when I got the fly rod, wading boots, and fishing vest. Don signed us on for a guided float trip on the South Fork of the Snake River—and I thought the fishing guide was as patient and understanding as any person could be with a hook snagged in his shirt, poised to pierce flesh and draw blood.

By the time Don and I married four years later, I was fully equipped, but completely ignorant of the gift that had actually been bestowed. The skis, the backpack, the fly rod—these translated into mementos of an endless audition, a constant state of preparedness, an interminable survival exercise. The decathlon of relationships. And I was no Ironwoman—*that* at least seemed abundantly clear. It was only after a decade of hiking and camping and fishing that I began to understand: Don had been fitting me with the means to feel at home, here in Utah or anywhere I found myself that had a mountain or a river.

～

Everything about the Snake River float trip became ritualized by the third summer: how many bottles of tonic and liters of gin we needed, what day of the week we left, when we launched, how far we floated. By 1988, there were six regulars in our party and no need for a fishing guide. The only two variables, really, were the spring runoff, which determined the amount of water moving downriver, and the progress of the salmon fly hatch moving up.

In wet years, the discharge from Palisades Dam can be high and fast enough to delay the trip until August or September, in which case we miss the salmon fly hatch that begins in Swan Valley along the thirty-mile stretch we fish, during the first week or two of July. The discharge levels also affect the river channel itself. Gravel and sandbars appear and disappear, seasonal deadfall may clog a regular take-out or block a channel altogether. Fast water at the wrong bend in the river may mean missing a promising bank or being flung past one of our favorite campsites.

In spite of these vagaries, the trip was, after three consecutive years, one I could consider reasonably predictable and therefore tolerable. Predictability was comforting for someone like me for whom the natural world was an arena of trial and peril. And predictability meant that an acceptable level of risk had been displaced by ritualization that in turn meant I could indulge in my favorite preoccupation: self-improvement.

How convenient it was to compare and evaluate my individual progress from one summer to the next when so much of what happened could be anticipated! My agenda, every trip, was full: I won't forget anything, like packing my contact lens case; I won't do anything klutzy, like piercing my thumb with a fish hook or dumping my box of fishing flies overboard; I won't make heroic gestures, like offering to row the raft. One year I even quit smoking before we embarked. Big mistake. Not the quitting, that is, but certainly choosing the out-of-doors as the proving ground. The next year, I pared down my expectations and only vowed I'd get through the weekend without crying.

On the Snake River trip of summer 1991, though, everything changed. Everything I thought I'd known about myself and what I required and what the world might expect of me shifted.

Could there be an admission more ruinous to my credibility? For we are all cynical now. We watch the evening news and hear people describe how disasters unnatural and not, or miracles, or chance encounters, have altered them forever. We smirk and make rude, urbane comments during the commercial break. The story makes us uncomfortable. The next night our favorite late-night talk show host delivers a satiric joke or two about it and our discomfort is ameliorated, our ridicule and skepticism vindicated. What our culture trusts are miracles that occur in psychiatric offices and detox centers and personal weight-training facilities—these are still our authorized shaman-ships.

My testimony though is not one of spectacular divine or technical intervention and transformation—unless among miracles you include a river, a raft, and a July day in Idaho.

੭

On I-15 from Provo to Pocatello you can see it: the terrace carved into the Wasatch Front, the coastline of ancient Lake Bonneville. There's plenty of landscape in the West more dramatic than this, a range of mountains with a shelf of earth several hundred miles long carved into it. Consider, for example, the Great Basin: the Bonneville Salt Flats in Utah and the Black Rock Desert in Nevada where the expanses of land are so flat and empty that the mind and body are fooled into feeling a giddy weightlessness. Or consider the Colorado Plateau: the thrust, fold, swell, slice, and fracture of sandstone evident in Arches and Canyonlands National Parks, representing eons of movement yet suggesting a timeless state of suspended animation.

This lip along the Wasatch, though, is a feature that invites a different experience of reading landscape. This reading comes with sound, and that sound is a groan and an explosive rush of water and rock; the sound that Lake Bonneville made when, about fifteen thousand years ago, it breached the natural dam at Red Rock Pass near Pocatello and gushed into the Snake River Basin. It was a geologic and hydrologic cataclysm; a flood with a maximum discharge lasting eight weeks that inundated a canyon rim to rim, heaved and deposited a field of basaltic melon boulders several hundred feet above the present-day Snake River, and created a backwash that scoured the Snake River headward, into the canyon we float through every summer.

After Pocatello the freeway cuts through the dark rubble of basaltic lava tongues furred with sagebrush. The placidity of potatoes, not the violence of volcanism, are what we usually associate with Idaho. And it's odd at first to hear spoken the Hawai'ian terms that have migrated here: *A'A, pahoehoe, kipuka*. But evidence of a hot spot in the earth's crust, which some geologists believe is now under Yellowstone National Park, is everywhere: in these once sluggish, now hardened, flows, in the ash and tuff flows that tower above us as we float—which we notice now and then when we release a trout and remember to look up.

A sound accompanies this aspect of the landscape as well: a low rumble up here, perhaps; down there, a deafening thunder as the tectonic plate carrying Idaho piggyback inches westward, the weight and friction melting the crust of the earth below.

But this geologic sound track is never as easy for me to imagine as the lapping or sudden draining of Lake Bonneville. After all, I've emptied a bathtub nearly every night of my life.

෨

Our small convoy arrives at the South Fork Lodge near Swan Valley, Idaho, before noon, on schedule. This is because for once, I've remembered to bring everything I was assigned. Last year we'd made three stops between home and the river to shop for items I'd forgotten. I'm feeling a little carsick from sitting in the backseat. Don and I rode with Katharine and Kirk, towing the dory; Virginia and Dr. John followed us, their four-man raft deflated and rolled, an unwieldy rubber pastry weighing down the belly of their VW van.

The lodge is a requisite stop: we need fishing licenses; we need to arrange to have the cars shuttled from our launch site to the take-out ramp downstream. But we don't need the Snickers bars and fried pork rinds we buy, and we certainly don't need anymore flies, but we get those, too.

The shop in front is bustling with impulse buyers like us: sport fishers pilfering the racks of junk food, swapping notions about which fly will knock 'em dead on the river that day. Since there are six of us needing licenses and not enough help at the counter to go around, and since we're planning to have lunch here, and since the clerk remembers us, he waves us out of the shop and tells us to settle with him later, and we gather up our junk food and our flies and our license applications and head into the restaurant.

Guy stuff dominates the decor in the main hall of the lodge. The pool tables have forced the dining tables and chairs to the perimeter of the room where they jostle for space against walls congested with animal trophies—moose, deer, antelope, trout. Conspicuously absent, though, are the sardonic signs common in backwater establishments: "Bigamy is one wife too many; so is monogamy." Or "Unattended children will be rounded up and sold as slaves."

A wooden plaque on the women's-room door says "Setters" (men are "Pointers"), but Virginia, Katharine, and I are usually the only women around to appreciate the distinction, not counting Linda, who shows us to a table—*our* table—in the cafe out back.

The same black-bear skin is splayed across the paneled wall near the bar, but the index card tacked by what's left of its right front paw is new. "Somebody stole the claws off of Spence's bear. $100 for information about who committed this &!*%ty crime!" Linda, who runs the lodge with her husband, Spence Warner, brings a round of her famous barbecued-beef sandwiches and a pitcher of cold beer. We fill out our license forms. We crack the usual stupid jokes and snort in our beers.

"Weight?

"Not applicable."

"Eyes?"

"Yes."

"Sex?"

"Who wants to know?"

A Reba McIntyre tune is playing on the jukebox. Barbecue and brew at the South Fork Lodge: the one time all year that I not only endure listening to country and western music, but actually like it—a little.

⌐

At the Spring Creek boat access, there's the prelaunch flurry of activity that always arouses my chorus of inner critics. *Everyone but you knows what needs to be done and is doing it.* Dr. John hands me a new pair of needle hold-ers, an indispensable tool for removing hooks from trout lips. I have lost my needle holder in the Snake River four years running. Now each of us has one of these surgical instruments hanging from our fishing vests like a military decoration. I thank John as he goes to work, cabling his air pump to the car battery. Virginia has already begun deftly piecing together the aluminum raft frame.

Kirk and Don are loading the dory, distributing and securing river bags and coolers in some exacting and rational manner. Katharine is assembling oars, joining the paddle half into the handle half. Only two parts, I tell my-self—not much of a contribution but something I can manage without causing bodily injury.

Virginia catches her first trout not five minutes from the boat launch. I am in the back of the raft with fishing line tangled around my ankles, still trying to decide whether to apply sunscreen over or under the insect repel-lent. She releases the fish, and seconds later her line is snapping neatly above her head again in tight serpentines, front and back and front, then unfurling with a whisper across thirty feet of water.

In my hands, on a bad day, the line is a thing possessed, lurching and rasping, knotting itself perversely around the fly rod. I hang up on willows and break my tippet and spend ten minutes on a blood knot that should take ten seconds. If I do catch a fish its anguish becomes my own; its handling, unhooking, and resuscitation a timed event I botch more often than not.

On a bad day, I forget into which of the two dozen pockets of my fish-ing vest I've put the 6x leader material, my box of flies, the oil-based oint-ment that keeps a fly dry. I lose time puzzling over the flies themselves, deciding which morsels of thread and tufts of fur and feather to tie on next: Elk-hair caddis? Midge? Hare's ear, renegade, blue dun, grizzly wulff? Scud or woolly bugger? Yellow-bellied humpy, yellow Sally, or yellow stimulator?

On a bad day, my fly looks like a fake. I know full well that trout don't get big because they're dumb. They get big because they're *complex*. I know that presentation of the lure—making the fly behave like a real insect either emerging from its egg and swimming about under the water or struggling for dear life above it—is everything.

On a bad day, novice fishers like me don't stand a chance, because there are certain hours, even weeks, when the fish won't willingly bite. During these times, real fishermen and -women keep at it, consulting one another, changing flies every fifteen minutes, moving on to another, more promising, spot. Pretenders like me reel in the line and sit down. And so it was on this day. The trout weren't particularly hungry, only bloated from the salmon-fly feeding frenzy we'd apparently missed.

It was something of an honor each summer to notice the first salmon fly crawling on someone's hat or T-shirt, and that distinction should have been earned by now. But whatever it was that amorous salmon flies required—some optimum of water and air temperatures, some interval of daylight and dark—was over. They were gone: hatched and mated, eaten or dead. All that was left were a few live, but expended, stragglers on the banks and thousands of dried casings, those eerie, empty pupal skins that the salmon flies shed after emerging from the river.

We stop on a familiar gravel bar for lunch. On every water-worn rock and twig, more casings. I smile. I've shed a few skins myself along these banks.

ᥫ

The rest of the afternoon I don't even pretend to want to fish. I wave to Katharine, lounging with a Willa Cather novel in the stern of the dory up ahead. Everyone else in her boat is intent on spotting risers along the bank, but Katharine points skyward where a bald eagle studies us imperiously from the blighted, upper branches of a cottonwood.

The South Fork is an important cottonwood riparian ecosystem, one of the largest in the West. This particular stretch of river has been designated an eagle-nesting preserve, and Katharine scans the sky constantly when we reach it, determined to surpass her 1989 record of fifteen sightings.

Now Virginia's pointing, too. Off the bow of the raft a mother duck and a dozen ducklings are paddling, comic in their sudden panic for cover.

"Merganser," she says, lifting her rod and resuming her backcast.

I thumb through my Peterson's field guide. Sure enough. Rusty-colored head and spiky crest. "Female. Definitely," I add.

Virginia grins, casts, retrieves. Casts again.

There's still not much trout action, but it's hard to be disappointed. A flock of Franklin's gulls wheels above us. A pair of raucous kingfishers darts among the onshore pines. A beaver ferries a water-logged branch upstream. And a stoic blue heron, strangely prehistoric-looking in flight, heeds our progress down river, landing, then swooping out from the brush, again and again, just as the raft overtakes him. We turn into a narrow channel, stalling in an eddy until the dory, which has dropped behind again, catches up with us. When it does, Don shouts something about a moose grazing a few hundred yards back.

But there isn't time to think about what we've floated past, because what we're floating toward is nothing but trouble. The channel unexpectedly splits around a sandbar, and it's Kirk in the dory on the passable side who notices that our raft is drifting right for a pile of deadfall. We won't clear the craggy, rubber-ripping log blocking the channel, and Dr. John hasn't the strength to pull the three of us and a loaded vessel backward against the current.

There's absolutely no sense in what I do next, but I'm suddenly hip-deep in cold water, digging my heels into river cobble and stalling the drift of the raft long enough for Virginia to toss her rod aside and jump in, too. Together we tow the raft to safety on the other side of the bar.

ॐ

That simply, my life is reset. We pick our campsite and unload our gear. We mix the gin and tonics. We light a fire. I dangle my only pair of shorts on a stick over that fire to dry them, replaying the moment I floundered then stood fast in the water, thinking, *Implausible. Ludicrous.* A 125-pound woman against one thousand pounds of passengers and their gear and the pull of a river current? But none of this nay-saying erases what has in fact happened: all of the stories I've told myself about myself have been rendered inapplicable.

As always, Don, Kirk, and John wander off with their rods to fish in the riffles until it's too dark to see. When the boat traffic stops, Katharine, Virginia, and I bathe in the still river, our ablutions in the bone-numbing water quickly devolving into the splashing, hooting, and squealing characteristic of seven year olds. Dusk comes. The fire seems brighter, more welcoming tonight than ever before. I sit watching it for some time entertaining a notion, a serious departure from routine, before I act—before I decide to try setting up the tent.

What was once a bewildering array of folds, zippers, and aluminum and fiberglass shafts seems to me now, well, logical. Katharine sets her book aside and comes over to help.

When the tent snaps taut, I say, "Ta-da," and I say, "A first," knowing somehow that this will be the last time I ever use that disclaimer to earn sympathy or a compliment. I am closer to home here now; only visitors have the right to ask for indulgence.

Tonight we eat Virginia's marinated pork tenderloin. Tomorrow night we will eat shrimp scampi. These are the extravagant meals we eat and in this order every summer on the Snake River. On the last night of our float, we will keep enough fish for our dinner, and only on that night when six trout seem part of an appropriate, even necessary, communion.

When the dishes are done and the fire and conversation have died down, we might hear a hawk crying upstream, hunting in the gathering dark. Then she'll be upon us, perched but unseen in a cottonwood just outside our circle of light.

EAST BY U.S. 191

I was to blame for introducing the topic of barfing on the drive up here yesterday. State Road 150 out of Kamas winds through the Wasatch National Forest on the way to Evanston, Wyoming. It is shown as a scenic byway on the map, but as one somewhat prone to motion sickness, I will tell you the trip is anything but scenic unless, that is, you're riding shotgun, securely belted next to an able driver such as Virginia. At one point I swiveled in my seat to thank Shauna and Barb for sitting in the back, and mentioned in passing a road trip my husband, Don, and I had taken not many years ago.

We'd flown into Washington, D.C., visited the neighborhood of his youth in Arlington, Virginia, and then pointed our rental car toward West Virginia and a family reunion near the coal-mining camp where his immigrant grandparents had first settled. That road, twisting and climbing, through the Blue Ridge Mountains, sparked his memory of the cave that was the backseat of his family's Pontiac Star Chief and of every stop along the way they'd had to make on his account, traveling to visit the relatives.

"I was sick there," he told me, and a few miles later, he'd point through the windshield and say, ". . . and there. Yes, I think I even remember that tree . . ." and so on, all the way to West Virginia.

Barb told us then about becoming ill one afternoon in the parochial school of her childhood; so ill that the nuns insisted she change out of her sour-smelling uniform and into the only spare clothing they had on the premises: a fluffy white confirmation dress. She'd been taken into the cloister of the convent itself, beyond that heavy door that all the children had been instructed never to open, never to pass through, and then to an available bed in a stark cell with concrete walls where she'd lain in silence for two hours beneath a cross portraying the Passion; one nauseated and frightened little girl; a future-candidate Bride of Christ.

Shauna, by her own admission, was a champion child puker. She walked to grade school alone, she told us, and every morning for years—how many she couldn't recall—she had stolen behind a particular bush situated along a prosaic residential street in her hometown and lost her breakfast. After some time her parents became aware of the problem and sought medical advice. The doctor was baffled. He prescribed chicken soup and soda crackers, which Shauna dutifully ate, and which of course came right back up.

Flash-forward: Shauna is twelve and her older brother has managed to strike terror in her heart—as he undoubtedly thought was his duty—concerning the fate of all seventh graders on the first day of junior high school. Shauna sits in her first-period class in the back of the room. She's placed her brand-new suede purse with the long leather fringes on the desk in front of her. She is nervous and uncomfortable in this strange new environment; apprehensive naturally about the rest of day, about the things her brother has said are done to "scrubs" like her. The room seems hot, congested. The clock, if it's moved at all in the past half hour, says she still has fifteen minutes to wait; fifteen minutes before she can slip out of the classroom, this ghostly white slip of a girl, and get to a rest room. She already knows she's going to be sick. She suddenly knows she isn't going to make it. And no, she doesn't raise her hand, doesn't want to draw attention to herself, doesn't think it proper somehow to interrupt her homeroom teacher. She's been an able student in those many lessons of ladylike conduct. And when what is inevitable happens, Shauna perfunctorily, unceremoniously, and inconspicuously lifts the flap of her new suede purse and pukes in it. Once, twice, three times. A dark stain begins to spread on the leather, but finally the interminable period is over. Shauna demurely leaves her seat and drops the purse into the first trash can she can find.

When she comes home from school that afternoon, her mother asks her about the missing purse, and Shauna tells her the only truth she can: she tells her mother that she lost it, that it must have been stolen.

It's hard to believe we're laughing over this story, but we are. Rolling eastbound to the summit of State Road 150, I think, *Every single one of us in this car knows exactly what this story is about; knows exactly what it was like.*

We do not, though—at least not at this early juncture—explore issues relevant to growing up female in America. We segue instead to a discussion about the sudden nausea produced by appendicitis. Three of us in the car have lost our appendixes. I marvel at this unexpected congruency in our personal histories. Virginia was walking home from her grandmother's restaurant at the onset of her attack. She threw up banana cream pie, and the next thing she knew she was on the table at a rural medical clinic, inhaling ether. "They still used ether in those days," she says.

Virginia is the designated Crone in our group. In the popular New Age parlance, the Crone is the third aspect of the ancient Triple Goddess, the first two being the Maiden and the Mother. As Crone, Virginia has achieved a certain age and status, a range and depth of spirit and knowledge, and is consequently deserving of our respect. We use the term for convenience only, though, and almost facetiously. Virginia is, above all else, our friend, and to call her our Crone seems obsequious and somehow at odds with the unpretentious person she really is. If we are indeed goddesses here, we choose not to flaunt our rank in the pantheon. And we will not be beating sacred drums or summoning our power animals by the campfire tonight—although this has occurred on a past trip and then because these more exotic activities happened to be part of the personal explorations of another friend of ours that one year. That is to say, we are not rigid in our agenda. We trust, I think, in some natural ecology that develops in our company over this weekend, with each woman contributing in her unique, ineffable way.

Jennifer is our botanist-cum-geologist-cum-wilderness guide. She is the one who owns the most extensive collection of U.S. Geological Survey maps, and the one who actually knows how to read them. A landscape architect by trade, she has her wildflowers and conifers down cold. And she can provide, at the very least, an educated guess as to whether the mountain you're looking at in the distance is granitic or sedimentary and give you some idea as to why you might care. These particulars are offered without a trace of arrogance, but as simple gifts of her vision and expertise. To walk the trail behind Jennifer is to see with the integration of a naturalist's eye and to absorb the often poetic vocabularies by which science explains the natural world.

Jennifer is also a dedicated mushroomer. This time of year in the Uinta Mountains the ground is still moist with runoff and blanketed with lush grasses and undergrowth kept a verdant green by afternoon thundershowers. I have never known Jennifer to return empty-handed from an expedition. And yes, we're all very spoiled: last evening Jennifer prepared a batch of *boletus edulis*—commonly known as King Boletus—a sauteed delicacy that, not twenty-four hours into the trip, we're already expecting from her at every meal.

Shauna and Barb, while part of our larger circle of Salt Lake City acquaintances, are new to this trip. The two are old friends whose steady stream of joking and banter characterizes their interactions with us and with one another. But theirs is a deep affinity that has been tested and survived times of conflict and disharmony. They tell anecdotes about their lives that are at once poignant and farcical; the sort of stories that keep me in a constant state of high alert, my pen moving across my notepad, transcribing them as fast as they are told. One such note from the drive up here yesterday reads, "Ask S and B whether I can use the barfing stories." As a writer, I strive to be forthright in these matters. There is, however, an unavoidable parasitic quality to my line of work, and a certain risk you undertake when you invite a writer into your life. My disclaimer is plain-spoken and succinct: "Just remember," I say, "you have all been warned."

༄

Don't get me wrong: I am a happy camper. I do not mind dredging insects, drowned or kicking, out of my coffee. I do not grouse about bathing in a stream that still qualified as snowpack yesterday. I do not hide if someone wants to take my picture, even though I have hat-hair and no makeup on, and even though I am wearing articles of clothing in half a dozen bright colors that any five year old knows better than to mix.

I would rather have my back propped against the trunk of an Engelmann spruce at a campsite anywhere in the West than cradled in a chaise lounge by a crystal-blue pool at a five-star resort anywhere in the world. I am a good camper, and I am a good sport—my mother says so, and she should know. The last time she (or anyone in my immediate family) even *thought* about going camping, Alaska and Hawai'i were still eligible for statehood. They all hate dirt *that* much.

You should know, though, that when I wake up in a tent I am not a very happy woman. I'm not happy about the pressure in my bladder and the many obstacles I can see to relieving it. I try to unzip the sleeping bag that is now, with the soft morning sun glancing across it, finally—finally—warm enough. The zipper jams five times on the way down. I kick myself free of the bag, and I feel the dull throb of bruises over my hip bones where the backpack harness rested the day before. I have a good look at the clothes I've slept in, blotched with spilled coffee and Crown Royal, soiled with campfire soot and grass stains and general trail grime. I put on my glasses, wanting that restorative vision of evergreens and lake and alpine meadow, and the lenses instantly fog over with condensation in the morning chill.

I fumble for my hiking boots, dump them upside down to check for live stowaways and slide my feet into those dank, gritty tunnels. I struggle to knot damp laces. I crab my way toward the door, dragging everything in the tent with me. I try to unzip the tent flap. I can't find the zipper tongue. I curse. Out loud. Twice. I tip my head back, trying to see under the fogged glasses, then snatch my glasses off and toss them into the jumble of sleeping bags, stuff sacks, and clothing behind me. The tent zipper jams three times before I've created an opening big enough to crawl through.

By now my bladder is screaming.

This morning Virginia is already up and out of the tent when I wake. I am grateful for this small blessing. Grateful because she'll be spared these unseemly first minutes of my conscious camping self. But more grateful because, when I wake, I find myself curled against her empty sleeping bag in the sliver of space I've granted her.

This tent sleeps three adults comfortably—unless one of them is me and the temperature has dipped close to freezing during the night. I lever myself onto my elbows and notice that two-thirds of the tent is vacant; the two-thirds, that is, that I'd relentlessly claimed and abandoned over the past few hours. Several luxurious square feet of nylon stretch away to my left. There is no room to spare to right where I'd driven Virginia to the tent wall and where I'd slept, spooned against her in the cold, probably all night, as I would have my husband.

My husband is not on this trip, although he offered to portage our gear and to cook for the privilege of joining us. Shauna tells me that Chris, her significant other, probably came closer to outright begging. This outing, you see, is legendary among our men. We aren't precisely sure why this is so; we never intended to cultivate a mystique. But once every summer a small company of women—this year we are six—packs up and heads for the hills. It's not that men aren't welcome; they're just not invited.

Boots on, lenses clear, bladder empty, I shuffle into the clearing—our downtown cafe, so to speak—where we meet every morning and evening for food and easy conversation and live entertainment. At dusk last night we were singing a medley of lounge-lizard tunes, a repertoire with an astonishing depth given the span of our respective ages, thirty-five to fifty-something. There are three tents in the outlying suburbs: Shauna and Barb live to the north; Jennifer and Holly, to the east; Virginia and I, across the stream to the south.

I am the last one up. Shauna is changing into hiking clothes. Barb has wandered off to the shallow lake nearby. Holly is sitting on a rock, meditating on the ragged, gray summit of Hayden Peak. Jennifer is slicing olives and cheese for breakfast quesadillas. Her dog Myekh—pronounced mica, like the mineral—is sleeping in a patch of sun nearby. Myekh's sides expand and contract in the gentle heaves of slumber. Her black lips are drawn away from her glistening white canines. Myekh is one of those dogs that you'd swear grins when she's amused and feeling playful, or as now, is utterly content. This is Myekh's home turf. Jennifer found her cold, hungry, and lost on the last leg of a cross-country ski trip up here a few years ago. Myekh's jowls are streaked with black and green like a commando on patrol: she's been rolling in the moose dung already this morning, a stunt that got her banned from Jennifer's tent last night—as it clearly will again tonight.

Virginia is smiling at me over her cup of tea. She has a slow smile, ready enough, but a smile that's earned all the same, that gathers itself with the energy of a small wave moving to shore. It is a smile I've come to love over the years of our friendship.

"Sorry," I say. "I brought the wrong sleeping bag." Rated for forty degrees Fahrenheit or above. What was I thinking.

Virginia smiles and pours hot water over the grounds in my coffee filter. "We'll share the space blanket tonight," she says.

༄

By ten-thirty we're ready for our day hike. Virginia reminds us to pack along our rain gear. We set out across the meadow to a trail that will take us up and around Murdock Mountain and into the next basin to Shepherd and Hoover Lakes. There are hundreds of these small glacial lakes formed some sixty million years ago when the Uinta Mountains rose. On the fishing map I have back home this prominent east-west range looks like a giant green sponge, its every available pore brimming with bright blue water.

We fan out across the meadow, Myekh running ahead of us, pitching herself headlong onto every heap of moose dung she comes across. At the trail we fall in behind Virginia—and Myekh. Myekh always leads off, it's her job. A few hundred yards down the trail, she'll start down the line, collecting pats from each of us, counting noses. Then she'll lose interest in herding us and dash off into the underbrush after a ground squirrel. Jennifer lags a bit, breaking out of formation frequently to hunt for mushrooms. When she finds the first King Boletus, we are jubilant—it looks like hors d'oeuvres again tonight—and before long Shauna is finding them, too.

Mushrooms, at least the kind we're after, are not a flashy sort of organism. They thrive in obscurity, hunkered beneath drifts of deadfall, tucked in thick nests of grass, or nestled under the skirts of the pines and firs flanking the trail. Jennifer and Shauna work the terrain like bloodhounds. Each time one of them calls out, the rest of us crowd around, as if by witnessing the mushroom being pried from the ground we, too, might develop their near psychic foraging ability.

For a while I follow Holly. This is a courtesy, a small kindness it makes me happy to extend: not too many years before I was the new element being introduced to the alchemy of this group. Like her, I was new to camping, new to backpacking. Like her, I felt underequipped—everything I had with me, down to the tin fork in my mess kit, was borrowed. I felt self-conscious, awkward, and decidedly off the vigorous pace of the pack. As Holly had last night, I'd heard Jennifer's speech for the first time, the one she delivers without fail to every newcomer: "These are wild mushrooms. There are no guarantees. If you'd rather not eat them, I will not be offended. It's entirely your choice."

But back then when I heard that caveat for the first time, I was at work reshaping myself, my concept of myself, as a writer and a woman and a human being. What I was after was an identity that encompassed the kind of self-reliance, resilience, competence, and capacity for celebration that I saw and sensed in the extraordinary women on this trip. I needed to trust myself. I needed to trust them. I ate that first bite of wild mushroom as though, lost in the wilderness, I'd found manna from heaven.

The trail levels out at a small pond. There are three people standing on the far bank, college-age, two men, one woman. One of the young men is skipping stones. He is quite good. The last one kisses the surface of the pond four times before it sinks. The young woman applauds. The other young man is silent, sullen. He stands, arms folded across his chest, a few feet away. The woman is very attractive and fashionably dressed—pressed white T-shirt bearing a Calvin Klein logo; pressed denim shorts with cuffs precisely rolled against her tanned thighs; hammered gold necklace; designer watch—she is, as *Vogue* magazine might put it, "very together" in a way I never was at her age, and never will be. When we pass them on the trail, I can smell her perfume: Georgio of Beverly Hills. I wonder if she suggested this hike. Or if it were one of the young men, whether she really wanted to come at all; and if she did, why; and if she didn't, what that moment felt like when she wanted to say no, but said yes instead.

I think about watching *Gilligan's Island* as a child, about all those years of angst and indecision: Who did I want to be? Ginger the sex kitten or Mary Ann the girl next door? I think about the long road of self-discovery and that one destination—call it self-acceptance—I never quite get to. I think about what Barb said last night by the campfire: "If I'd only had the chance to be around women like us when I was twenty . . ." She never finished the sentence. But Virginia did: ". . . it sure would have saved me a lot of time."

I walk behind Holly so she isn't the last one in line, eating nothing but dust. But after a quarter of a mile or so, she asks me to move on ahead. "I just need to go at my own pace. I'll catch up," she says.

ᔐ

The pond to our backs is rimmed with water lilies suspended on a flawless plate-glass surface. The still water mirrors the arrowhead tips of the firs encircling it and the occasional gray jay winging between them. Say the words *serenity, tranquility,* and this is the image I would hand you.

It is a day of itinerant sun: In a blink, the white-hot light is gone, and a drop cloth of shadow drapes across the basin. Dense banks of clouds with gray underbellies scud overhead. Not a hundred yards away, Hoover Lake roils with an insistent chop, lapping against the shoreline. I want to understand the anomaly of landscape and air current that makes this possible; that renders this pond placid, and the lake, so near it, uneasy, restive.

Virginia, Barb, and I have brought our fly rods, but the wind is stiff and persistent; there will be no fishing after our lunch. Last evening Virginia gave Barb her first casting lesson. I worked from the bank a few yards away, launching twenty-five feet of line to a skittish trout or two that, judging by the size of the rises, were no longer than four inches. Guppies. Then again, a little practice never hurt anyone. I listened to Virginia deliver a now familiar litany about the proper arc of the rod tip—ten o'clock to two o'clock; about the rhythm of the cast, that precise cadence of pull and pause, of push and release.

"See how high Dawn holds her line?" Virginia said. "How flat the arc of her rod is? It's actually like using a roller brush overhead to paint the ceiling." Virginia and I grinned at one another. This last sentence was a nod to me from my mentor. A man will always say that casting is like using a hammer, but it's not; not the way any *woman* I know of hammers. So I'd come up with the painting analogy to explain how the mechanics feel to us.

After a while Virginia set her rod aside and stood behind Barb, pressed against her back, her left hand on Barb's shoulder, her right on Barb's rod. The two of them rocked together, forward and back, forward and back, Virginia modeling with her own body that concert of movement between muscle and fly line that seems so elusive at first. When Virginia finally stepped away, Barb's body continued to rock, but its shape had been re-sculpted. And though the motion it had adopted was not yet its own, its former awkwardness and uncertainty had been erased forever.

We sit in the clearing, talking about nothing at all, and everything in the world that matters. Not our loves and fears and losses. We do talk about these, but only later, when nightfall creates the illusion of privacy that moves our tongues and unseals our lips.

Here, now, in the daylight, we tell our daylight stories. We talk about the mortar that holds us together, those little joys and defeats we hardly think to mention to anyone else. Shauna straggles in late for lunch, right hand bristling with the stray garbage she's collected—other people's Styrofoam cups, crushed cans, and Ziplocs. In her left hand she holds the most perfectly formed King Boletus we've seen yet. Shauna sits beside Barb and tells us about her dog, Sam, who came bounding toward her on one of their morning cross-country ski outings with a pound of raw bacon clamped in his jaws. She ordered him to drop it—*Yeah, right, Mom*—and Sam promptly swallowed the entire slab of meat in one great gulp.

As Shauna saw it at the time, she had two options: one, go back and find the dismayed camper from whom Sam stole this bacon, 'fess up and pay up; or two, ski like hell out of there. She started kicking down that trail, hard, even so imagining that the camper was a young Boy Scout who would now, thanks to her—and Sam, of course—have his own great story, a mystery, to tell for the rest of his days.

Jennifer is sketching a still life: stone, grass, and a dark pool of trapped backwater from the pond. Holly is already asleep. One by one the rest of us lie back on our rain gear, our improvised tarps of bright yellow and blue. Behind my eyelids I see the six of us stippled by shadow and light, a magnificent tableau *sans souci* that I think only a Renoir could hope to evoke, were it to be rendered on canvas.

An hour later we are back on the trail, headed for camp. I walk behind Virginia, managing, but only barely, to keep up with her. In two weeks she and Jennifer leave for Nepal on a six-week, 240-mile round-trip trek into the Himalayas. Destination: the kingdom of Mustang, home to an isolated community of Tibetan refugees that only last year opened the gates of their fortress city to Western visitors. The two friends have been on a self-imposed training regimen for months, hiking the mountains of northern Utah together, gradually increasing their tolerance for distances and elevations.

Virginia aims the tip of her fly rod at a wildflower along the trail. "Here, Dawn. Tell me what this is," she says. I stoop to have a look: the flower is white with four delicate petals. Nothing ostentatious here; a flower with an honest face. I shrug. "Wild geranium," she says. The lesson continues. Virginia points; I sing out: "Purple aster. Monkshood. Gentian. Lupin." I'm pleased to get so many right. Mouse-eared chickweed. Bistort. White yarrow. Penstemon. These are names, not by which I lay claim to what I see, but by which I feel connected to it. Language is the way I make love to the world, and naming, the way I come to feel a belonging to it. Indian paintbrush. Buttercup. Bluebells. Shooting star. Pussy toes. Common names, humble names, given by travelers from a time and a place I'll never know, then given again by the woman walking a few paces ahead who knows how much they mean to me.

At the meadow we disperse to hunt for firewood. Shauna, who has a knack for finding lost belongings in the woods, returns with kindling and a neon-green baseball cap with a bald eagle and the words *Utah Heritage*

Jamboral, A New Frontier embroidered on it. I have no idea what this organization is or does—most likely something innocuous—but the word *militia* pops into my mind. And on the heels of that, the question my mother asked about this trip before I left town: "What will you take for protection?" I told her a tent; she, of course, was thinking along the lines of a submachine gun.

A few minutes later we meet up with Barb and Holly at camp. I hear Holly thank Barb for waiting at the trailhead for her. "I'm not sure I would have known which way to turn for camp," Holly says.

I am instantly angry with myself for forgetting her. On my first trip with the women to the Bear River, I lagged behind, found myself alone on the trail following indistinct boot treads in the dust, knowing that soon I'd have to veer east toward our camp, but not knowing at all where that veering should happen. As I came up a small rise, I saw the branch of a tree spanning the trail before me, and on it, curling and lifting in the warm August breeze was a flannel shirt I recognized. The marker Virginia had left behind.

"Sure. No problem, Holly," Barb says. I tell myself, *For godsakes, Dawn, give it a rest. Cut yourself some slack.* Both women are smiling. Barb says, "I remember how it feels to be lost."

~

Tonight Jennifer has introduced us to two new varieties of wild mushroom, *suillus brevipes* and *lactarius deliciosus,* the latter from the genus of gilled mushrooms that give off a milky juice. I am in love with their Latinate names, the way their consonants and vowels spill across my tongue and collide behind my teeth, long before their flesh ever reaches my mouth. After the hors d'oeuvres, after a dinner of steamed vegetables over rice, and when the dusk begins to settle, our company sets off for a short hike up to the base of Murdock Mountain. Jennifer, on a scouting mission the previous evening, had discovered a brilliant wildflower garden there, as well as a splendid vantage, she says, from which to watch the sun set on Hayden Peak.

We follow a brook that is, yes, babbling down the hillside. The water is slightly clouded. Jennifer tells me the fine white silt it holds in suspension is called glacial milk. When we reach the alpine meadow above our camp, Jennifer remembers the bottle of Crown Royal I bought to share on the trip and insists on going back to camp for it herself. I am pleased and more than a little surprised: the liquor was an afterthought of mine. No one here is much of a drinker. But I'm embarrassed, too, because I'd imagined that pint of gold as a kind of votive centerpiece to an evening such as the one we're about to share. And I had, as I'd paid for it, wondered if the bottle was a contrivance, my way of engineering a role for myself in this group. Sometimes I think too much. Now I can see the scotch for what it is, and will be: a simple contribution, a bit of good cheer to be passed among good friends as the sun goes down.

The barren, pallid hulk of Murdock Mountain brings to mind the rounded back of a sleeping hog. At its base is a vast field of colluvium, those massive boulders tumbled from above by the inexorable tug of gravity. Farther down are the other boulders Jennifer has described, engulfed by wildflowers, a gaudy and riotous display, an inconceivable explosion of color and shape. A fireworks finale on the Fourth of July. We find our seats among and on the rocks facing east toward Hayden Peak. Somebody calls for the hooch. The bottle changes hands, the sun drops, and the night stories begin. Stories of deep wounds and of welcome healing. Of connections made and connections missed. The stories of our lives.

The certain progression of alpenglow color begins. First comes the incarnadined flush of orange-red light, then the mountains burnish to ochre. To salmon. To pink. To blue. To purple. To black.

A jet airliner rockets overhead. I watch the passage of its strobes—left wing, red; right wing, green; tail, white—and a second or two later I hear its roar muffled by the miles of atmosphere between earth and sky. I wonder if the sound feels sad, never catching up with the light. I think of what Holly said to me today about going at her own pace. I have to remember to tell her: you're absolutely right. I'd passed her on the trail, but she is, as it turns out, way ahead of me on this one. Sometimes I still push too hard. My body gets tired trying to keep up with my mind, with my desires. Here is where I part company with the Buddha, though: Desire is good. Desire keeps us moving, learning. But we *are* mortal: we can only do so much. Pacing and patience are everything.

Barb says, "First star."

Shauna says, "Planet. Only stars twinkle."

We all smile.

Virginia asks us, if we could choose, of all the people living or dead, whom would we would most want to know, to be around, to study with. Her vote is the late mythographer Joseph Campbell. Holly chooses Carl Jung.

"How about you, Dawn?" Virginia says.

"I don't really know," I say. But this is a lie. Something about my answer clogs up my throat. I think it will sound grandiloquent, too convenient— yes, contrived—and therefore somehow false to the ear. But here is the truth. I am the love poem Ronald Pinkerton wrote to me in the sixth grade—anonymously, in green ink. I am the anguish my niece shares on the phone when a love affair is ending, and she thinks her young life is over. I am a child in a lonely bed singing herself to sleep. I am the mushrooms growing wild and the constellations scrimshawed between the stars. I am every story ever told to me, and the stories I will tell.

Here is what I want to say to this company of women: I am learning already from the best teachers that ever lived. Every one of you. Right here. Right now.

WEST BY THE MOTHER ROAD

I. ÁCOMA

If my earliest childhood memory can be trusted, it's this: I'm toddling in ever diminishing circles around a lone tree beneath an empty, blue sky. A rope tethers me to the tree because my parents fear I'll wander off the edge of a New Mexican mesa while they set up our tent. How like them to worry so.

I must have been frustrated—three year olds are, constantly. So much to touch, but always over there, up there, out there, just beyond reach and permission. I must have been . . . overheated, yes, and scared. But beyond discomfort, what else did I know, wandering in that tightening circle, scribing a spiral into the soil and coming at long last to the end of my umbilicus, to that tree at the center of the world?

Did it feel like home? Did this home, the desert, enter me in every head-over-heel step, move into me with its furniture: the evanescence of wet sage and creosote, the music of dove-song and snake-rattle, the rumors of coyote and tarantula?

༄

No one can agree. So the story, like most everyone's family stories, like the history of humankind, is a collaborative, though hardly a cooperative, venture. I exaggerate: everyone agrees we left Albuquerque for Los Angeles in 1959 driving a blue Plymouth. But it might have been 1958. Everyone agrees that Bluebird, the Navajo rag doll I've cherished for a lifetime, was purchased on that trip at a coffee shop in Gallup. My eldest sister has no memory of buying the doll for me, but my father insists that it is so.

Fission nearly occurs over the route we took. My father finds a road atlas. He turns to New Mexico and for a several minutes he and my sisters stab at what are today interstates, but which in 1959 (or 1958) were two-lane highways if they existed at all. There were several trips to California from Albuquerque, my father says finally. Which route depends on which trip. Which trip am I interested in?

I'm confused momentarily, thrown off stride. My father's question implies that a story rich in detail will unfold behind the right answer. Then I remember: We're a family long on theory and short on story. There is no illuminated manuscript to explore. The whole of our history amounts to little more than marginalia.

I'm interested in The Move, I tell him, I'm interested in what everyone remembers about the Mother Road.

Five minutes later, it's suddenly time for dinner.

࿏

Route 66 was somewhere under me, under Interstate 40 westbound out of Albuquerque. I drove a rented white Nissan but imagined my family in the blue Plymouth. I squinted at mesas in the distance as though squinting could bring the past into focus. I was on the way to the past all right, but not mine. I was on the way to Ácoma.

According to historian Ward Minge, tribal elders say the name *Ácoma* means a " 'place that always was, '. . . a home or even an eternal resting place." Archaeologists confirm habitation around 1200 A.D., but tribal legends move that date back to before the birth of Christ. Either way, I'm disposed to believe the pamphlet I picked up in the hotel lobby that calls Ácoma the oldest continuously inhabited site in the United States. I wanted to see what a place like this looks like.

More than that, I needed to see.

The afternoon before I'd driven to Idlewilde Lane, parked across the street from the first house I had any memory of. I squinted then, too. Did I think I'd see my oldest sister's first kiss under a weeping willow in the front yard or my face in the window, standing on a chair, watching the snow fall? Did I—yes, I guess I did—hope to comfort them all? My mother crying constantly until she is sent away to the hospital for a rest? The two year old I was, uncomprehending, yet certain, as children are, that they are the center of all things, of a mother's happiness—and her misery?

Sitting there in the Nissan, I saw one sure thing, old as I am old: a spruce my father planted in the front yard. My father, who sometimes calls me by the wrong name, but who remembers planting that tree and fertilizing it regularly with the ammonia he brought home from work forty years ago.

༄

A shuttle bus deposits us on the mesa at the pueblo of Ácoma where we meet Jeri, our guide. Jeri and several dozen other families live at Ácoma without electricity and running water but with, as Jeri says, a peace of mind she couldn't get in Albuquerque. She tried leaving, she says, but she missed the mesa, missed the quiet.

A pueblo 357 feet high in the middle of everywhere is a quiet place. Now. But not on January 22, 1599, the day Juan de Oñate's men arrived to avenge the death of one Juan de Zaldivar. The Spaniards burned the town and killed six hundred Ácomas. About seventy warriors were confined to a kiva, murdered one by one, and pitched off the mesa. Five hundred other captives, most of them women and children, were marched to Santo Domingo for trial. All males more than twenty-five years old were sentenced to twenty-five years of servitude, after having a foot amputated. Males between twelve and twenty-five and all females were condemned to bondage.

"Any questions?" Jeri tells this story of atrocity without embellishment, without any emotional discharge whatsoever. It is the same expression and voice she uses to tell us about pottery and bread kilns, about the cisterns, about the stout thirty-foot ladders cantilevered against the sides of the adobe houses, leveraged so that even a woman, fleeing to the safety of the roof, could pull one up behind her and strand her attackers on the ground.

Centuries of relative peace and self-sufficiency; centuries of siege, subjugation, and suffering. There is a doubling to everything in Ácoma. Every song of joy here has a sorrowful descant. What I realize at last is that Jeri isn't emotionally detached from the litany she delivers. This is her tourist face, her tourist voice; this is a demeanor she chooses purposely; a voice that is a shield, a face that is a shield, preventing us from taking the last thing Ácoma has, the one thing Ácoma has been able to keep: the story of Ácoma.

San Estevan del Rey mission church was built on the mesa between 1629 and 1641 by Fray Juan Ramirez. There is little inside the sixty-foot-high, ten-foot-thick walls: a dozen pews, a painting of San José with a few miracles to its credit, a simple altar on the chancel and above it a primitive and colorful fresco of saints.

Our group grows subdued. I look up at the thick roof vigas, forty feet long and fourteen inches thick each; fifty trees cut from a forest thirty miles away and hauled here by Ácomas for the greater glory of the Spanish god. It is cold in here. An adobe sarcophagus. Outside, a forty-foot-high wall retains the graveyard south of the church. It has been filled and filled and then filled again with earth laboriously hauled from the valley below. Ácoma ancestors rest above and below one another, several strata of what have been a durable and abiding people.

There are pottery sale stations every few hundred yards. The white clay Ácoma pottery is renowned for the intricacy of its designs, painstakingly painted with filaments stripped from the leaves of yucca. Concepción, who is the oldest woman I've ever seen is selling her bread. She smiles and nods and slides dollar bills into the pocket of her apron.

A few minutes later we get to the station where Jeri's pottery is on display and her brother is working. He takes the loaf of Concepción's bread from Jeri and hands his sister her lunch, a burrito.

The pottery is beautiful. The bread is soft and fragrant. But what I want isn't for sale. What I'm most aware of is what I can't pay for and pack out of here: the sound our feet don't make as we follow behind Jeri. Underfoot, everywhere that isn't sandstone, are several inches of flour-fine dirt. I begin to like the sensation of sinking in where I walk. Even through hiking boots I start to appreciate what setting down roots in a world without cement might be like.

At the end of the tour comes a choice: I can take the shuttle bus back down to the visitors' center, or I can climb down the Camino del Padre, a narrow, near vertical stairway of steps, footholds, and handholds carved into the side of the mesa. This is when I notice another striking thing about Ácoma. I haven't seen a refreshment stand or a public rest room. Not a bench or a trash bin. And, moreover, there are no guardrails to keep the unwary from stepping right off the edge of the mesa; not a single sign any-where forbidding this and warning that.

Released from my culture of precaution and forewarning, cut loose from that tether at long last, my sense of relief is as profound as it is old. Climbing down the Camino del Padre, fitting my fingers and toes into the stone where centuries of fingers and toes have gone before mine, I feel more confident and reliable than I probably should.

I am still a visitor here, but for a few minutes anyway I am also some-thing close to right at home.

II. SEPULVEDA

In midwinter in Utah a part of me is still impatient for overripe oranges to fall. I remember a vestigial orchard in the schoolyard where I played; how the boys improvised war games with soft fruit, how the girls gathered windfall in our skirts until a teacher scolded us for the indecent display of petticoats and underwear; how we came in from recess sticky, our fingers and tongues sweet with juice.

Sepulveda. A place-name borrowed probably from a wealthy Mexican landowner who settled here. But a name in which I hear the Latin root that makes *sepulchre* and *sepulture*. Burial. Funereal. And I hear *veda,* Spanish for *stop.* An interrupted burial? Or better, a disinterring, an unearthing.

ꙮ

The addresses changed, but the houses were all the same: wall-to-wall continuous filament carpet, bilious green, snagged and thread worn in high-traffic areas; ugly linoleum in the kitchen, chipped and buckling in the corners, stained with the ghostly shapes of recently departed appliances. Three bedrooms, two baths. Every room a different color as though the previous owner had purposely selected the gaudiest paint formulas, the real slow-movers, colors guaranteed to require a minimum of five coats (not counting the primer) to cover. In the backyard, bare dirt, packed and hard as a box of old brown sugar, colonized by a few obstinate weeds.

Fixer-uppers: These were our homes in the San Fernando Valley, other families' failed suburban experiments. Built in the late fifties and early six-ties, they were certainly not houses that people had grown old in and died in; not *those* kind of fixer-uppers, houses with history. Not the kind of house that the widow sells a year after the funeral when it's clear her son-in-law isn't going to make it by often to mow the lawn or change the washers in the faucets; not a house grandchildren remember; not a house with one disreputable but nonetheless adored mutt—Spud or Sport or Sparky—who will one day be buried in the backyard. These houses, the houses we lived in in the suburbs of Los Angeles, had at most two or three previous owners, all short-timers. These houses didn't need cellars and attics in which to store trunks and trikes: when the past was gone, it was *gone*. And front porches? No one stayed long enough in these neighborhoods to care who walked or drove by; these houses weren't for welcoming passersby. These houses had *back* porches, but front *stoops*.

These houses, our California houses, were tract homes. Down the street, a few doors away, was our house again, the replicate. Maybe some attempt had been made to disguise its lack of individuality: a portico, a fretwork of two-by-sixes decorating the side of the garage. All the same, it was a house like ours. Riding by on my bike, I felt a curious dualism: an undeniable connection to the other lives within, moving about in spaces that mimicked our own, yet a wave of mild revulsion, too, seeing this dwelling that housed a family of impostors living in a parallel dimension.

My father was the optimist. No prospective domicile was in a state too sorry for his earnest money. The puce and mauve and black walls, the bare yards, the slumping fences—these were the challenges by which one was proved worthy of home ownership.

The only problem was, my father wasn't terribly concerned with achieving closure. What interested him was not the *fait accompli* but the *cause perdu*. Consequently there was always a project half complete when another was launched, always a room we closed off when company came: plumbing was exposed or rectangular holes gaped in Sheetrock where something, who knew what, would manifest.

My mother had never had what she considered a real home; my father's devotion to the provisional meant that in fifty-six years of marriage her perception never changed.

∽

On a spring morning in 1959, my father left Saint Louis to take a new job in Albuquerque. By the time he turned the grill of our Plymouth onto Route 66, my mother would have been seated on the bottom stair crying. I was three months old; my sisters nine and fourteen, and there was this Missouri house to sell, and an entire household to pack. The sewer was backed up, and the basement was flooded. She could smell yesterday's bacon grease in the sleeve of her bathrobe. The question was, Would she stop crying before the plumber arrived? The question was, When it comes right down to it, who cares?

Maybe my father was in Springfield by the time she made the beds; clear to Oklahoma City when she finished giving me a bath that night. Did he call home from Amarillo? Did he open the map on the motel-room bed and trace the Mother Road from Lake Michigan across the country where it sips finally on the Pacific Ocean? Did his finger wonder about the towns along the way? Did he mispronounce Tucumcari when he said it to himself, out loud the first time? Was he already daydreaming, as he drove west to Alburquerque, of the house he would someday buy for us in California, that Promised Land at the far end of the Mother Road? *Just a fixer-upper for starters. Just a house that maybe needs a little attention.*

⌒

It's impossible to do anything well sideways at seventy miles an hour, although this has never stopped me from trying to read road maps flayed open on the front seat and steer at the same time. It's stupid. No question. But how can a little lost qualify as a reason to worry traffic by pulling off in the emergency lane? I passed a guy on Interstate 80 between Wendover, Nevada, and Salt Lake City last October with a paperback book propped against the steering wheel. It was dark, so he had the dome light on. Now *that's* what I call reckless. A person could ruin his eyes trying to read under a light like that.

All right. Stupid. But sideways at seventy is when a map makes the most sense to me: unfolded in the car in full view, while I'm actually moving toward some intended destination, when I'm actually *in* the process of getting lost. The only exception is when I'm lost on a freeway within the limits of any city, and then it might as well be a treasure map I'm looking at, all of the crucial landmarks cunningly encrypted: *Follow Interstate 405 until you see the scorpion that stings the mountain at midday, then exit.*

The irony is, I grew up on freeways of the worst kind, the California kind. I'm technically a veteran. But all those years, I never paid any attention to where I was being taken. My grade school, the Pinecrest Academy, materialized every morning at eight-thirty; the neighborhood grocery store, Hughes', two or three times a week. The dank barn of a rink in Culver City where I took ice-skating lessons appeared on Saturdays after an hour's drive from the Valley like the end of a bad dream. In fact I fell asleep coming and going on any trip that took more than thirty minutes one way—a symptom of the passivity I'm convinced only freeways can instill. Another being this bafflement I suffer now as an adult driving on them myself.

Here is what I learned as a child. To get somewhere my mother learned the names of two off-ramps: From and To. In the case of my father, knowing just one would do; you drove in circles and cussed until you located the second.

Unfortunately our family left California only a few months after I'd been issued my learner's permit, before I'd driven enough to formulate my own navigational strategy. But part of me—even the small, frightened part that suffers chronic disorientation—still believes if you can't take a freeway directly to a place you want to go, you have no business going there at all.

This afternoon, on the map in the seat next to me is the hesitant pathway I traced in blue ink from my motel room downtown to the San Fernando Valley. Today, even sideways at seventy, it makes no sense. Something tells me it will never look like the way home.

_ɕ_

Plummer, Swinton, Odessa Avenue. Three of our California houses are in the San Fernando Valley in the suburb of Sepulveda. All are within a few blocks of one another. I turn and double back, turn and circle around, until a familiar house finds itself in the rearview mirror.

Plummer to Woodley to Mayall to Swinton. Plummer to Gothic to Halsted to Odessa. Did these street names ever _mean_ anything to anyone? Here, where the postwar developers were throwing up tract homes and making road cuts faster than history could possibly provide any meaningful connection between place and name?

No. Here, place ceased to exist decades ago. It all became property instead.

On Odessa Avenue I park the car and do something I've only seen people in movies do: walk up to the door of a house you used to know and ask a stranger to let you in.

She does.

_ɕ_

Brenda lives alone with her dog who is also friendly. They're happy to show you around your own house. Brenda has seen the same movies; she's just never had the nerve to do what you have.

The big chalkboard in the kitchen where your mother helped you learn long division before the bus came is gone. Here is the dining room where she used to make out the Christmas cards. Here is the living room where the TV stories were told and the family stories were not.

Here is your bedroom where you tried to become Petula Clark because that's what California does: convinces people that who they are and where they are isn't enough. Your bedroom is Brenda's office now. The bookshelves your father built are gone, but Brenda is a writer, too, like you. It is some consolation.

This, you tell her, is where you crouched in the earthquake. And here, you say, is the trapdoor.

You don't really say that. The woman is a complete stranger after all. But the fact is, this house has several trapdoors. One by one they swing open beneath you, and you fall into remembering.

It was first thing in the morning, you say. Everyone still in bed. Except for your mother. What you don't mention to Brenda is how surprised you were to learn that your mother had started sleeping on the couch.

෴

What was it like?

A surprise.

A surprise is exactly what it was like. Earthquakes aren't tornadoes or hurricanes or blizzards or brushfires or volcanoes after all. They're a complete surprise. Something like an avalanche perhaps, but even then, well—there *is* snow piled up everywhere you look, isn't there? The point is, once you understand that the face of the planet isn't solid, but is *always* moving and that your parents are not fixed entities, but are *always* changing, nothing is ever the same.

Later, you will not be able to remember what an earthquake sounds like. You will not remember the sounds the earthquake must have caused: the thud, the shatter, the crumple, the slam, the creak, the pop, the squeal, the crash. You'll think it odd, surveying the condition of your home, that you do not remember actually seeing any objects airborne; that you didn't notice the refrigerator square dancing with the range or the tsunami in the swimming pool.

If you're asleep when it happens, the first thing you'll do is find shoes; you never realized until now how much glass the average house contains.

After you find your shoes, you'll be out of ideas, but your mother will already be mopping up the kitchen floor—during the aftershocks. This image will haunt you until several years later when you can afford psychotherapy. If you locate your pet, you will have looked in the most uncomfortable, inconspicuous, or incongruous space you can think of relative to the size and customary habits of its species. The cat may be hiding in the dryer—in the lint trap.

When you and your neighbors are instructed to evacuate because the integrity of the reservoir's dam may be compromised, you begin packing. But you do not take anything that will make sense when you unpack a few hours later. You will take a drawer full of cancelled checks and reconciled bank statements, the television with the poor reception, the clothes you meant to box up for the Salvation Army two years ago. You'll watch your neighbors packing, too. Later you'll remember seeing one of them load an aquarium into the trunk of the car and reassure yourself with this thought: *Some people are even bigger idiots than I am in an emergency.*

That night in a motel, if you're lucky enough to find a motel, you will watch average citizens on television trying to understand an awesome force and their utter impotence; this miracle, that senseless tragedy. You will not be able to escape irony. In developing nations, suffering is the by-product of natural disaster; in American suburbs, it's irony: the one house left standing after a landslide; the straw run clean through a two-by-six during the cyclone; the freeway overpass that didn't collapse on your father because he overslept and missed the carpool.

For some time to come, you will feel aftershocks. You will sleep with your shoes on and not well at all. Years later, in another country, in a hotel a few blocks from where a new subway line is going in, a crew will detonate an explosive underground, and you will feel the unexpected vibrations through the floorboards of your room; you will hear a pane of glass rattling, as loose in its glazing as an old tooth in a socket.

And suddenly you will remember everything you learned in the house on Odessa Avenue.

❧

Somehow in the few seconds before you tell Brenda good-bye, the conversation slips, like a thrust fault, from earthquakes to the topic of food supplements. At this time Brenda tells you that she and her dog are both taking blue-green algae regularly and feel better now than they have in years.

This is good news, you tell her. Very good news indeed.

III. KA LAE

We are not birds after all, and birds are not us. Though journey can be a story and a way of finding memory and home, sometimes the one right destination may be all that we need.

At the end of the Mother Road we climb into the sky and fly toward morning, west over water to Hawai'i. The disagreement began on the ground somewhere between Punalu'u and Nā'ālehu.

It was a day in February of the year I turned forty. We were on our way to Ka Lae, The Point. I'd become intrigued by heiau—those sites where ancestral Hawai'ians sent up prayers for fish, for taro, for love, for rain, and for courage; platforms or enclosures of lava rock often remained, separating sacred ground. There was, I'd read, a heiau called Kalalea at South Point, but I knew nothing more.

My husband, though, insisted we'd been to Ka Lae before. I was just as sure he was wrong, that I'd never seen this place, that I'd only visited Hawai'i one other time with him, briefly, and that South Point had not been a stop we'd made. He had been here before, of course—with someone else. How difficult it can be sometimes to keep our memories sorted out.

A road, you see, is never just a road. A road starts as a journey and becomes a story—or an interrupted conversation. But the road to Ka Lae was even more: at 18.54 degrees north latitude, it was the farthest point two married Americans could go south in their own country.

To South Point the road was barely wide enough for two cars to pass in opposite directions, and twelve miles on such a stretch can seem like a very long way. The grasses on either side of the car were browsed to ragged stubble; I could almost imagine we were back on the mainland, driving across Wyoming. The heliotrope was permanently twisted to the ground by the persistent makani. The ocean wasn't yet in view but respect for it was: all of the tin-roofed houses were perched on stilts. I thought: *Lucky for us we live in Utah on bedrock at the edge of a memory of old water where the land doesn't end, where the landscape reminds us of what can last and why.* I thought: *We'd never have survived this long, the two of us, living twelve feet in the air with a current of trade winds always under our feet. One of us would surely have blown away by now.*

When the road forks, we follow the sign that says VISITOR CENTER.

It is a rusting trailer, is all, with three steps up. Three wooden steps that the salt air wants to cure and the humidity wants to rot. Inside the trailer there are many things to touch—shells, musical instruments, konane—but not much to buy. Postcards. A few books. I do not see any ili'ili stones, though. So I go to the woman in the muumuu who is shaped like a papaya, whose skin is the color of copra, whose teeth are as white as sand.

Who says, My name is Leimomi, which means necklace of pearls. Who smiles and bends and brings the ili'ili stones up from under the counter. Who says, I put them away when no one seemed interested. Who tells me the story then.

The black stone is the mother. She is from Pele, a lava stone with round lava pebbles like ova embedded in her flesh. See?: her children. The white stone is the father. For the children, the ili'ili, to be born, you must put the black stone and the white stone in water together.

Leimomi demonstrates and smiles. She is quiet, looking at me, and then she says, "You've been here before, I think."

Never to Ka Lae. To Hawai'i, just once.

"No. Another life, perhaps. And now that you've returned, I won't say *mahalo* to you, because *mahalo* means good-bye. To you I will say, *a hui ho,* good-bye for now, because you and I, we'll meet again."

At South Point my husband and I sit for a while on lava thrones worn round and smooth by water and wind and time. After he leaves I watch the waves flatten and spread across a patio of lava, releasing the heat held in the black rock.

I lie in the warm sheet of water to think. I lie on the grass inside the heiau to dry.

When I look for my husband later I will find him, as I often do, with another fisherman. This time he'll be standing on the edge of a cliff with an islander whose line is hundreds of yards at sea, learning a new way to turn hope into flesh.

⌒

Tomorrow morning I will still be thinking about the other story Leimomi told me. What she said when I asked her if she'd seen the Night Walkers here, seen their torches, heard their drums; when I asked her if she believed that the spirits of the old ones returned to the heiau, to the places they'd known.

Oh, yes, she said. Yes. But the young ones can be just as noisy. In my home in a basket I keep the bone of an infant taken from its grave by a scientist. The bone was happy as long as my children were young and the house was full of their laughter. But now that they are grown and gone, the bone cries at night. It will not be comforted. I have been working to trace its provenance, so I can take the bone home again.

On the way to the airport tomorrow afternoon, I will see messages professing immutable love spelled out in white coral on black sand. I will think of the Bonneville Salt Flats and messages of longing there, black on white.

In Hawai'i I am *haole,* a white woman. A stranger. In Utah I am a gentile, a nonbeliever. A stranger. But this is only one version of the story, and it's an old one. In the new story, in both places, and elsewhere, I am home.

Map, Landscape, and Story

DOUGLAS CARLSON

On your chosen site, let memory speak.
—ELEVENTH-CENTURY JAPANESE
GARDENING MANUAL

MY GRANDFATHER on my father's side was a gardener—by vocation. After emigrating from Sweden around 1900, he cared for a series of modest estates from Massachusetts to Vermont to southwestern New York. When the estate gardener gave way in the 1950s to "landscape firms"— seasonal help employed to do the mowing and trimming and digging and weeding, all under a supervisor's eye—he became a gardener for a company that produced metal office furniture. What a factory gardener did is anyone's melancholy guess; I suspect he mowed the strips of lawn around the buildings and put in occasional flower beds—hand-me-downs from the times of factory towns when landscaped space, that escaped remnant of the natural world, was planned into workers' daily lives. Whatever he did, when winter turned soil to ice, he went inside and worked on the line. And when soil became stone as the green spaces were paved over, he went inside to work for good.

Yet his passion for gardening remained, taking root around his home. An ordinary, small front yard like the rest on the street, an ordinary house, an ordinary driveway alongside leading to the garage—those predictable squares and rectangles could not disclose the back. What was undoubtedly once a simple, rectangular lawn that sloped up slightly from the house had been transformed into two flat semicircles. The lower was connected to the upper by a set of stone stairs under a rose trellis. Each lawn was bordered by beds of columbine, peonies, and hollyhocks and by a honeysuckle hedge that closed it off completely from the neighbors' view. At the far end of the upper lawn, almost entirely hidden in the low branches of a pair of arbor vitae, was a lawn swing.

In 1953 my grandfather had a severe heart attack. And, as was the case in those benighted days, he was told to rest completely—first in the hospital, then in a hospital bed in the living room. After months, he improved to the point where he was allowed to sit up, then stand, then take a few steps. In March of the next year, probably feeling the "green fuse" of spring, he asked my grandmother to get his shovel and rake from the garage. In his living room, among the doilies and old photographs and overstuffed chairs, he pretended to dig up and rake out a flower bed. Then he got back into the hospital bed and died.

It became my task after he died to mow his lawn—something I both loved and feared. The dread came from my grandmother, whose mourning over him apparently continued throughout the many years she survived him. Often when I came into the house for a drink of water or to use the bathroom, I would surprise her at full-throated grieving. Worse, after each mowing, I was obliged to eat fancy cookies while sitting at the dining room table in front of a lace place mat and a delicate plate. She, always on the verge of tears, would sit and try to talk with me—of him, of what, I have no recollection. But it was definitely too much for a twelve year old who already had learned an appreciation of the Swedish art of restraint. The joy came from the gardens. I would allot myself a certain number of circuits with the push mower, then sit for a while on the lawn swing, then mow, then sit. Of course, I had seen such gardens in pictures, but now, as a mower of lawns, I possessed one.

A passion like my grandfather's becomes legacy. So when my father returned to his hometown and bought land, he became a gardener too, but of a different type. He was a teacher and a physicist. His gardens were made to be eaten: work converted to food converted to energy. His were gardens of rows, angles, and order. He gardened and my mother canned. Rows of beets, beans, and peas became rows of jars of beets, beans, and peas. Teachers didn't make much then; his becoming a vegetable gardener who grew flowers only as time permitted was probably by necessity. But whether by necessity or design, two gardeners raised two quite different gardens.

While at my grandfather's house, I relished the magic of the step up under the trellis into a private space with scent and color and imagination; at my father's I sullenly hoed beans in the sun. Not that his garden wasn't a beautiful thing in its way. Each spring an acre was plowed and dragged. At the northwest corner, my father began a path with his rake. With great care, he described a perfect square within the larger rectangle of the garden. Within the square, the smaller vegetables grew; the larger, expansive ones—potatoes, corn, and tomatoes—were relegated to the outside.

To anyone else, this was the logical garden. I knew better; actually my father had made a baseball diamond. The careful pathway he raked became base paths; carrots, lettuce, beets, and spinach made up the infield; the outfield stretched away to the corn. Imagine my emotions when forty years later I watched Ray Kinsella's dead father emerge from a cornfield onto a ball field in the film *Field of Dreams.*

After supper, I would gather round stones into piles in that northwest corner, which became home plate to me. One by one, I would toss them up and belt them with a crude bat I had turned on a lathe in wood shop: screaming line drives into the potato bed, long home runs over the corn. The rules were simple, and I was honor-bound to follow them: an out was any stone I popped up or overspun into the small vegetables; a double reached the potatoes, a home run went where home runs always go.

But here, I must confess. This was not *entirely* a lonely kid making up summer games to amuse himself. I remember clearly a certain pleasure when an occasional stone would dip down and rip through a row of beets or Swiss chard—never on purpose because of the rules of the game—but I apparently found some perverse joy in damaging the plants. Clearly I saw my father's control over his garden as more evidence of a world out to control me. I fought back as any kid would.

But a third-generation gardener was bound to emerge with his own garden on his own terms. The years 1969–1975, what we're now calling the Vietnam years. I was married with a son, trying to teach freshman comp with honor, facing every professor's dilemma then: should I be responsible for changing my male students' status from II-S to I-A just because they can't write complete sentences?

We bought a house. We were middle-class poor—teachers *still* didn't get paid much. I entered into an agreement with an elderly neighbor to work his vegetable garden in exchange for a share of the food. He was at least eighty-five and had gardened for his entire life. His gardens were my father's gardens—but without the baseball diamond. It didn't work. He drove me crazy. No matter how I prepared the soil, dug the holes, fertilized, watered, planted—it wasn't right. Of course it wasn't. Imagine my grandfather from his living room bed: don't push the shovel down that way, you'll hurt your back; don't dig that rake in so deep; turn it over so the tines are up to smooth the soil. My neighbor and I tried for a couple years. Then I retreated to my own small backyard, by now abandoned to the demands of two sons who needed a space for Wiffle ball, touch football, and Frisbee. So I mowed.

Like a flying stone slashing a lettuce patch, I mowed through peonies, hydrangeas, iris, and lupines that the former owner had planted. I put up fences around the property and mowed to within four feet of them, letting the land grow into a border of feral columbine, evasive goldenrod, grasses, sumac shoots, and brambles. Beyond this barrier, events were happening that repeatedly brought us to tears of rage and sadness. Within this boundary, I created a place where my sons could play and that, once a week, I could shred into submission. This was a garden too, and gardens are, after all, about control.

Lawns are about total control—without imagination. I can look back now and remember mowing my father's lawn. With friends, he was building his own house the summer I was eleven. Since the land had been cleared to the dirt and he hadn't time or money to make a proper lawn, he decided simply to let the grasses grow back and keep them mowed. One of my daily jobs was to bring his lunch up a long path from the house we had rented for the summer, through an abandoned pasture, to the building site. On the way I was to fill a bag with clover seed that I scattered each day on the lawn. For years I pushed a mower through a confusion of sweet smells and honeybees.

But this Vietnam mowing was far different. While the decisions of Johnson, Westmoreland, and MacNamara were beyond my power to change, and my draft-age friends' fates were determined by a lottery, at least here was something I could control—with the crudest of technology possible. No plant was a match for my spinning steel blade and roaring ferocity.

෴

In 1979, my wife and I went with a realtor to look at a small cottage on the shore of eastern Lake Erie and about ten miles from our home. The place, empty for several years, was a wreck: windows were broken, the roof leaked, a fallen tree had destroyed the porch and bedroom. But these problems didn't prove to be the worst. The cottage stood thirty feet from the edge of a bluff that was about to begin some serious erosion. How could we have known then? We made the dumbest and best decision of our lives. We bought it.

For most of recent time, the space our cottage occupies today was water. Other times it was air—or mud, or silt. Geologic time seems to be measured by the news of what filled various spaces at various times. Three hundred fifty million years ago, a huge sea, fed from rivers that eroded the surrounding mountains, covered most of New York State. Residue from these rivers created the Catskill Delta, thousands of layers of clay and silt that compressed to form the shale, siltstone, and sandstone that we call solid ground. But as the seawater receded and, much later, the glaciers passed over, new rivers and valleys were cut from the rock. Siltstone and shale returned to clay, which flowed into the basin of a prehistoric lake. Twelve thousand years ago that larger lake receded to form the present Lake Erie and exposed the old lake bottom, a bed of clay mixed with glacial residue. Someone built a tiny cottage on this pile of clay around 1930. The pile was then and remains now a solid clay mass twenty feet deep resting on a ten-foot layer of glacial till. What we bought was that cottage and some very unstable land.

Clay is lazy, fat, and leaden. Its pores are small so water moves downward through it with unbelievable slowness. Even during midsummer, moss clings to the bluff's face, an indication of the unusual amount of water still burdening the soil. And what we didn't know was how much this water had increased, that the decade before we bought the cottage was the wettest in more than a century for the Great Lakes' coasts. Excess groundwater creates instability; instability causes erosion. Groundwater moves through barely permeable clay to even less permeable glacial till, where it enters a small layer of silt called a lens. The till stops the groundwater's downward progress, so it follows the lens horizontally to the bluff face, creating seep zones and causing the face to fall away.

But at its crest, the bluff is under more duress. Rain continues to add weight to the clay; pressure increases on its pores; an already unstable system deteriorates further. Shear strength, a soil's ability to hold itself together, decreases. Meanwhile, storms throw waves, sometimes more than ten feet high, against the bluff's toe. All is out of balance, a condition that natural forces will not tolerate.

That first year we lost fourteen feet of land. Six the next. Our neighbor to the east sank a six-foot, steel break wall in cement. Our neighbor to the west built an intricate bulkhead of I-beams, railroad ties, cable, and tons of dirt. I didn't do anything. The next spring, except for the twisted, useless metal they had, our shorelines looked the same.

It wasn't difficult to see that our bluff, if left alone, would eventually solve its own problem. A near-vertical wall wouldn't march inland indefinitely; a gentler slope would begin to emerge. And each spring, pioneer plants—wild raspberry, goldenrod, thistle, and coltsfoot—would make another try.

First we needed some time; then we had to hurry the natural process of reclamation along. In the fall of 1986, I tore down the porch (most of which was suspended over the bluff in midair) and the bedroom (with the roof that never did stop leaking). Then, with an extraordinarily clever friend and advisor, we lowered what was left of the cottage onto wooden skids. When the ground froze, we brought in three come-alongs, a lot of chain, six hearty friends—and moved the cottage back thirty feet. I guessed that we had bought about five years.

Then I made a garden.

The text for my bluff garden might have come from a paraphrase of that old garden hater, Henry Thoreau: "That gardener is best who gardens least." Working the ground was out of the question since anything I did would simply be washed away by the first rainstorm, and I saw no reason to introduce some new cover species to struggle in that miserable soil when certain plants had already shown a willingness to grow there. I simply gathered seeds, even whole plants, and dumped all these aggressive weeds on the flatter areas.

I got lucky: we had a dry winter. The land that fell away didn't slide all the way to the beach; it formed the beginning of a ledge instead. And the herbaceous plants gained some valuable company—sumac and locust seedlings. From there on it was easy; each season I added brush and cuttings from yard work on other parts of the property. Each June, I trimmed the tops of the quickly maturing seedlings, driving their energy into their roots. For the time being, we could sit on our deck and look over a wild tangle of color and life to the waves beyond.

Thank you, Henry. But, as well, you teach us that this fragile balance can't last long.

Finally giving up on trying to stop the inevitable loss of his land, our neighbor to the west bought property across the road and moved his cottage to safety, unintentionally creating something rare: vacant lakefront property that no one would ever build on. I began watching with interest as maple and locust seedlings appeared in the unmowed lawn, as goldenrod, aster, and thistle flowered during the first fall. I planned some succession studies to learn what happened when a garden invented itself. Then something happened that changed our relationship with our cottage permanently.

On a day the next April, a plague of loud and huge machines invaded. I had been bathing in new sunshine, listening to the cries of killdeer and redwings where there had a month before been only an occasional gull, to the splash and retreat of waves released from ice. In an instant all sounds of spring were shattered, and in four hours, I lived next to a fresh, raw gully leading to the lake (the developer called it lake access for property he was selling), seventy-five feet wide and gradually deepening to thirty feet as it reached the edge of the shoreline bluff. Not a plant remained. Some gardening.

∽

Having been devastated by technology again—first hearing horror stories of napalm and tanks, then watching bulldozers—I began reading on the topic. In the introduction to an otherwise businesslike bibliography that I found, *Technology in Early America,* Brooke Hindle brought me up short with this: "Perhaps technology was not so much a tool or a means as it was an experience—a satisfying emotional experience." The presence of this genuinely new (for me) idea enabled me to take a fresh look at gardens and lawns. At man, nature, and control.

In the beginning was the desire to gain control of nature. The means—religion, magic, and technology—probably developed in complex, unpatterned ways. But John Collins in *Primitive Religions* makes one distinction: "The attitude [while doing magic] is one of manipulation—of putting the components of magic together in a proper, efficacious manner. Because of this mechanistic nature, the emotionalism associated with religion is generally lacking in magical practice. What is found is usually a detached, impersonal feeling." The self-reliant magician replaces the praying supplicant, which implies a sequence in which the left hemisphere of the brain gains precedence over the right as people become more independent, less superstitious. Then technology, more rational and successful than magic, eventually displaces it. Yet the desire for control remains, to be satisfied through sometimes useful and sometimes gratuitous acts of technology that—almost magically—defy nature. Something has been handed down.

As Bronislaw Malinowski wrote, "Thus in his relation to nature and destiny, whether he tries to exploit the first or to dodge the second, primitive man recognizes both the natural and the supernatural forces and agencies, and he tries to use them both for his benefit. . . . He never relies on magic alone while . . . he sometimes dispenses with it completely. But he clings to it, whenever he has to recognize the impotence of his knowledge and of his rational technique." Modern man remains reminded of his impotence each time nature turns on him through, for example, erosion, storms, his own death. And we've been conditioned to believe in the new magic, regaining control through the technological fix.

And what developed from my neighbor's "beach access" gully, his triumph of technology over nature? A fine return on his investment: he sold three building lots across the road. He also left behind a new, grotesque study zone for me to work on the following summer.

Using a pile of one-inch PVC pipes I bought for reconnecting the plumbing, I separated the gully sides into three horizontal sections of ten feet each. Then I laid more pipe up and down the slope, dividing each section into ten-foot grids. I had the soil from each of the three horizontal sections tested and each week counted, by grid, the plants that grew back the year after the first bulldozer attack. At the bottom third of the *V,* the steepest section, white deposits of salts discolored the surface. The land had turned to the antithesis of earth: a pH of eight, no organic matter to hold nutrients, minerals only, silt waiting to float on the rain into the lake. The soil analysis disclosed what I already had guessed: low in phosphorus, 1.4 percent organic matter, off the chart in magnesium and calcium. In any ten-by-ten area, fewer than fifteen plants—maple sprouts of the year and coltsfoot—struggled. In the middle area, some pioneer plants—hedge bindweed, black medick, goldenrod, and ragweed—survived where some clay remained and where the gulch's feeder streams permitted. But even these hardy pests were sparse, about a hundred to a grid. Finally, at the top where the grade was less steep, other plants thrived. Chicory, dock, and Queen Anne's lace gave the impression of a struggle that the plants could win: a country roadside in late summer, but only after the seasonal herbicide application.

This atrocity offends me in three ways. A green place of variety and life is denied us. The destruction of a shoreline buffer allows nutrients and silt to run directly into the lake. And the whole idea is wrong because it doesn't work. Only the nimblest can stumble down the beach access's washes in dry weather. No one tries after rain. Left defenseless, the land succumbs easily to rain, wind, and waves. Beach access soon becomes beach, then lake bottom. Even a beginner in the dirt-pushing business, keen to do *something* with his big, new machines, should have anticipated all this.

Slowly I began to understand that it was this same garden-by-bulldozer mind-set that, in my own backyard, sheared the perennials that my wife loved, that imposes a lawn on nature, that mows through memory. I find no compensation for the loss. Too late, I try to make the gardens my father and grandfather made, but my wife and I have lives that increasingly keep us from the land that might once have grounded us. We'll rent or sell our house, and we'll wander. We'll make a garden of whatever the landscape we live in permits: hanging plant, window box, squash bed, or flower border. We'll call that place, for the time being, home.

Introduction

Thirty years in the same job, fifty in the same region—and a strong need for change came over Donna and me. A signal change it was too: from the dairy farms and rolling hills of upstate New York to the wheat fields and plains of the Midwest, from the confrontational hubbub of the New York State University system to a small Lutheran college where nearly all remains tacit. And having developed a taste for motion, we dropped off our belongings at our new home in Moorhead, Minnesota, and headed even farther west, to Yellowstone National Park.

Thus we found ourselves on a high porch outside the third-story apartment we had just rented for the week. Fifty feet below, the Yellowstone River rushed by sounding to us exactly like what it was, a hurrying stream. And since hurrying water had become an unfamiliar sound to our newly trained, flatlander ears, we listened as we composed that ubiquitous free-verse poem: the grocery list. Then I slowly began to realize that, because we had just traveled eight hundred miles in two days, the stream was sounding more like tires on the interstate, or the wall heater in the motel room we had slept in the night before. The sound of the river was becoming known to us by what *was* known.

Across Paradise Valley, the Gallatin Mountains, snow already on their peaks, glowed in the fall sun that warmed our faces. Something as stationary as a mountain felt good to the eyes after the car's fleeting landscapes. We debated English muffins or dry cereal for breakfasts; we sipped our wine; we were settling in.

An hour later, we crossed the river and were headed toward the entrance to Yellowstone when Donna turned around and noticed that she could see *"our* house" from the park entrance. I knew what she meant, and I also knew that we had probably set a record for finding home. When I came back to the car a few hours later, after a saunter along a small stream, I said that I'd "like to get started for home" before the snow began. She understood.

We talked a bit about our uprootedness as we drove home through soaring lines of mountainsides that took our thoughts up and through acres of burned lodgepoles. If our efficiency apartment in the Absaroka Lodge wasn't our home, what was? We own a house in upstate New York that has become home to three college hockey players. We own a tiny cottage on a bluff overlooking Lake Erie; since we've stopped using it, *Eptesicus fuscus,* big brown bats—a half-dozen of them—have made it their home. Our one-year home on the northern plains is someone else's real home, but it feels like real home to me when I reach out the door for *my* paper then read it over coffee while watching the rising sun return the color to *my* yard. When my one-year visiting-writer appointment in Minnesota is over, we'll have another home, as yet unknown, for our list.

Just the week before, a homeless man had been murdered by one of his colleagues in a park a few miles from where we live. I suggested to Donna that "homeless" was a misnomer. The victim certainly had lived a horrifying, poverty-ridden, dysfunctional life, but he did have a home—two in fact. He spent days in a tent and slept in an abandoned car for safety and privacy.

I recalled that years ago a friend of Donna's died in childbirth. I was doing shorebird research that summer and so visited the same beaches each day. And each day I saw the husband, lying on a beach towel, his head inches from a portable radio. In his grief, his house was surely no home. We were expecting *our* second child then, and I shuddered on the rainy days when his spot on the beach was empty. Where did he go?

We had spent the night before we got to Yellowstone with a friend in Billings who took us to his favorite eatery, the "Suds Hut." When the friendly waitress learned that we were strangers, she had asked, "So where do you guys call home?" I wanted to say "Anywhere."

Or "Everywhere."

Discussions of place often identify it with story and suggest that the more stories per place one remembers the closer he is to "home." As this present essay was conceived with its loosely defined subject of "dwelling places," I was living not far from where I grew up and in the same house where we had raised our sons. A million stories. An easy task. But the more stories I exhumed and examined, the more frustrating the work became. No matter what memory I chased or what image I delved into, the result was a question: why would you stay in one place for so long? My answer:

In western New York, my library of choice was the Lockwood Library at the University of Buffalo; it was big, but I could find anything quickly. The second day on my new job at Concordia College, I walked into the Carl B. Ylvisaker Library. The on-line catalog fought me; the stacks confused me. Forget doing research, I couldn't find the bathroom or a drinking fountain. I couldn't even pronounce the library's name. I felt foolish. And old. I was reminded of the terrible turns in health that Donna's mother and father took when they were removed to hospitals and nursing homes. Change *is* hard.

And then there are the made-up reasons. The kids—a move during adolescent years is dangerous. The failing parents—*someone* has to take care of them. The possessions—who'll close up the cottage in the fall, who'll weed the garden and tend to house repairs, what about our stuff? And finally I'm left with the first law of motion: "Every body continues in its state of rest . . . unless it is compelled to change that state by forces impressed upon it."

Some psychologists separate the forces that drive stress into two types: life strains and life events. I was tired of the responsibility of a decaying house, the repetition of a mind-numbing job, and especially the predictability of daily life. Recent life events moved our move along: the kids left home, several valued colleagues were "downsized," our home was burglarized and our gardens repeatedly vandalized. When I listened to them, I found that my stories told me that my life and work and home had become disappointing, stale, and unpleasant. Instead of writing, I was whining.

In *Placeways: A Theory of Human Environment*, Victor Walter defines place as a location of experience that "evokes and organizes memories, images, sentiments, meaning, and the work of the imagination." Bad places evoke bad images and memories, and a home becomes a bad place when these negative evocations weaken the imagination. Walter's reading of French philosopher Gaston Bachelard ties home to place. For Bachelard, "The home gathers images, cementing memory to imagination. . . . [W]e build houses to support [and shelter] daydream, and the home acknowledges our daydreams." The murdered "homeless" man's homes had failed him: violence dominated his images; spray paint and other drugs obliterated his memories; his imagination died long before he did, his life having turned from daydream to nightmare.

For us, the same was happening in ways less dramatic but no less real. So we quit our jobs, rented our house, and began the process of redefinition with the premises that "home" didn't have to be the same as confinement, that life was not merely an unpleasant tape loop of "homelessness," and that expressive places will become sheltering and supporting homes as they become, in Walter's phrase, "containers of good feelings."

Part One—Home on the Range

Chautauqua County, New York State, various houses and apartments, off and on for fifty years.

Barnstable County, Massachusetts, various bay-side cottages, every June for twenty-five years.

Billings and McKenzie Counties, North Dakota, various motels near Theodore Roosevelt National Park, multiple visits in 1997.

We were, after all, at Yellowstone to write, and it was, after all, October. So when a snowstorm closed the park roads three days after our arrival, we weren't surprised or even disappointed. We sat in our rooms and watched squalls drifting up and down the faces of the mountains that we faced across the valley, sometimes obscuring the foothills, sometimes teasing us with glimpses of near-summit peaks. And we talked of places where we felt, at one time or another, "at home."

Three places emerged as important and, we knew, would find their way into my essay: upstate New York for its longevity, Cape Cod for its poignancy, and Theodore Roosevelt for its newness.

༄

We had been to the Grand Canyon, so erosion was no surprise, and we had seen Badlands photographs. But still our first view of Theodore Roosevelt National Park was a shock. We had chosen to approach the north unit from Watford City—driving south through a mix of rolling prairie and occasional buttes. We were beginning to wonder, as the brown-and-white road signs counted down the distance to Theodore Roosevelt by tens, just how bad these Badlands could possibly be. Then just a mile from the park entrance, the buttes that crowded the west side of the road parted—and bam—red scoria, brown and yellow clay, blue bentonitic clay, black lignite, dark green/light green juniper, silver-green sage, red/green/brown grasses. This was not a couple of introductory, weathered buttes but a full-blown swath of violent erosion (if an action lasting a half-million years can be called violent) that extended to the horizon.

I slammed on the brakes and backed up; the confusion of black skid marks on the road showed I wasn't the first. And we sat and stared as trucks and cars drove by, ostensibly without interest. How could they? Here we were: stunned to silence again. But I quickly realized that this first-time experience was unlike most others. The first time I saw a male magnificent frigate bird, a humpback whale, a cottonmouth—these were moments that incorporated motion in an already familiar setting. Here the moment wasn't at all momentary; we humans could pass by, sure in the knowledge that this unsurpassed view would be around the next day, year, or decade pretty much unchanged except for the occasional fall of pieces of scoria, chunks of clay. As we walked the trails and drove the circles in subsequent weeks, land formations became familiar: like houses on a street, furniture in a room. They became familiar so quickly that when we drove the southern circle or walked a circular trail in the reverse direction for the first time, we became disoriented with the unknown backsides of things to misguide us.

That first trip was superficial; everything was too new to our northeastern eyes that had grown up accustomed to green and rolling hills, cow barns, and small, dingy towns. Hiking was out of the question—the temperature in nearby Dickinson was one hundred degrees the day we arrived. But a week later we left the sanctuary of an air-conditioned car and walked on Coal Vein Trail in the south unit near Medora. I was scrambling up a small butte for a better view, slipping and sliding on the silty clay surface when my feet finally let go and I went down—both knees and both elbows and nearly some face. First my brain reminded me of something I had just read in the trail guide: the holes in the clay (that I was staring at from a foot away) were common homes for black widow spiders. Then from a deeper memory, a strong sense of déjà vu of having walked here before. Later I remembered some research I had done for an earlier essay. A book called *Body, Memory, and Architecture* by Kent C. Bloomer and Charles W. Moore built on earlier work about perception by J. J. Gibson that considered the senses as perceptual systems. One such system is the "haptic" sense, or "the sense of touch reconsidered to include the entire body rather than merely the instruments of touch, such as the hands. To sense haptically is to experience objects in the environment by actually touching them (by climbing a mountain rather than staring at it). Treated as a perceptual system the haptic incorporates all those sensations (pressure, warmth, cold, pain, and kinesthetics) that previously divided up the sense of touch." So first my feet and legs noticed, then my eyes: I *had* walked here before, but fifteen hundred miles away.

Our Lake Erie cottage teeters on the edge of a clay bluff of thirty vertical feet. To the northeast is a twenty-foot-deep gully cut into the clay by an unnamed stream. To the southwest is a larger gash cut into the clay by a fool and his bulldozer—a failed experiment in shoreline development. To get down to the lake and back up, I had to negotiate one of these three approaches. So it was the clays—the yellow, brown, and blue clay of the Badlands and the brown clay of New York—and their stories and their shared metaphors that connected these two different landscapes.

The Badlands' clay story is a bit more involved than the story of the clay my cottage was built on. As the Rocky Mountains were being formed from a massive land uplift sixty-five million years ago, they were simultaneously providing eroded materials to form a broad alluvial plain to the east. At the same time, volcanic ash was being blown or carried by streams into standing water where it decomposed to become the blue layers of bentonitic clay. These depositions continued until the Pliocene period (5.2 million years ago) when episodes of gentle erosion by slow, meandering rivers began and continued until the close of the period about three million years later. Then the advancing continental ice sheets began to block north-flowing rivers, such as the Little Missouri that flows through Theodore Roosevelt, and sent them on a steeper descent, into the Mississippi River basin. Rushing now, and cutting deeply into the soft layers of sedimentary rock, the Little Missouri and its many tributaries worked quickly and effectively for six hundred thousand years to create the Badlands' precipitous edges, its violently disordered terrain, its heart-stopping beauty.

The result is a landscape of buttes and conical hills with horizontal clay bands of varied colors interspersed with black strips of lignite, rust-colored strips of iron oxide, and brick-red strips of scoria—formed when lignite occasionally burned and fire-hardened the clays. I've become familiar enough with some individual Badlands buttes to recognize them. The clay bluff at my Lake Erie cottage is brown, all the way down. If I were shown a photograph of it, I'd be unable to distinguish it from all those many similar ones that line Lake Erie's southern shore. But whether scrambling up or sliding down, I'd know that clay is clay. And whether eastern clay or western clay, it will fill with water and sag, slide, and slump—reaching a sort of clay entropy, level and featureless once more. This common fate they share.

⁓

But for now, western New York has hills, albeit low and gradual ones. Every day on my commute to work, I climbed four hundred feet, from near the Lake Erie shore to the snow ridge, an area of hills at around twelve hundred feet. The drive covered ten miles. Without a doubt, this lack of topographical drama in our former lives was an important reason that Buck Hill, a few feet short of the highest point of land in the park, became our favorite spot in the south unit of Theodore Roosevelt. From here, our morning coffee stop, we faced generally southward over a small table of grama and buffalo grass whose edge is twenty feet away. There the land falls away over a series of drops, ledges, and slopes from twenty-nine hundred feet to twenty-five hundred feet in about one-quarter mile. The flat valley below is more than a mile wide, dotted with low, juniper-topped buttes and cut by coulees that mark Paddock Creek's tributaries, which formed the valley. Otherwise the valley floor is grassy with bare areas of silt at the bases of the larger buttes. Then the land rises again over more buttes and hills to nearly the same height as Buck Hill. The result is a two-mile-wide bowl with a one-mile-flat bottom, some interesting sides, and a lot of sky. It is the antithesis of western New York topography: it is free, unpredictable, wide open, and generous. Here we sat in the grass and drank our coffee, looked out over the valley, talked over our morning walks, and made notes.

Often our talk turned to what was becoming a theme for us: how we kept coming across pleasantly remembered things in this unknown land. So we might be taking turns with the telescope watching wild horses graze or a huge, old bison snooze and be recalling northern juncos—how they flew up in front of us on a ledge just below the ridge at Theodore Roosevelt National Park's Wind Canyon in the same way they scattered into our Lake Erie cottage's gully on those rare, fresh, fall days back east. Slate-gray tails, darting white outer-tail coverts, and bright-yellow leaves—this image is treasured whether the leaves are North Dakota's cottonwoods or New York's wild grape. Or we might have talked of the walk to the Little Missouri and of picking up wafer-thin pieces of ice arranged by the same rules-of-crystal that arrange the autumn ice in the splash pools along our mudstone-and-shale beach on Lake Erie. And walking back along the outwash grasses we might flush a distant cousin of the cottontails that ate every crop of lettuce or peas I ever planted. These stories were comfortable and familiar, home-away-from-home stories. But the place invented itself for us as well.

One morning coming down off Buck Hill, we rounded a switchback and were surprised by three mountain bluebirds. They flew out of a juniper draw, directly in front of the car and onto a butte across the road. I went ten years back to another place that took its identity from a mountain bluebird that stopped there in front of my binoculars. These were a male and two either female or immature birds. Plenty of blue. They landed on a sandstone ledge that extended beyond the butte's clay walls. A typical butte: about thirty feet high, a lignite strip about halfway up, some iron oxide and sandstone for color, rill weathering for texture, and now a story for identity. We watched the bluebirds with delight until they took their color back into the dark green of the draw. Then I walked the butte's perimeter. Bison tracks were everywhere; the silty clay sides were worn away by bison rubbing. Grandfatherly love temporarily overcame National Park protocol, and I gathered a handful of bison hair to send to our granddaughter in Maine. The butte at the foot of Buck Hill. The butte where we first saw mountain bluebirds. The butte where we got bison hair for Lydia. If stories name places and make homes, how many good ones does it take?

The evening of the bluebirds we went back to Buck Hill as had become our habit. In fading light we scoured the park for its nightly offerings of mule deer, coyotes, pronghorns, chattering prairie dogs, and singing western meadowlarks. We usually finished up at Buck Hill near sunset to see wild horses, bison, and that night, elk. We watched as two dozen females and two males grazed in the valley and turned golden in the raking light.

Then we saw the bull: first only his huge rack as he walked along the bottom of a coulee, then his huge bulk as he climbed out. His body glowed in the sunset, and his antlers seemed to give off a glistening light.

The place where we saw elk at a distance at sunset.

We drove to the base of the hill toward our motel home past a familiar silhouette. And as I write these words five hundred miles away with the Yellowstone River and its magpies and its white water and its yellow cottonwood leaves, I can close my eyes and see images of a home: the valley of Paddock Creek, shadows cast by a lowering sun, elk, mountain bluebirds on a butte.

❧

On a wonderfully crisp morning we came to a favorite turn in the road into the park where we could see the Little Missouri for the first time that day. In morning light, the prospect shimmered: on the near shore, cottonwoods and green ash with a scant but welcome late display of yellow, the shallow river reflecting a deep blue, warm brown grasses on the floodplain, another row of trees, a snowy-appearing slope that was actually alkali, and a line of buttes that rose 350 feet above the river. As we were marveling at this layered landscape, we noticed two deer, knee deep, fording the river. I was about to comment to Donna that there was something unusual about them when I realized they weren't mule deer, but the less common (for the park) whitetail. And what I had noticed wasn't the unusual; it was the ordinary. Here was a species I knew intimately. After all, I had killed three of them with my car in the Kabob swamp.

❧

I came upon the Kabob swamp in a narrow way, forced onto a tiny, bumpy road as the only alternative to dodging semis on a state highway on my way to my former teaching job in western New York. So my view at first was narrow and purposeful: get to work. I drove that route for way too many years, yet over those years it did teach me to drive slower, to watch for wildlife, and always to pay attention to the landscape I pass through.

Cassadaga Creek begins as a south-flowing outlet of Cassadaga Lake at thirteen hundred feet above sea level in Stockton Township, Chautauqua County, New York State. Four and a half miles to the south, at 1280 feet, it begins to meander through Cassadaga swamp, a low, flat area of approximately fifteen hundred acres; two miles later and after a fall of thirty feet, it emerges near the village of South Stockton. A road laid out in the 1830s bisects the swamp north and south. Locals call the road the Kabob Road and the swamp the Kabob swamp, or simply "The Kay-bob" (with a stress on the first syllable). No one knows why for sure. One story, told by a local raconteur, goes like this: the Kabob Road was a corduroy road; poles were set crosswise on the road to keep wagons out of the swamp's muck. Local Indians coined the word *kabob* when they ". . . went bump, bump over the poles, chant[ing] in unison 'Ka-bob, Ka-bob, Ka-bob' a word that soon caught on with the white population. Although they never knew exactly what it meant, it seemed appropriate."

While no more or less important or interesting than any others like them, the creek and its swamp were a part of my life. For twenty-five years, I drove over the Kabob Road to and from work; I believe I felt every emotion possible along the way: joy, depression, boredom, excitement, grief. I hit three deer and barely missed hitting at least a dozen others. I stopped to watch flocks of up to thirty wild turkeys cross. One morning I sat, immobilized, watching and hearing a snipe's display flight. More than one night I had to stop and wait for blowing snow to let up. Without realizing it, I noticed changes: houses burned, houses built, lots cleared, fields grown into woods. And defining this place became important, leading me back through local histories and microfilms of old newspapers to, eventually, the records of the Holland Land Company.

In 1797, the Holland Land Company, a group of Dutch bankers, bought a mammoth tract of land that included a five-thousand-square-mile parcel that is now western New York State. To survey and sell this land, the company divided it into ranges running north and south and into towns running east and west. The resulting grid identified townships six miles square—Kabob, for example, can be found in range XII, town 4. Where possible, the company further divided townships into sixty-four equal lots. Thus, space was identified.

Space begins the transformation to place when a landscape is added. For this, a human is necessary. Surveyors in the 1790s felled trees along the perimeters of the townships and described the land by noting tree species and, occasionally, soil composition, steepness, and agricultural value. A second, more detailed, survey followed the lot lines. Field notes from range

XII, town 4, for the first survey are dated 1797 and for the second 1807—three years before the first settlers built a dwelling there. Surveyors described the land a third time around 1840 when the Holland Land Company sold its holdings in Chautauqua County to the Chautauqua Land Office. Field agents identified and described unsold lands and property that had, because of nonpayment, reverted to the company. For two heady weeks I held these "lot" reports that the surveyors made. Each lot's survey was bound separately, with a leather cover and string binding, each book four-by-six inches. Many contained crudely drawn maps—the scrapings of lead pencil on rag paper by firelight after a day of reconnoitering—imposing human observation on a grid. The size of the booklets' pages and the purpose and idiom of the writer made a series of found poems like this one for Stockton township, lot 17.

West line first 80
rods mostly maple
Elm dark Soil Black
Loam 2 feet in Depth.

4 or 5 acres
Between the Two Creeks
of Butternut flat
of choise land

North Line
mostly Hemlock

East line to the forks
mostly Black ash
good soil fit for
plowing or Meadows

South line mostly Hemlock
some ash soft
maple Soil of
Black muck good.

A landscape emerged that I would recognize as I walked it, more than 150 years after its description.

The Kabob's stories would complete my understanding of the place, the setting for *my* stories. And I learned that the Kabob's stories reflect what happened whenever pioneers made contact with the natural environment. East of the Mississippi, anyone's drive to work might pass through similar tales.

ᔥ

In 1818, a pioneer could buy a twenty-five-acre parcel of land in the township of Stockton for fifty dollars. But by then, money still hadn't migrated in any quantity to western New York. No one worked for wages, and pioneers used the barter system. The only reliable cash crop—ashes from the oak, beech, and maple that the pioneers felled—returned little on the investment.

Yet in 1818, a pioneer could make fifty dollars (more than six hundred bushels of ashes) in one day. Kill a wolf. Wolves had become an emblem for all the natural obstacles that pioneers had to overcome. Wolf forays near homesteads occasionally netted a sheep or two, and if your entire flock numbered a half dozen, the loss would be devastating. Imagine a pioneer family lying awake, listening in terror to the howls of wolves going about their nightly business.

Bounties were set: the state and county each offered twenty dollars for a grown wolf, ten dollars for a pup. Most towns offered ten dollars as well. Wolf hunting and trapping paid well. In 1817, Chautauqua County paid a total of $580 for wolves; in 1818, $710. Then the familiar result of European contact with a balanced environment can be seen in subsequent legislation: the county reduced bounties by seventy-five percent in 1820; after 1834, no bounties were offered or paid. Yet before settlers successfully extirpated the wolf from Chautauqua County, one of the more romantic events of the county's early history took place. By 1824, the town of Stockton settlers had had enough; they organized a hunt to rid the Kabob swamp of wolves. On October 2, 1824, around four hundred men from all over Chautauqua County descended on the Kabob, surrounded it, closed in on the center, and, having made the circle small enough, shot anything that moved.

After all the game had been dispatched that could be seen, a committee of three or more was sent within the enclosure to search under old logs and fallen trees to ascertain if any game had fled to any of these places for safety. Here's an eyewitness account.

After the return of the committee, the men, by orders, moved towards the center of the inclosure, bringing in the game, consisting of two large wolves [another source claims three], one bear, several deer and a large number of rabbits. The men were evidently disappointed in the number of wolves captured, but after speeches from a number of the officers, the woods rang with their hearty cheers, and they resolved for another hunt, which took place in about three weeks, killing one wolf and several deer and other small game. The third hunt was in May 1825; but no wolves were found, and only a few deer. In June 1828, the fourth and last hunt under this organization, like the previous two, caught no wolves.

The county had offered a large bounty for the scalp of the wolf, fifty dollars or upward, and by resolution, Gen. Barker, Elijah Risley and Walter Smith were elected a committee to forward the scalps, and obtain the money, and expend it in ammunition, provision and whisky to assist the men in future hunts.

The image of four hundred men loaded up with "provision and whisky" and thundering through the swamp persists. As I drove to work the first day of deer season each year, I counted a couple dozen pickup trucks parked along the road. Hunters leaned against most of them, unarmed, drinking beer from cans in the heart of the Kabob.

All along the Kabob Road, signs are nailed into the hemlocks and birch that identify the woods as a "cooperative hunting area," owned by Hammermill Paper Company and administered by the Department of Environmental Conservation. In a bizarre twist of ecological events, Hammermill, which owns twenty-five thousand acres of land in three western New York Southern Tier counties, has become concerned with the potentially disastrous effect that huge deer herds might have on their timber. With the help of the Department of Environmental Conservation, they can now direct hunters to their lands—to harvest the deer whose numbers, without predators, are rapidly becoming a serious problem. Having completed the work the 1818 wolf hunt started, hunters now must take on the role of their earlier victims.

The Kabob wolf hunts tell the history of the swamp, of the land around it, and of the entire Northeast. As I drove through the Kabob, I passed survivors of the hunts: the human beings with their cows and dogs, the deer-turned-pest, the carrion crows, the unseen and adaptable ones like crickets and tree frogs. Walking the Kabob, I tried in vain to reenter the past. A path led into the woods. Another survivor of the hunt, the deerflies that had driven me away on my two previous attempts, swarmed my head and face; but beyond occasionally finding their way under my glasses and into my eyes, they couldn't solve my defenses, gloves and a hooded sweatshirt, tied securely—on the hottest and muggiest day of the year. Within two hundred yards, a few minutes' walk, the woods became something out of the ordinary. First-succession birches gave way to mature hemlock, and pioneer weeds gave way to ferns. We returned to an older world. Here, a woods of hemlock and beech, with maple, ash, basswood, and cucumber, survives. My companion, a bird-watcher, ticked off the bird songs as we walked: Canada and black-throated green warblers, veery, white-throated sparrow. When we heard a barred owl call, she told me that they were sometimes active on dark, misty days. The thick ceiling of hemlock and beech shut out the light from a forest floor lush with bracken, marsh and sensitive fern, shining club moss and mushrooms. The trail widened and meandered along a small ridge at the floodplain of Cassadaga Creek. Formerly an Indian road, it was originally pressed, not dug, into the earth. We talked about the past, the gloom, the imagined mysteries, and the wolf. We left the trees and the ridge and slogged through muck and small swales and a carpet of sensitive ferns to the creek bank. We stood and watched the slow motion of the water, brown from last night's thunderstorm. Alongside us, red Canada lilies stood above the ferns; we felt the hemlocks' darkness behind us. Only thirty minutes' walking time from us, cars bumped by on the Kabob Road. Here, in a misty swamp, we felt something exotic and foreign that tied us to the past and completed our isolation. I told her about the Holland Land Company's booklets and their maps. But we also saw stumps left behind by chain saws; ORV tracks ran through the floodplain; we heard an airplane. The woods of Kabob's pioneers can be only imagined.

Early descriptive accounts of the Kabob mention—in addition to the wolves—black bears, wildcats, and pine martens among the large carnivores; and porcupines, otters, and weasels as animals present then and now scarce or absent. As a commuter, I passed new forests, mapped and manageable things that are allowed existence only as they continue to offer service.

Now on any given morning, an opossum, returning from a night of backyard hunting, may make a fatal error in judgment. A factory worker from Cassadaga, bleary with morning, runs over the opossum's hindquarters. The animal drags itself to the shoulder of Route 60 and dies, meat and viscera laid bare to the sun. In no time, a succession of saprobic fungi, like pioneer trees reforesting an abandoned field, begin and end their short lives, excreting enzymes and absorbing their chemically softened surroundings. Fungal species replace one another on a changing landscape as substances—sugar and organic acids first, then starches and protein, then finally more resistant material—are depleted, and the carcass continues on its way to becoming a pile of chemical hash. Meanwhile, bacteria, with their enzymes, help fungi in the decomposition process, making matter digestible and soluble while converting elements present in compounds in the opossum—carbon, nitrogen, oxygen, and sulphur—making them available to the biosphere.

All this goes unnoticed by man until the assault by a common byproduct—the odor that attracts *Phaenica sericata,* the blowfly. On a good day, six hours after a female lays her eggs, a fresh batch of maggots will hatch out and begin devouring the microorganisms that are causing decay. By the next morning, the carcass will swarm with them. Other diners—carrion beetles, flesh flies, rat-tailed maggots—climb aboard. Crows come to tear flesh, pluck out the eyes, and eat some maggots. At night, a foraging dog might nose around for a meal or simply roll in the wonderful stench. Eventually little remains of the opossum but some matted fur lying in a dark stain. The hunts have ended and the wolves are gone.

☙

Even in the wildness of a national park, even west of the Mississippi, a familiar story brings a new story to mind. October 6 and 7, 1997. The roundup. An Associated Press eyewitness account reported:

Smooth, efficient, effective—but not nearly as much fun as the "old days."

That's how wranglers describe Monday's roundup of wild horses at Theodore Roosevelt National Park.

Clear skies and a bright October sun warmed the North Dakota Badlands as two helicopters headed out about 8 A.M. About 15 wranglers saddled up and headed to the top of a rise just south of the park's corral north of Fryburg.

The wait was on.

The silence was broken by the sounds of song birds and the whirl of helicopters in the distance. After nearly two hours, a voice over a radio said, "I hope the elk get out of the way."

The spectators saw a helicopter bob over the hilltop. Shortly afterward, horses could be seen galloping down the draw. They were led by a lone rider and trailed by the rest of the wranglers and two helicopters.

Three days after the roundup we talked to a ranger at the north unit about the event that happens every three years or so. Her enthusiasm was marvelous. We were inside the interpretive center surrounded by artifacts, photographs, and careful explanations about the land and its animals, written by scientists for nonscientists. But this was real. She had been there, felt the rush, seen the animals up close, heard their breathing and the collisions of their wild bodies. Listening to her talk, I remembered thinking what it must have been like in the Kabob in the fall of 1824: shouting men, panicked animals, gunfire.

These are the results of the 1997 event.

South Unit—nearly one hundred horses rounded up and corralled, thirty-three culled out for sale, thirteen thousand dollars in total sales (which goes to the expenses of the roundup). One night just after sunset, we came across a couple dozen horses. They all took on the same gray-brown color. Their manes fell across their faces as they grazed. Their tails barely moved in the breeze. About the auction, Park Superintendent Noel Poe said, "It didn't appear a lot went to the canners. We were kind of pleased."

North Unit—about 190 bison rounded up, one hundred went to various plains tribes, five to the Jamestown buffalo museum, and one to the Sully's Hill Game Preserve. Processing included implanting microchips and testing for disease. The day after the roundup, we came upon a herd of at least fifty bison in the south unit. They blocked traffic, they butted heads and brawled like college kids in a bar, they glared at us with their feckless eyes, they shed their matted hair, and they shat giant mounds everywhere. Wonderful.

The management of these animals is, of course, absolutely necessary. Badlands ecosystems can no more handle uncontrolled animal populations than can New York State ecosystems. Only Yellowstone attempts to maintain a large, free-ranging bison herd, a herd that wants to come off the mountain each winter to graze. This migration resulted in the slaughter of more than one thousand animals in 1997 because local ranchers hold the position that bison might spread brucellosis to cattle herds. So even the largest of parks have problems, and compared to other parks, the Theodore Roosevelt units are small: 24,070 acres for the north and 46,158 for the south, acreages that combined still wouldn't equal ten percent of the land affected by the 1988 Yellowstone fires. One is often aware of either traffic sounds on Interstate 94 or the fences that contain the park. Further, many species—bison, elk, bighorn sheep—were reintroduced into the park. Whether by shotgun or helicopter, humans must take the role of predator or, more politely, manager. A diminishing possibility of diversity has migrated west with the pioneers, from Kabob to Medora. A loss of plant and animal diversity, weathering, a leveling of land forms, fewer stories.

⌇

Toward evening the snow lifted to the highest peak, the sun came out, and Yellowstone's mountains released their captives. Lines of snow-covered cars and trucks passed our windows like a spring freshet. I had been reading Paul Schullery's natural and cultural history of the park and had learned a few things about those people inside those cars and trucks. I learned that Yellowstone broke the three-million visitor mark in 1994. I learned that during the same year some of those three million accidentally killed animals with their cars: fifty-one mule deer, forty-nine elk, nineteen coyotes, twelve moose, eleven bison. And I learned that, according to a survey from the 1980s, the third most common activity in the park was "shopping."

But I wondered about those people snowbound for a day in Mammoth with the elk and the steam from the hot springs and the snow squalls. Had they been frightened or had they merely blundered through? Had any found a home?

With my binoculars, I could see from our north window a bit of the northern elk herd resting and grazing inside the park. Cars drove by with their lights on; elk grazed in the low light of the setting sun. I had learned a few things about those elk. I learned that long before there was a Gardiner,

Montana, elk migrated down the slopes and into the valley for the winter. I learned that in 1962 Yellowstone National Park killed 4,619 elk as part of their population-management program. And I learned that after that program ended and "natural regulation" began, the population had increased from five thousand in 1967 and had stabilized at about twenty thousand. Less attainable was what I could know about elk and humans together: at Yellowstone and in the Badlands.

"Natural regulation," Yellowstone's 1968 hands-off policy toward animal populations, is awash in controversy that has already claimed a forest's worth of paper. Over the elk herd, politicians, bureaucrats, and scientists fight each other and among themselves. Will a burgeoning elk herd destroy the woody plants of the park's northern section? Have they driven out the beaver for good? Will reintroduced wolves keep the herd down?

And what is the future of the fenced-in Theodore Roosevelt herd? When does a wildlife sanctuary become a park? Or a zoo?

The night before, we had walked the cold and rainy streets of Gardiner. As we left the commercial area, we noticed yards surrounded by wire fencing, gates on the walkways, shrubbery wrapped in chicken wire. Clearly the elk still entered the valley in winter. That afternoon we had stopped at the Mammoth Visitor Center, where elk lounge on the travertine ledges of the hot springs and graze on park headquarter's lawns. When we got back out to the car, I stepped in a pile of elk shit so fresh I nearly lost my footing. No matter how humans decide how it will be between elks and us, we share a home.

Part Two—Homeostasis

I wake up in the middle of the night. I roll over to my back from my right side. A hand grabs my neck and the back of my head. My arms and legs flail. The bed moves violently. I manage to say to my wife, "Donna, something's wrong with me." I sit up and swing my feet over the side of the bed. The hand pulls me directly backward. I catch my fall with both hands and push forward. And I'm standing or, rather, staggering between bed and dresser. I reach out and grab the dresser and the hand goes away. I have no idea where I am—this new Minnesota home, this stranger's bedroom, this new life. Sweat is pouring from my body while I shiver from cold. My wife is fully awake by now. She flings open the window and a blast of prairie wind hits my drenched face and chest. The terror subsides. She's carrying a damp washcloth for me and the hand has gone away from my head and, seeing the washcloth, I can manage a wry and frightened laugh. We go back to bed and watch the Weather Channel until dawn.

Three weeks of sleeping sitting up and two doctors later, I found that I had something called positional vertigo. My understanding of it, no doubt flawed, is this. Small calcium chips had broken away from the cochlea in my inner ear and floated into the semicircular canals. "Rocks in my head," a friend said. At certain positions these chips settled into the cilia that take care of balance for me. Disturbed, the cilia sent all kinds of bad news to my brain: the room is spinning, your bed is turning upside down, your old friend the horizon can no longer be trusted. This happened whenever I turned from one side to another, or tilted my head back to read a book title on the top shelf in the stacks, or simply began to lie back. At the Heartland Clinic in Fargo, I endured a "maneuver," which is a medical term for getting flipped all over the place, and which apparently floated the chips back to where they couldn't do harm. I probably have this all wrong too, but I'm reminded of a bath toy my kids used to play with. You push a button and the tiny suspended balls float up into the hippo's mouth. So I'm fixed—but not completely. The evil hand that kept coming back to grab my head and toss me around the room hasn't returned since the maneuver, but I still occasionally feel, to use a good, vertiginous word, loopy.

Actually, I've always had a fear of heights, but one that I could think away. Partway into a flight, I'll sit back and enjoy the view; after the first day, I'll walk directly to a hotel-room window and watch the yellow cabs struggle, so far below that their fares are featureless; I've seen photographs of myself, relaxed and smiling at the brink of the Grand Canyon. But now the fear is founded. At Scoria Point in Theodore Roosevelt National Park, I bent over to pick up an interesting, fossil-like specimen, took two stumbling steps forward and then caught my balance—looking over a two-hundred-foot drop. The next day I walked the rimrock north of Billings with the poet Jim Peterson. When his Welsh corgi, Dylan, got too close to the edge, I could feel my legs begin to buckle. The North Dakota/Minnesota prairie land I had moved to was looking better all the time, a safe place to step back a while from all my edges. It was as if my illness, the uncertainty of my personal and professional changes, and my graceless aging were coming together under the workings of a familiar metaphor.

Many years ago, I wrote this short poem on the occasion of a good friend's death.

LEARNING TO LOVE THE DEAD

We sleep to the sounds of dead friend's names
wake to the space they filled.
Each day they speak from some common thing.

They tell us every room we enter
has no floor.

And looking back over ten years and thousands of words in dozens of essays, I reluctantly conclude that, from my cottage perched on an eroding clay bluff, I kept writing and rewriting those last two lines in one form or another.

One of the best of the old Firesign Theatre albums is called "Everything You Know Is Wrong." This is vertigo of a different sort, but vertigo nonetheless. In early incarnations as a figure of speech, "vertiginous" brought to mind inconsistency and giddiness; in our more brooding times, existential uncertainty and doubt might be more apt connotations. Those things that make balance possible are undercut, suspect, or just plain dysfunctional.

On one of our walking routes we discovered shortly after we moved to Moorhead, we can wind our way for a mile or so through the houses of our development and emerge at an amazing spot: the edge of a vast sugar-beet field and the intersection of Cass County Road No. 76 and River Haven Road. From here I can look south down a road so straight and flat that it extends beyond my vision. It is an aspect without edges, a safe place to revisit former and less sure homes.

૭

Several boxes of notes traveled to the prairie with us, and I wanted the one with the musty, closed-up smell. Here were ten years of journal entries written at our cottage each year from September—when fishing, sailing, and swimming stopped—to January, when I couldn't get the inside temperature to a livable level. As I read these notes, I was able to go back to a time when it was still possible to think about ways to correct imbalances, to reach a momentary, sublime equilibrium. But as the entries progressed, I read more of erosion and less of stability. For example, I wrote that a December storm in 1985 was typical of lake-effect storms, those of early winter that occur when cold air passes over the unfrozen lake, a foot of snow fell; wind blew more than sixty miles per hour. But this storm was special because of the dramatic seiche caused by high westerly winds pushing water ahead of them until lake levels at Buffalo were seven feet above normal. Ten-to-twelve-foot waves released nearly twenty feet of water against the land.

By the next afternoon, I was able to drive to the cottage to see the results. The snow had stopped but not the wind. My first concern was our boat, which I had turned upside down and tied to stairs seventy-five feet from the gully's entrance. The boat was gone. Forever.

Waves ten feet high smashed into the bluff at the mouth of our tiny stream, narrowed their force, swept upstream to the stairs and withdrew, roaring, clearing the stream to its bed. A withdrawing wave occasionally met an incoming one; the explosion sent sheets of freezing spray over me, driving me to higher ground.

The news from the crest was no better. The bluff's face was cut back to under the new flower box I had made the summer before and attached to the deck's edge. I stood and watched the nightmare below. Each wave, brown and filled with debris, cracked against the bluff, throwing spray at my feet. Whole trees danced about like driftwood. I watched a stump three feet in diameter roll off the top of a crashing wave and slam into the bluff. I found myself instinctively backing away.

I recalled making the flower box on a July afternoon: cutting the boards, laying them out, planning and thinking, taking my careful pace from the sun on my back and the lazy waves. In September I had transplanted some sea rocket from the beach into the box, hoping to save the seeds. Now these seeds, insubstantial and slight, would be the only survivors.

I felt rage, the urge to throw everything within reach into the water and watch it disappear. But the rage was a wave; it came in, did its damage, and rolled back into the lake.

Then I felt helpless. I knew the waves would kill me if I got into them. I knew, too, that the flower box and the boat were already becoming symbols for my life, viewed from a distance, feckless and absurd. How quaint these little activities were: repairing the transom on a boat that now lies somewhere twisted and beaten, or measuring the parts for a flower box that won't outlast the seeds it holds. I saw myself through the indifferent eyes of the storm.

Then came the signal event of the cottage: in the fall of 1986 we saved the place by moving it. The process was simple—which is easy for me to say because I didn't have to think it up or solve the problems that arose. A talented and clever friend, Jim Currie, did that.

1. Tear down the bedroom wing. Shortly before we bought the place, a huge locust tree had fallen on it, crushing the roof and part of the north wall. My father and I rebuilt it.

2. Tear down the deck.

3. Lift up the building with house jacks and knock out the pillars that held it up.

4. Build a skid of four-by-six-inch lumber and attach it to the bottom of the building.

5. After dismantling the plumbing, lower the building to the ground.

6. While waiting for the earth to freeze, borrow three come-alongs and lots of chain, round up "volunteers," buy beer.

7. Pull.

Oddly, few of the details of the preparation or move found their way into my journal; mostly I recorded the changes of weather, numbers of migrating ducks, and observations from beach walks. Only four entries were even a bit introspective. Rereading them after a dozen years, I was surprised at the turns they took.

～

16 Sept 1986
land 57°/water 67°, NE wind 10–15, frost warning inland

A quiet Tuesday after a busy weekend. Flock of fifty Canada geese about a mile out. Lynn and Sharon Matson here on Saturday to take down the cherry tree and to enjoy some pleasant debauch. Sunday, Jim Currie for early plans to move. He says it can be done; I see huge problems that he could solve, not I. It looks as if all my energy will go into the move, thinking about it and doing it. And it seemed, before Currie came aboard, more an act of destruction than preservation. On Saturday, Lynn and I took down the cherry tree on the point because with each wind its roots would shift and weaken the bond between it and the clay it grew in. We went to a lot of trouble to save a stump high enough to put the martin house on. The martin house is the last big project my father undertook; it's a beautiful piece of work, carefully planned and executed: single storey, sixteen apartments, shingled roof. I can only imagine the discomfort and frustration he went through to finish it—his mind still agile as his body failed him. So we climbed a ladder to take down the tree, felling it inland where it landed on other, younger cherry trees—the old tree's next generation. I worked the next morning, taking off fireplace logs from the bottom up. But I had to give up when I couldn't reach any higher. I couldn't clear the crown away; it still hangs there. At around ten feet, I counted seventy rings—my father's age. The connection, which I don't understand yet, established itself. The seventy-year-old felled tree rests in the arms of its children.

11 Oct 1986
land 69°/water 63°, cloudy and calm

Hard to concentrate here. The neighbor's house is back by the road, poised on a sixteen-wheel flatbed to be moved to where the woods used to be. And today I tore down the bedroom walls and ceiling. Tuesday I'll cut away the floor. Thursday I'll clean out the skirting and maybe take down the cedar trees. Then the frightening stuff begins.

I started work with little enthusiasm. My first job would be to tear down something my father and I had saved. The technique was what Currie calls chainsaw carpentry. The tools—a pry bar, a maul, and a chainsaw—can disorganize any structure, quickly. Eight hours of feverish, unskilled labor later, the room my father and I rebuilt was reduced to a pile of wood to be burned, for fun, on a January day. A week later, using the same tools, I'll take apart the floor. I worked alone. I talked to myself, planning out loud, solving the small problems with an imagined audience. And all the while I thought of my father. He had helped me build this room; he solved the problems, telling me what to do, restoring a structure that I had to tear down. No restoration for him: his strength gone, his voice fading.

30 Oct 1986
land 47°/water 57°, N wind at 5, cloudy

A winter wind turns my face red. From my walk, a flash of fifty snow buntings. Ducks have moved in: grebes—30, mergansers—100, loons—

15, goldeneye—4, bufflehead—2. The lumber is here for the move. Today I tear apart the deck. So much happening so fast that there's no time for feelings. We try to attach the skid on Sunday afternoon. Tuesday, sitting talking with Currie at the table, I saw a female pheasant walk across the deck. And today I tear it down.

The deck is gone—it took less than one-half hour to destroy it thanks to years of dry rot. My only tool was a sledge hammer.

Sitting in my writing chair remembering things that happened on the deck and knowing that those things can't happen again. But how lucky we did this. No more, ever, will my wife and sons and I huddle under a blanket and fall asleep listening to the waves. But we *did*. How pointless it would have been to buy something new and hoard it for our adult plans. Everyone should have at least one child—and one place on the water.

This connection between my father and his illness and early work on the move continued as I pulled apart the deck. Not a deck exactly, ours was originally an inside floor of a covered sleeping porch, now exposed to rain and snow. Its tongue-and-groove structure never stood a chance against the fungus, bacteria, and slime mold that thrived inside boards that were continuously damp. My work—again with the pry bar and maul—led me to thinking of my deck becoming food for living things that I couldn't see. While we lay in the summer sun, killing our epidermal cells, below us, fungus and bacteria were breaking down cellulose molecules, turning carbohydrates to simple sugar and water.

The bluff below the deck had eroded up to two feet beneath it, so I worked at the edge of disaster, at times swinging the maul and sending boards spinning into the air, down to the beach 30 feet below (beach fire later—I wanted to burn everything I tore down; between the dry rot and me, everything would disappear as much as it can in a chemical world). We would start again. All the while, thoughts of fathers and sons haunted me. Around me, change and age found different forms. Images and poems raised themselves up, and I blasted them away with the maul. What erodes, rots, is torn down, grows old, can't be revived. Start over. I can't make my sons young again or my father strong. The more I thought, the angrier I got; I didn't know—I still don't know—what to fill all these new, empty spaces with. Working alone is dangerous, falling into thought too easy. I went inside and found a bottle of schnapps left over from summer. I drank a toast to good times on the old porch and to my changing family. Then I promised myself some company for the next phase of the project.

18 Nov 1986
land 37°/water 49°, light rain/snow

Next-to-last entry for the year. Next entry will contain the results of the move.

First snow inland—Nov 10

Drained the pump and tank. Water fought me, didn't want to leave. Blood in the veins.

First snow here—tonight for sure

Big flocks of mergansers. Grebes in close. Gulls all over, but no black ducks.

Cross supports make the room impossible to move around in. Stuff is everywhere; the couch is standing on end. I have just enough room to sit next to the window in my writing chair and try to remember all the times I did this. Same old waves. Same old gulls.

Went for the final beach walk. Nothing.

I tried a poem earlier called "Dry Rot." But I've forgotten how to write poetry. Nothing to do but start again. Chainsaw whine. Cherrywood smell. Father's hands.

I sit here looking down on the water for the last time. And I have nothing to say.

෴

The journal entries for 1986 end there.

The cottage got moved. Currie was brilliant, and right all along. My father, with his physicist's mind, must have admired the plan. We fastened the chains to the skid and to various trees on the property. Six good friends ratcheted the come-alongs, and the cottage slid thirty feet over the lawn. Halfway into the four-hour job, a wet snow made things even easier. The cottage was saved, memory dislodged.

My father died 18 March 1997.

෴

My father had an early diagnosis of Parkinson's disease, then "atypical Parkinson's disease," then "multisystem dysfunction." Whatever. Two awful things happened to him. First he lost his balance. He would be shuffling along with his walker and suddenly all hell would break loose. He would spin wildly, careening off furniture and walls, ending up in a heap of abrasions, contusions, and fractures. Then he lost his language. Professor Carlson couldn't talk; this most convoluted physics lecturer, this dreadful punster, this multilingual/goofball/language person was silenced.

I saw my father dead. Maybe I saw him die—I don't know because it was a death free of technology (monitors and such), a death to which the old-fashioned and religious word *passing* nicely applies. But it was a death nonetheless.

This death's landscape featured mouth agape, partial removed, eighty-year-old molars intact, hair white and downy, and the terrible topography of bones after a long and desiccating illness. As I watched I remembered helping him in his shower and the ponding of water in the triangular depression formed by the scapula, clavicle, and first rib. He was, along with my mother, the human I have known the longest: my profoundest memory. I don't intend a eulogy here but must admit a looming presence—part of home—gone.

༄

The school mascot of Concordia College, where I teach, is a guy dressed up to look like a corncob; the college nickname is the "Cobbers." The local high school is called the "Spuds." This is good and honest, more real than "Spartans" or "Bombers." Most of my students grew up on the prairie or in prairie towns. They think about their homes a lot—talk about them in class and write about them. And there's a good reason: their homes are either in jeopardy or they're already gone.

History here is brief: four generations. Some of my students have great-grandparents who might have gathered up bison bones to clear the way for sod-breaking plows. Then the next generation, my father's, farmed their land. And there was drought, and depression, and crop failure, and low prices, and a new truth about farming: bigger is better.

A major benefactor of my college farms fifty-five thousand acres of potatoes. A good-sized farm at midcentury would have been five hundred acres. Has the potato king displaced one hundred homes? Probably not. Not exactly anyway. Paul Gruchow grew up on a 1950s prairie farm in Minnesota. In his collection of essays, *Grass Roots,* he describes his family's 160-acre farm as a motley of corn, wheat, oats, soybeans, flax, a hardscrabble house, outbuildings, goats, sheep, chickens, pasture, fencerows, a marsh, and people: Paul, his mother and father, sisters Kathy and Paulette. In 1980 when he went back for a walk on the old ground, he found 160 acres of corn. Nothing but corn.

My students' families are selling off or moving off their farms; most of my students—as much as it might hurt them and their families—won't go back (*if* there's a farm to go back to). Even public schools have lost the chance to give kids the identity of home. A weekend morning paper told me that D-G-F had beaten U-H by a score of 78 to 64. D-G-F is a school made up of the former schools of Dilworth, Glynden, and Felton. This is called consolidation, a by-product of dwindling population. Another by-product is a loss of history and home. Three schools—probably named after railroad executives, but for people nonetheless—have lost their names and are called the "D-G-F Rebels," and, therefore, share an improbable cultural identity with the University of Mississippi. In this flat and safe haven for family values, the concept of home is undergoing dramatic change.

During those classes when we have talked about our homes, I've often thought about my father, the area he was tied to, and the land he owned. His home, 159 Westman Road, Bemus Point, Chautauqua County, New York, is hand built. His hands. In a farmhouse one-half-mile north, his mother died—in 1936, of influenza. He grew up in that farmhouse—and after college, graduate schools, and teaching here and there—he came home. He bought some land overlooking Chautauqua Lake, made a garden, built a house, and lived in it for forty-three years.

I object to any metaphors that suggest this dwelling was an extension of his self or a re-creation of his father. The day his father, my grandfather, died, my father and I had worked together on assembling the heating ducts of the new house. But some sentimental, bad-poem connection of fathers and sons and blood-in-the-veins/heat-in-the-ducts doesn't work. This is a house. I laid awake in fear listening to the mysterious sounds of its settling; I missed its security during my freshman year in college; and until the day I can't walk anymore, I'll be able to walk its rooms blindfolded. But it's still a house. Other people live in it now, like bats in our cottage or hockey players in the house we left behind in New York—happily and at home.

In 1996 my father moved into the Gustavus Adolphus Nursing Home, "home" there being a place where his self resided and not his possessions.

Then he moved inside his head, proving the point. Then, of course, he died.

Part Three—Home for the Holidays

I went home for Christmas—to my father's home. With its efficient, egalitarian grave markers flat to the ground, the Sunset Hill Cemetery, where he is buried, is itself easily buried by any amount of snow. The day my wife and I visited, it presented a pleasant, upstate–New York snow-covered hillside dotted with a few, very few, spruce and old oaks and over-layed with winding roads. No gravestones rise up here to remind you of death. In fact, the cemetery under snow is difficult to distinguish from the Sunset Valley Golf Course across County Route 76. Except for the Christ-mas wreaths. Hundreds of them: artificial spruce branches, red ribbon, plastic holly and berries, white painted cones—efficient wreaths placed ostensibly over the graves of the dead whose loved ones shelled out the $22.95 to buy the wreaths and have the cemetery staff "install" them.

Knowing which section to look in, we tried to find my father's marker, but with no gravestones or trees to guide us, we managed to push aside a foot of snow from strangers' graves. We were about to give up when we came upon one of those pictographs common to snowy fields: small ani-mal tracks, the graceful imprint of wings like two open fans, a small confu-sion in the snow, a dash of red. I had two thoughts. The first, sentimental and pleasant, was a wish that my father's grave be so marked: with a natural and true statement of death and beauty, not some dumb wreath and a slab of metal stuck into the ground in a row next to hundreds of other rows of other slabs. The second thought took me into night on a cold and feature-less hillside. I imagined the fake wreaths gone and added an owl and a field mouse. Then I tripped myself up by thinking of the prairie we had left just a few days before—at sunrise, two crows seeing us off, low and long morn-ing clouds over a distant shelter break and horizon line, wheat-stubble field stretching toward us and away on the other side. That flat and stable land. Then I tripped myself up again by thinking of rollovers.

The rollover, along with deer hunters accidentally shooting human be-ings, is a prevalent and gruesome occurrence that prairie folk seem to con-sider with a stoic sense of inevitability. Here's what happens. You're driving home after midnight, tired from too much work or too much beer, down an endlessly straight and flat gravel road. You lose concentration or you nod off and you're in the loose gravel on the shoulder. The ditch drops away quickly from the raised road, about six to eight feet. The front tire of your truck catches and, wham, you're a rollover. Someone will find you early the next morning. If you were wearing a seat belt, you might be alive. But you probably weren't. Your name will be in the *Fargo Forum*.

Predator and prey, life and death. There I was about to make a solemn speech but being nudged into working on a joke about rollovers and my father rolling over in his grave. Then the speech got mixed up, and the joke got lost in the memory of one of his favorite lines, repeated often.

Anyone at any dinner table: "Do you want a roll?"
My father: "No thanks. I'll just sit here."

It was a confusion of places and words. It was vertigo. It was a good start.

༄

Near where my father grew up and where he built his house is the Bemus Point Cemetery, not one-tenth the size of Sunset Hill. Stones here date back to the 1850s and seem almost randomly placed among the cedars, blue spruce, and Norway spruce that date back nearly as far. The same snow that covered the ground-level Sunset Hill markers had made gentle white mounds of the more modest tombstones. We walked directly to the spot. On a slope overlooking Chautauqua Lake and within a triangle formed by three old cedars are two stones, a space, and a stone one-by-one-by-two-feet that reads "Carlson/Otto A (1883–1954) and Wendela G (1880–1936)." The other two stones mark the graves of an aunt and uncle; the space was clearly intended for my father and mother. But family decisions often go far beyond which in-laws get the kids for Thanksgiving dinner, and my father ended up in the matriarchal plot. Yet if the grave is the final home and the spirit is free to wander, *here* is my father's resting place.

Some cedar limbs had broken off during the storm; golden-brown cedar sprigs littered the snow; a foot lower, the petunias I had planted the spring before were blending with dirt and decay; and below it all, 150-year-old cedar roots wrestled with my family. A flock of geese honked overhead, but I didn't look up because I knew where I was. I knew they were Canada geese, and I knew what they looked like, and I knew the lake they were headed to because I had skated over it, swum in it, and fished it.

Late each summer afternoon in 1953, my maternal grandfather, my "morfar" (mother's father in Swedish), and I rowed a half mile down Bemus Creek and into the same lake the geese were flying to. We rowed out of the creek mouth and into a shallow bay bordered by a wild, swampy point ending with a sandbar that stretched into the lake to the northwest. To the southeast, rushes grew along the shoreline and into the water. We fished at the edges of weed beds in six to eight feet of water. Morfar made the rounds, trying each spot until they started to bite or we pulled anchor and rowed to a new bed.

I know I caught fish; a shoe box in my parents' attic held grainy black-and-white photographs of a skinny, serious boy holding stringers of bass bigger than his arms. But although I remember the bump, the trembling rush away, and the game of landing a fish, I best remember what happened during the long periods between the action. I recall little talk; perhaps Morfar was reluctant to use his second language on a boy. In silence, I played with the iridescent blue damselflies, sometimes two or three at a time, that landed on my pole tip and darted away when I dipped it into the water. One quiet sentence would break the silence—"I tink I'll have a smoke"— in his heavy Swedish accent, my favorite iambic trimeter line. Morfar lit his pipe; it gurgled and crackled as the smell of Velvet tobacco curled around us.

We fished. He tapped the pipe out on his palm, refilled and relit it, scratching a kitchen match on the gunwale. Late-afternoon sun slanted into the water outlining ridges of ripples in silver. Then the damselflies stopped coming back, and the match glowed brighter on Morfar's face when he relit his pipe. We fished shallower and closer to shore, following lines on the water of reflected lights from a solitary cottage's windows. Occasionally we heard the deep gurgle of an inboard and saw its red or green running lights out in the middle of the lake. Then we were alone again with the silence, the darkness, and the shore lights' reflections. After we fished by feel for a while, hoping for big bass, we gave up. Perhaps shivering a little from the night coolness, I held a flashlight on the grasses at the southern shore of the creek mouth. Once inside the mouth, guided by cottage lights, Morfar rowed to the dock and tied up. That home was bright and dry and warm.

༄

I could see between the cedars that the lake was still partly open; without trying, I could see mergansers, buffleheads, and goldeneyes diving. I imagined gulls and black ducks standing on the ice's edge. I waited for something to jar my certainty and balance, but it didn't come. Not that time.

So Christmas wasn't *all* about death after all. There was time with memory and with family and friends, the treasured nuances of their presences and voices. But a first fatherless Christmas should reveal something; odd that the strongest memory of that sort that I would carry away would be that sense of balance I felt in the Bemus Point Cemetery.

The baggage I carry back into that town is so twisted and confused that I can't think clearly enough to write while I'm there. Each Tuesday and Thursday afternoon of the spring semester before we moved, I drove to the landing where a ferry crosses Chautauqua Lake, and I scribbled away at *this* essay, this essay about home. I read through old newspaper clippings, drove by former homes, even peered in the windows of the gym where I played basketball—which is now, I was amused to learn, apparently an activities space for a retirement home the school was converted into. I collected pages of notes and details, but none of those words written in and about my hometown will find their way into this, or any other, essay.

Then out of nowhere comes a simple moment of peace.

Driving to New England and trying to understand, we got to talking about dreams. Mine are like anyone else's, I suppose, a safe and honest way to connect my exterior world with my interior one. About a month after he died, I dreamed the first time about my father. The entire family—my mother, sisters, wife, sons—were crowded into the tiny bathroom of his house where I was trying to repair the window. He was away doing errands and was long overdue home. As the seven of us jostled for space, we talked about how worried we were. Since then, I've dreamed of him at least once a week. Virtually plotless, the dreams are simple: my father and I are in his house or yard; each dream raises the issue of falling. At first he spun and fell; I lunged to save him. Then he toppled less and walked more. I worried and steadied. Most recently, he's shed his walker and has been running an old man's shuffling run. I jog alongside. "Careful, Pop."

He's safe now, I'm apparently deciding, balanced at last. I'm my own father now.

⌘

By the time we got to New England, we were awash in memories. Here our two sons live with two remarkable women. Here we said good-bye to them as children and drove away to a safe distance to wait and watch as they put in their college time, grew and changed and followed remarkably similar paths: Kevin the writer-turned-television producer and Jeffrey the musician-turned-theatre sound designer. We came to rest in Kevin and Anne and Lydia's home in Kittery, Maine. Jeffrey and Rachel had battled from Connecticut through a northeaster. Those four drank coffee and talked in the living room. Donna read to her granddaughter. I sat alone in the upstairs bedroom that was ours for the week, savoring the balances and imbalances downstairs and around me. I saw how, in the woods behind Kevin's house, the snow of a day past melted in the way peculiar to New England in early winter—first from granite outcrops and the tops of old oak roots. Familiar patterns. Leafless hardwoods stand aside to reveal conifers and oak trunks, black against white hillsides. Now and then a bent-over birch intervenes with its suggestion that all this ascending straightness has its counterpart. We learned to know these New England landscapes well—and to love them as extensions of the beloveds who made their homes there and who made countless trips a joyful necessity.

I found the disk that I'd transferred old notes and scraps of writing to, fired up my laptop, and dove in. The words came from times of letting go and change. The tone was lonely and unsure. Home and family, after all, were being undone. I had found, in researching shore life in the north Atlantic, a good image for the disturbing changes I was going through: the hundreds of tide pools I had peered into on the Maine coast. I had written about how plants in tide pools use sunlight to make sugar and starches out of carbon dioxide and water, releasing oxygen for animals to breathe. The oxygen makes the breakdown of organic matter possible, releasing energy, carbon dioxide, and water. A perfect balance. Except at night when darkness shuts down photosynthesis while respiration continues unabated. The amount of carbon dioxide in the water diminishes in daylight while oxygen accumulates. But at night, oxygen is used up, and carbon dioxide accumulates while combining with water to form carbonic acid. If the imbalance continues without correction the next day, the oxygen depletion and acidity will kill everything. The balance of the pool—really a series of imbalances being corrected—reveals the true nature of balance among any living thing: diatoms, invertebrates, or people. The comfort that image offered remains.

In a folder labeled "fathers and sons," I found this fragment among a dozen or so pieces written about Nubble Light, a lighthouse a couple miles from where I sat.

The moon, just beyond full, yellow and aging, rises over Nubble Rock. The red line of Nubble Light burns into water and wet sand. But I've had enough of scenes like these: the moon dragging the sea back and forth across the beach, a lighthouse far away blinking in pain. I turn away from the window and send my son to the deck to write a poem about what happens when two lights on water cross, when fog undefines each edge.

Rocks wear away under waves that climb their old, black, basalt sides and fall away. I watched all day and tried to speak but couldn't find the words. My son has written my poem. My eyes are shut, my mouth silent. Without knowing, we've been waiting for this for all our lives.

Not very tight, the editor part of my brain told me, pretty melodramatic and stagey. And I recalled that it didn't *really* happen just that way. But there in the bedroom, with the family below, New England outside, and memories swirling, I revisited the feeling of the words with more than a little surprise at the poignancy they held for me.

The area separating honest emotion and sentimentality is one I know I've arrived in when I start getting weepy. Sometimes it's good to just get in and wallow; other times a little reflection is called for. This time I put away my computer with its encoded memories and headed down the stairs. I stopped halfway so as not to interrupt the conversations. Donna was walking in from the kitchen with Lydia, holding her up with both hands as Lydia walked her tiptoe, unsure walk. There was an undercurrent of voices and music. There was the lighted tree, the gift wrap and toys lying about. I was back in that dangerous and poignant area again, wishing that *transcendent* was a word that would survive past the millennium, wishing that we could take a time-out and write a page or two of old-fashioned, romantic prose, but knowing that someone or something would have to move in space or time to undo the balance of the moment. So halfway down the mountain, as it were, I took another step.

Part Four—Home Is the Sailor

Maine was bliss for us, but our journey home wasn't quite done. Cape Cod, with its water and sand in constant motion, seems the antithesis of the prairie. Nothing stays in place. The instant of high tide is followed instantly by the beginning of the ebb. On the outer Cape the land is said to migrate—so much so that, without plantings to hold it down in the nineteenth century, it actually invaded and occupied a Provincetown schoolhouse to the height of the desks. Cape Cod would complete our traveling outward, and it would complete our traveling inward as well—one more grave, one more storm, one more home.

In the summer of 1969, we sailed over Cape Cod Bay on the *Kittiwake,* my Uncle Alden's altered Cape Cod catboat with restepped mast and jib added. My wife and I were crew; the skipper was my aunt, her eyes still filled with anger over my uncle's death. We sailed over the deep blue-green dwelling of bluefish, horseshoe crabs, and kelp. And my uncle's ashes.

I had gotten to know him well in 1965 when my wife, my sister, and I went to Cape Cod the first time. Before then, he was a bit of a mystery, not spoken of much by my family. We visited him at Sea Song, his cottage colony near Provincetown. That first year we sanded the *Kittiwake*'s hull and caulked her. The next year we remodeled the front second-floor apartment of the beach house. Four of us convened each morning in that room: the black lab Bonnie, a world-class gull chaser; the terrier mix Cookie, a world-class food processor; Alden; and I. Being much more efficient and knowing what had to be done, my wife and sister worked elsewhere at preparing the cottages for the season. I drank coffee, Alden drank a concoction of Jim Beam and fruit juices mixed in a blender, Bonnie and Cookie panted and dreamed of gulls or table scraps. We talked, sauntering from idea to idea, reluctant to start work that we were ill-suited for, and watched Provincetown across the bay: the Pilgrim Monument, the steeple of the Universalist Meeting House, white beach houses, tan line of beach. We watched the tide come in filled with waves and food and unmatched blue light. And often we talked straight through until the bay emptied itself sandbar by sandbar. In the short time I knew him, he became a mentor, teacher, and second father. His recklessness and worldliness balanced my own father's caution and provincialism. His education was inclusive while my father's was specific. Although brothers, they held differing views on such issues as civil rights, the Vietnam War, religion, and ethics.

I pieced his life together from his stories: the scrapes he got into as a liberal student editor of the Cornell University *Daily Sun,* his connections with the New Deal Cabinet, his two careers: program director at NBC radio and owner of a TV advertising firm. When his partner ruined the advertising business, Alden lived inside a whiskey bottle (as the saying goes) until his doctor pronounced the sentence: quit drinking or die. With money she made as a cabaret singer, my aunt bought him the beach house, a gift that saved his life. And Alden moved to Cape Cod, learned to regulate his drinking, and became a happy man.

His stories from New York suggest the chaotic life that led to his self-medication. During a winter of lawsuits and recriminations surrounding the failed business, he would return home to Long Island and become incensed with the starlings that monopolized his bird feeder. But instead of shooting them, he sat in the snow and shooed them away until they gave up and the cardinals, chickadees, and nuthatches returned. At a party, Arthur Godfrey, the old-time radio and television star, made a pass at his wife; Alden sucker punched him. This was the same man I watched spend fifteen minutes capturing and releasing a hornet rather than swatting it. He was, finally, ill-suited for the things he had to do in New York.

In his Cape Cod stories I looked for signs of a bitter man, cheated and driven to exile. There was no trace. He loved to stand on the beach at the end of a summer day to look at the thousands of footprints made by vacationers at play, totally absorbed in the joy he imagined that each print contained. After a lonely, off-season day, struggling with his accounts, trying to survive the winter financially, he went for a walk on the ocean side to clear his head. During the walk, he stopped, looked down, and saw a washed-up sand dollar. He sat down and laughed at the irony until he cried. When his rickety Peugeot station wagon had accumulated enough sand inside to attract his attention (usually a medium dune's worth), he would wait for a blustery day, drive to the highest point of land, open all four doors and happily take a long beach walk while the wind tidied up as best it could.

Certainly these winds and tides and waves that ultimately dominate the tip of Cape Cod were part of his cure. The last bit of solid ground was left behind by glaciers at High Head, just inland from Sea Song. All is sand from there to the tip at Provincetown, and the Atlantic with its gales and Cape Cod Bay with its high tides and winter storms are never more than a mile apart. East of Sea Song are first the Atlantic, then the sand dunes of Provincelands, and then Pilgrim Lake—a freshwater pond formed when a narrow sandbar built up and shut off a harbor in Cape Cod Bay. In 1869, the sea was closed off and a road put in. Between the road and the bay, my uncle lived the last years of his precarious life—on a sandbar barely above sea level. And he often spoke of the vitality and comfort he took from such wildness and insecurity.

Only later and gradually did I learn what he meant. On our first trip to Sea Song, my wife and I went for a walk on the tidal flats. At the Cape's end, the flats feature large pools and asymmetrical sand islands that sink away as the tide rises. Hopeless rookies that we were, we went out too far and, heading back, waded through pools that became alarmingly deeper. Suddenly, it seemed, we were wading up to our waists from sandbar to sandbar. Then swimming. On that same trip we walked the beach one moonless night. Sensing something at our bare feet, I turned on the flashlight and discovered that we were walking through hundreds of scuttling sand crabs. We screamed the screams of frightened landlubbers and ran. We were learning. The Cape might hold a place for us, but it wouldn't come easily.

Shortly after Alden's death, a particularly acrimonious rift between my aunt and me took this treasured place from us. After she died, we learned that, because of our differences, she had changed Alden's will and cut us out completely. Having already composed several drafts of a resignation letter to my department chair and dean, I was devastated. I was resigned *to,* rather than *from,* a life of teaching freshman composition. And to a life without Sea Song. My only consolation was that Bonnie and Cookie got twenty thousand dollars each.

So I waited thirty years to go back to Sea Song. We had been coming back to the Cape twice a year for family stays at Eastham, a few miles down the bay from Sea Song, and I had driven by the cottages many times and noted the changes, but an undefined fear and a natural reticence kept me from approaching the new owners. Not knowing what to expect, I finally, in June of 1997, intruded on the friendly couple who live in one of the beachfront units and run the bay-side half of the business (it had been divided a few years after its sale). We chatted—I told them what I knew of the history of the place; they talked mainly about beach erosion. Indeed, the bay seemed dangerously close to their front deck. When I walked the beach, I remembered raking the seaweed daily that high tide left behind and piling it in front of the beach house where it captured drifting sand and built a dune at least eight feet high. Alden planted beach grass and salt-spray roses to hold the sand in place. The dune was gone now, and the bare beach sloped away to the waterline. This bay, the tides, the waves, my uncle's ashes. But no epiphany. Nothing really had changed. The forces that controlled the land were firmly in place no matter who held deed to what.

One such force, a second northeaster, was already starting to move up the East Coast when we got to the Cape from Maine. Winds blew in the thirties for three days straight; gusts reached sixty miles per hour. It was glorious—then perfect when we turned on the Weather Channel and saw that our northeaster had dumped two feet of snow on the route that we had planned to take home through New York State. We were stuck in another home, the Wellfleet Motel, for three extra days of brilliant sun and booming surf.

I made one final visit to Sea Song to close that book. Shuttered against the winter with scraps of plywood, buildings too close together, high-tide debris—bits of fishing net and Styrofoam flotation, plastic bags, broken boards—lurking under the decks, it looked tacky and trashy compared to the deep blue of the bay and the pure white of the wave crests. On the beach house, I could see the high-water mark left by waves that had pulled down the snow fence that was supposed to protect the sand that was supposed to protect the buildings. Just a bunch of cottages and a beach house with a name. Not for long, Sea Song—maybe a couple more winters.

I remembered again the dune I helped Alden to build, now a flat and featureless beach picked clean by the storm. Then I had a good memory. When Alden and I were working on the kitchenette of the second-floor front room, we needed to replace a small wall section with a sheet of Formica—a one-hour job, even for us. No, Alden thought it would be a good thing to create a Mondrian wall. We collected different-colored Formica pieces from old projects and bought yards of metal molding. We customized the two-by-four stud supports and made our masterpiece. It took three blissful days. We knew it looked awful, but we didn't care. Out there, nothing lasts anyway, just wind and water and stories.

∽

My wife and I lived four days in the power of the storm, letting it dictate each next move. At Newcomb's Hollow, ten-foot breakers with tops flying madly back out to sea created a boiling confusion of water and foam as violent as I've seen. The scene repeated itself all along the ocean side—Marconi Beach, LeCount's Hollow, White Crest Beach, Race Point. And always, out beyond the surf line, the rich blue of the water set off wave crests and gulls. To add to the spectacle, hundreds of gannets flashed white and black along the waves, soared upward, and dove with the force of mortar shells crashing.

On the bay side at First Encounter Beach, we watched the tide come in as the wind swung around to the southwest. Combined, wind and tide forced the bay over the winter berm. Behind us, the marsh quickly filled in above its grasses. The freshening wind blew a rain squall ashore and whipped up ragged waves in the marsh where just hours before there was dry land. The sun returned and turned the shallow marsh water a dramatic pewter. A full double rainbow formed concentric arches from marsh to bay. Fifty-mile-per-hour wind shook the car. Sand and spray rattled against the windward doors and windows. It was quite a show, the Cape at its best . . . unless maybe you're homeless in Provincetown, or a fisherman caught offshore, or just old, alone, and afraid of the wind. Or an alcoholic living by himself through a Cape Cod winter. The moment, thrilling and beautiful as it was, had passed. My footing had proven unreliable, even worse than clay. I remembered other Sea Song stories—of deception, anger, confusion, and finally despair. The Cape and its sand will do that to you: tides rise and tides fall, a wave reaches in and pulls the land from under your feet. But, as Alden loved to point out, every twelve hours the bay fills up again.

∽

During the height of the windstorm, we drove to Kingsbury Shores, a hillside of cottages whose highest point holds Chase's cottage—the one we've rented for twenty-five years and truly a "home away from home." We parked alongside the cottage for a while. Donna worked on composing a couple photographs of the storm-twisted sky, the boarded-up cottage, scrubby pitch pine, and brown grasses. I shut my eyes and walked inside in my imagination. Open the back door into the galley kitchen . . . directly in front of you a small window opens onto the bay . . . if you keep both door and window open on a breezy day, the cross draft will put out the pilot light on the stove top . . . walk to the window and turn left into the living room—a motley and beloved collection of mismatched furniture, books, maps, photographs, and the huge window. This is the window I look out from whenever I need to: enduring traffic, longing for a meeting to end, listening to a speech, or lying awake and waiting for morning. This is what I see. White chairs have been scattered about the gray and weathered deck in ways determined by conversations or the positions of the sun. Beach towels are draped over a couple of the chairs and the railing. After this burst of color, the scene comprises—depending on weather and time of tide—shades of greens and browns and blues: the honeysuckle and pitch pine, the sandbars, the bay and sky. And our only reliable "landmark"—the target ship, the *James Longstreet*. Built in 1942, the *Longstreet* had a short and dull career as a cargo ship and after two collisions was towed to Cape Cod Bay and sunk in shallow water—most of her hull exposed at low tide. Then she was shot at, practice for navy guns and missiles. For us the target ship was never the rusting hulk she, in fact, is. She became a feature that measured fogs and rains: "You can't even see the target ship today." She told us the direction of squalls. We could tell which bay beach we were on by our relationship to the target ship.

Photography over, we walked to the head of the stairs that lead to the beach. Spray reached halfway up the forty-foot bluff. Waves broke over the bottom ten steps. No beach walk. No beach. We had been trying for three days to spot the target ship, but in spite of the clarity of the air, we failed again. Driven back to the car, our reference point gone and our land eroding beneath us, we began to talk about years at the cottage, perhaps looking for some new anchorage for our time there.

༄

One of the things we used to do on the Cape was to fish. I approached it in my usual obsessive way, reading every book I could find, talking with bait-and-tackle sellers, studying tide tables and ocean charts. And like so many others who had only a couple weeks a year to fish, I usually got skunked. Kevin, at age eight, had it right: "You're a good fisherman, Dad, but you never catch any fish." I like his recognition that style does count for something; that's important for the obsessive person. But I think we both understand now that catching fish was never the real point of fishing; trying to catch fish was: hiking down the beach to a likely spot, casting and retrieving (or feeding crabs with live bait), watching the pole's tip with the childlike hope that the bouncing will be a striper and not the surf. Being there in a place where being there is enough.

But I did hook one good fish during my career. It happened one early June sometime in the 1980s. From the cottage deck, I was looking at the target ship through a telescope when I saw the unmistakable boil and confusion of water stirred up by feeding bluefish. I grabbed my pole and a Hopkins lure and raced to the beach where I commandeered the tiny rubber raft Kevin and Jeffrey were playing on. I paddled out to the spot, about a hundred yards from shore, and cast. It's said that bluefish in a feeding frenzy will strike anything, and I had proved this wrong several times. But not this time. A huge (I swear it) bluefish nailed the lure the instant it hit the water and started to take out line. I set the hook, tightened the drag a bit, and took a couple turns on the reel. It was then that I realized what was happening. The bluefish was pulling me out into the bay—and at a pretty good clip. I could feel its power pulse down the line and into my hands. This was a big fish. And my boat was small, so small, in fact, that my feet were dangling over the edge, now in the midst of a school of feeding bluefish. Not thinking too clearly, I tightened the drag way down and pulled the tip back hard. What that maneuver was intended to accomplish is unclear to me now. What it actually accomplished was to snap my line and allow me to figure out that paddling like mad to shore was my best next move. There was no saving face.

I tell this little story not to lead off a series of yarns but because it's the only halfway decent story we could remember from more than twenty-five years at Chase's cottage. There were events like bicycle spills and broken windows and sunburns. And there were wonderful memories of natural beauty and family times: sunsets shared, beach walks, seafood dinners. But no stories with those elements we ask of a story: a beginning, some tension, an ending. And, of course, the larger and unfinished stories continue; after all, a family grew and changed and changed some more. But nothing to recount around the dinner table.

As we sat reminiscing, we understood that the stories that defined our homes weren't necessarily of the classic and dramatic kind but, rather, simple images that have remained in our memories, enriched our lives, and improved over time. To revisit Bachelard, "the home gathers images, cementing memory to imagination . . . [it] acknowledges our daydreams."

The boys expressed disappointment that the fish got away. Donna was indirect. "Welcome home from the seas," she said.

Where I Live(d)

✳ ✳ ✳ ✳ ✳ ✳ ✳ ✳ ✳ ✳

WENDY BISHOP

Not just looking and listening, and certainly not imagining,
but moving constitutes the western experience. . . .
—NANCY MAIRS

Life can only be understood backwards, but it must be lived forwards.
—SØREN KIERKEGAARD

Where I Live(d): A Meditation on Place, in Parts

I THINK ABOUT a musical friend of mine—when he starts to tune and strum the guitar, he shakes his gray long hair and mutters, "What do I know? What do I know?" At first I thought—"Is this humbug? Does he know any music worth listening to at all?" Eventually, I learned that he knew too many songs, songs from his past, songs from the radio, songs downloaded from the Internet. He learns songs by ear and saves them by hand—making scribbles of notes and notations—and then plays them in a touch-and-feel-and-hear-and-say-and-sing collage, leafing through a manila folder of lyrics and paper reminders until he finds the place to enter the music for a while. Like me, he's experienced, knows many, but can't hold all his songs in short-term memory. Like him, I shake my head and say, "What do I know, what do I know?" And realize I don't know what I know. So I turn a page. I play.

༄

Fukuoka, Kyushu, Japan, 1953
Ventura, California, 1956–1971
Davis, California, 1972–1979
Kano, Nigeria, 1980
Flagstaff, Arizona, 1981–1982
Tsaile, Arizona, 1982–1985
Flagstaff, Alaska, 1985–1989
Tallahassee, Florida, 1989–

༄

I dwell in the West while in live in the East. I dwell in my head. At my writing desk. In my genes. I dig into my past to anchor my present. I dwell in my imagination. In these explorations.

༄

Unwriting My Life in the West
Familiar Tectonics

Writing the Perfect Poet

Propositions on a Lost Name of a Street

It's Not the Heat, It's the Humidity—It's Not the Cold, It's the Darkness

Hummingbird in the Garage

An Etiology of Endings and Beginnings

Where the Hummingbird Sips, There Sip I: An Appreciation

Hummingbird at Heart

Someone's in the Kitchen with Wendy

(Mainly) Middle-Class Suburban (Mostly) White, or Making Sense of Suburbia

Souvenirs

Autobiography

ᘓ

Unwriting My Life in the West
TO GO WEST[1]
      —Directions for Sean[2]

When living overland in Florida,[3] take a trail
by the nearest rock cairn, switch back loops
under last cottonwood,[4] climbs and vistas
into whale-backs of mountain crests.[5]

Go west in sunset by lost buffalo cliffs, by
corral where dust swirls into a rattler-strike.[6]
Conjure Swedes swinging off the train in
Flagstaff; they strip and sun in sacred
mountain light, as we watch.[7] West at
night, down Salt River Canyon: desert
primrose exhales in darkness.[8] Beyond my
tent, owl examines unmoving cactus.
Hitchhike west, shake bedrolls at dusk near
a hot-tar highway, elegantly empty of cars.[9]

To find a private west, seek Sierras,
share cold death in empty wagons[10]
or be blessed by a sunrise of stars.
The west knows each hippie who sang in

sulfur waters of natural hot-springs.[11] West
is EST. Fad, fancy, folly, down vests and
wool socks, hair shirts, sideburns, men and
women idle and who worked too hard,
country bars and unhappy hours, mine
tailings, broken blueglass bottles,
paychecks and horse-snort bone
tiredness.[12] There's a certain off-putting
ornery languor: west is all west, the first last
frontier, flimsy with trailers, highest hopes
lost to earthquake, lava, dust bowl, water
diversion, flash flood.[13] But to others, west
is salmon-dart-certainty in the coldest pools.[14]

To go west, I'm ten on the beach, saltwater
in eyes and excitement of undertow.[15] I'm
thirteen on a car trip east, sweating over
manners and a dose of relatives.[16] At
eighteen hike into Yolla Bolly Middle Eel
Wilderness. Suburban-brown-grass-coastal-
hill bred—I hate this, because scared, but I
can never go back to flat or easy.[17] By
twenty, navigating fog, climbing hills out of
Napa with soon-to-be-lost friends.[18] In
Capay Valley, I walk the moon into a broken
down barn, smelling forever, night fields of
buttery hay.[19]

Manzanita is west, and poetry. A college
photography professor who turned his VW
microbus into a giant camera, sliding side-
door for shutter, embodies *my* '70s. The
arteries of LA present themselves when I
close my eyes: familiar cluttered
hopelessness in so much space.[20]

To go west
be alone, when the red rock opens to a long
plateau,[21] grizzly trails down tundra hollows,

interstate signs promise *cheap food, cheap*
jewelry, restrooms ahead,
dammed waters lend color the foolish blue
of stellar jay feathers.[22]

To go west
find fast, if momentary, friends, swig a beer
midday in high altitude heat backpacked in
on a honky-tonk memory.[23] This ledge of
sky was never owned by the thousands
who, at hopeful early morning, like you,
passed by.[24]

∽

1. My Florida writing room faces west, toward an often barely visible
sunset. Sometimes, humidity down, skies clearing toward the Gulf Coast,
the sky burns a California brush-fire red, out of control. I stop, walk outside, stand, watch.

In 1989, when I moved to Tallahassee from Fairbanks, Alaska, a newly
minted but later-in-life Ph.D., I was aiming to land again in California
where I had grown up, run away from for ten years and now wanted to return to. Alaska was northwest and brimming with flotsam characters of my
Pacific Basin past, 1960s edge people, the Viet vets who couldn't go home
again, the Isla Vista and Berkeley organic gardeners who found in per-
mafrost their last and best challenge, the Oakland spiritualist, the Grass
Valley seeker, the Whittier misfit who found an Orange County acre first
too small and then impossibly expensive. Up the accordioned coast, Ore-
gon, Washington, and farther northwest, they drifted like clouds.

Florida was reviled throughout my Ventura, California, childhood as a
flat, hot, and hopeless place where my paternal cousins, aunt, uncle, and
grandparents lived. Sarasota. As inexplicable to me as Superior, Wisconsin,
the city and state they had left. Sarasota, imprinted on my memory like
hand-tinted postcards, where the oranges didn't taste as orange, the ac-
cents twanged disturbingly, the air was heavy with water and the Gulf with
warmth, where they hadn't heard of skateboards and the Beach Boys.
Florida, only to be approached with some necessary disdain (and twelve-
year-old excitement).

Tallahassee, I was relieved to find, did not have the more southern

Florida flatness of my Sarasota memories. In the blur of a job-interview drive through a town of knotted, narrow roads, sun slid into my eyes in February like a butter knife into warm butter. I wondered if I could allow the Alaska range or the Sierras—brash, new, rough mountain chains—to diminish to these slight rolling inclines of only bicycle seriousness. I decided that I was circumnavigating—that this was one way to return. Somehow. And of course, it paid. California rarely pays. At least not in the way seekers after and with/in it need.

My Florida house delivers the largest patch of west-facing sky I could find. Outskirts of a former plantation, a rare moment of cleared cattle pasture now filling in with "eastern" brick houses, oaks out back burdened with Spanish moss. I swap them in memory for California live oaks studded across grass-brown, steeply rolling coastal and then Sierra foothills, woman-bodied, clefted and grown wild. Hills just past Oakland that tumble down into the great Central Valley. Oak shade is as black as slow, night-caught breath during the valley summers. Crops growing audibly. The smell of onion and tomato processing and rotting rich hays.

There is a slight slope below this window, running down past the swimming pool, the oleanders I planted in memory of California oleanders; the fence—that falls and lists, swollen with years of humidity and insect life and punch-drunk from the arrival of a thousand-pound tree limb, heavy with water, the shattering exclamation point of a hurricane warning–sized storm; the next neighbor's yard; and three more suburban roads that lead down to Rhoden Cove landing on the undulating flank of Lake Jackson, which hosts the slow-moving blue herons, the confetti of cattle egret, the Tabernacle Choir of summer frogs.

2. Sean enrolled in my poetic technique class at Florida State University one semester. He fell in love with the poetry of Gary Snyder, with the unrolling, unruly Beat line, with personal excess (some mornings he was more "present" than other mornings). He made me feel a little old (well, of course, I am a little old). He resurrected my memories of the 1970s through his enthusiasms—writing about hitchhiking, about doing anything to get a girl he imagined himself in love with to notice him. A Floridian who grew up on an East Coast island in a working-class way, roofing houses with a construction crew until he was as tan as a dark beer, Sean couldn't fully understand my longing for the West, although he liked the poetry and the informality that causes me to ask every student to call me by first name.

He'd slump through an office hour making me laugh. I was half in love with him, of course, half in love with his rangy, crazy energy, his imaginary San Francisco, his belief that life could still "just happen" in the 1990s. He graduated, went back to the island for a long nail-hammering summer and then west to work on a writing degree in Flagstaff, Arizona. I know he got as far as Flagstaff. He wrote a letter saying so. I never answered, until today, if this is an answer.

3. Several times I've explained my life this way: I live overland in Florida the way I went overseas to Europe in 1971 as an eighteen year old. I brought back packages of Twinnings tea and Toblerone chocolate, entranced with the otherworldly gourmet packages in two languages, with the suddenly seen Old World. Returned, I found the teas and candies and soaps and vegetables in Safeway stores. I just couldn't see them before.

Until I lived in Florida, it was hard sometimes to see California.

In Florida, I drive to work, worrying about teaching and writing, my children and dog left behind, my day before me, and then I turn my head and I stare.

I stare at the screenless shack on the crumbling asphalt road in Panacea, the folks parking in a grove of palm-tree trunks beside a small, white Baptist church, the ramshackle Suwanee Swifty convenience store that just seems to beg for a daytime robbery. I'm more aware of danger and poverty in French Town, an African American neighborhood in Tallahassee, than I was in the villages of Nigeria where I lived one year in 1980. And, while I love the food at Sonny's barbecue I know it isn't "authentic," but I really don't want to go to the Gulf Coast and eat at Posey's Bar, oysters, white culture, and the heat of July all overwhelming me, or out to Nicholson's Farmhouse that I've heard described as old-fashioned, diners eating chicken and mashed potatoes and slaw together while the "help" works hard and late in the frog-noisy summer-night kitchen.

I'm not a native Californian—but ages three to twenty-seven made me who I am and who I remain—someone whose molecules go out on the Pacific tide and bob there dreamily. It's as if all the long afternoons I sat in a broken-down van at a cliff overlooking Rincon Beach watching my sometimes boyfriend, eventually first husband, Chris K., surf and pirouette on a long, flashing surfboard, it's as if this still takes place in inland seas inside me. I remember almost too easily the first breath of young adulthood, heady, filled with down jackets, mysterious distant snowfall on the Sierras as seen from that too perfect, ecologically minded bicycle city of Davis, California, where I shaped my days from 1972 to 1979, years and a location that continue to shape me.

4. To unwrite myself back into the West, I always travel via the Southwest. After a year in Nigeria, I ended up in Flagstaff, then in Tsaile, Arizona, teaching at Navajo Community College. This, at twenty-nine, my first successful attempt to relocate seriously (as opposed to travel to) more than two hours from the Pacific. There was something reassuring about the emptiness there. The butte- and sheep- and hogan-filled roads between Teec Nos Pos and Roundrock held the same emptiness of the hills behind Ventura where public grazing lands were rented out to Basque sheepherders. Cottonwood, piñon, spruce, ponderosa pine. And the red rock frozen into sandstone waves in Canyon de Chelly brought with it, somehow, the peace of the Pacific. I could look out and down, one thousand feet into the canyon, see the summer sheep camps or ancient Puebloan cliff dwellings, taste air lifted back up to me by the antics of ravens, and feel in alignment again.

5. Summer 1995. M., my third ex-husband, and during that last reconciliation attempt my roommate—another fact that makes me purely Californian though he is not—and I took our children back to the West for the first time in ten years (we had met in Navajoland). You'll see mountains, I promised our kids. At the first big road cut in Texas, they asked in some excitement: "Is this it?"

Behind Ventura, ranges of hills sleep. Beyond Davis, the Sierras, sharp, craggy, lie in wait across the entire horizon.

One morning, driving from Ojai to Lake Casitas, taking the back route to Santa Barbara, the mountains with their endless folds of fogs stopped me. This is what it means to be alive, to come around a precipitous curve in a VW Bug, to get out and inspect what some imagined creator left behind.

6. I never really saw whales or rattlesnakes. But they are part of the vocabulary of California that makes it what I miss. I was always almost seeing a whale (being nearsighted doesn't help). And the ranches and ranchettes triggered tales of rattlers. Whether with sixth-grade friends as we played in

refrigerator boxes in drought-dry hill grass or in college, trudging behind a college boyfriend, Kim, up and down the pastures of his Humboldt County family ranch, there was—across time—the perpetual pleasures of boot leather and rattlers, tails and tales.

7. To unwrite my life in the West, I have to unpack and set aside the days I taught at Northern Arizona University (remember, where Sean more recently disappeared to). I spent one long year writing and teaching writing in that railroad town before following Brad, my second husband, to the reservation where he had found work. I had already spent five years in Davis on Olive Drive, about fifteen feet from the railroad tracks, so I still woke happily to railroad clamor. And I had learned that I no longer had to go to Europe because in the 1980s the Europeans were coming to the Southwest. They loved the Hopi and Navajo, the sacred mountains, the Grand Canyon. They'd swing off the train at Flagstaff during a stop and strip all their clothes off except for tiny blue or red bikini underwear, men and women, blond and dirty but smiling their way into the western sunsets of their TV program beliefs. They'd twirl beatifically in the sun and the space and board the train again just before AmTrak pulled out. The western Route 66 towns—like well-mannered farmhands—ignored them, all the way to California.

In Flagstaff, I launched myself across the Southwest. I was half invisible there, a writing teacher who couldn't believe she was getting paid for her work, like an adult. But each vacation, the long umbilical desert drive back to California.

8. Most people I knew in California had, like me, arrived from somewhere else, but, also like me, at a young enough age to know nothing else, to claim some form of an immigrant past. Some, like my parents, arrived through the armed services, bouncing from Korea/Japan across the Pacific Basin to Washington and on to envisioned eventual retirement in San Diego, rolling up short some three hours north in Ventura and thirty minutes south of the more preferable, to them, Santa Barbara, a city of some history and (painful) class (consciousness). Ventura was just carving itself out of the orange groves, relying heavily on its impeccable beaches.

My friend Kate makes a point of her third-generation California pedigree (as does Joan Didion, and their relationships to writing sentences are equally serious). The people who overpopulate California are more like me than like Kate. Accidental, rooted in the *experience* of California more than in their place there. They move, they drift. Tumbleweeds. So, for a time, the Southwest was a way to keep the California of my growing-up years— not yet too expensive, pretentious, or overcrowded—into later years.

In the Southwest, I met M. who arrived west as a Chicago easterner and with some care and investment learned the names for things. Beyond knowing freeway and interstate numbers and exits, like any near-California-native, I knew little of desert primrose and the entire bewitching ecology of cactus, organ pipe, and jumping cholla. I began to earn the West by learning its names, left as people moved on, alphabetic memorials in the dryness by the side of the wagon train–rutted trails.

9. This part is the story of a woman learning her own freedoms in good company. In California, people did things. Drove all night, Davis to Lompoc. Hiked into backcountry in tennis shoes. Dropped acid by a duck pond. Played Frisbee in orchestrated contests refereed by dogs that wore red bandannas. They went to Lake Atitlan on a whim. They always appeared in the park the day the band played for free.

Kim took me hitchhiking, first down arterial central California, out into the desert-warmed highways of the Southwest, to walk across the border into the dust of northern Mexico. Torreon to Veracruz, to visit his aunt who lived there: a jumble of sunsets, dysentery, and the memory of washing a single dull-green skirt in a sink, again, again.

10. I wouldn't give up the Donner Party, Joaquin Murietta, or the sadness of Sutter Fort for anything. Such stories once told are never left behind. Bigs are big—death, cannibalism. Smalls are sly and disreputable—claim jumping or selling the last rotten egg in town as easily as selling your soul. And then the cold breath of stars blows it all away, and Californians begin again.

11. That's not to say it was always easy, the early 1970s. I remember a day at Wilbur Hot Springs where the Capay Valley ends and climbs to Clearlake. A mad psychiatrist had revitalized the springs (lost in poker hands several times in the 1880s and '90s), filled the house with people of

consciousness and a collection of thrift-store hats, and demanded that each and everyone there wear one, celebrate the body (dip in hot sulfur springs naked), and eat food that was teeth-crackingly solid and correct—brown rice, goat cheese, sprouts that tasted metallic despite their cultivation in glass jars and northern California sunlight. Young goats would lick our fingers. An uptight organist, Curtis, who came with Chris Lee's medieval-music ensemble to trade music for a free day at the baths, never got out of his gray slacks and pointed black organist's shoes. I saw him blanch as two women holding hands, wearing Indian-print shirts and nothing else, walked by. Refusing to age, hearty white-haired men howled unpleasantly in one corner of the bathhouse. Pot smoke fretted the atmosphere. Red skin. Someone smiling. Someone crying. It was easy to feel left in and left out.

12. In Florida, I wear a silver belt buckle. I've gravitated back to wearing vests and boots. I say "Howdy" to the people coming down the university staircase. They say "Hey" back at me. We scratch our heads. They know how to look fresh in the summer heat.

I can't abide anything much besides jeans anymore. How would I help Will change the irrigation pipes in his "ranchette" almond orchard, or trail after Kim as he catches Robert, his old white horse, up in the Garberville pastures, or maneuver breathlessly on the hiking trail behind Chris K. as we stare in the Muir Woods at the dripping, pungent redwoods?

How could the lepidopterist, his girlfriend—the cellist—and I arrive safely at the mine tailings where he would hunt butterflies with a net, naked and wearing a pith helmet, having taken mushrooms and sunburning vaingloriously? There was quite a strain of nakedness, and it strained me. I was always too shy for my West. But I tried. I dug blue bottles out of the foundations of the burnt-down cabin. That took blue jeans, as did eating Mexican food in Woodland—that is, as did anything worth doing.

When you're dirt and bone tired, I believe your soul dreams you back to where you were once very happy while it makes the necessary repairs. The rich river lands of the Central Valley, flat and promising, yielded and then broke lots of promises.

13. A Californian adoptee is a foolish thing. Loves the foolish, the un-fettered, the uncivilized.

In Florida, I'm entranced by the Alligator Patrol Trucks, the manatee, the fire ants that war with lawn owners, the canopy roads dripping with small traffic jams, the way March heat melts you to your bones before it stings you with skin cancer. But I'm also glad that my shrink is gay and my neighbors don't understand me and my kids' friends sometimes come by and stare at me for I might drink wine unapologetically at any hour of the day and stay home suspiciously to write. Even as I make fun, I warm to the part of Florida where everyone's a prospector—looking for a way to stay as alert as a lizard until the end of their days.

14. Moments of refundable happiness: waking up and knowing it was a beach day in high school; sleeping all night the first night to the sound of Pacific Ocean heartbeats with Chris K.; setting the tent up successfully, alone and able one Christmas Eve in Big Sur after Brad left me flat; watching a water ouzel on my first camping trip (these memories, like most, don't come in order) dive through a cold stream in Yosemite—learning its name *and* seeing what it could do. Imagine a world where birds swim under water. It's true.

15. It's a lie. My father and my oldest sister, Judy, tell me to trust them, to let them hold my hands and go out into the surf. The surf is stronger than their promises and tears me away. I tumble in sand-filled shallow water, snort, scare. Four years old and I'll never trust the ocean purely again. But, like all things I don't trust, I want to and do claim oceans. I wish I "did" oceans, too. But I hate sand in bathing suits, get impatient even with the Gulf Coast body-warm waves. I respect oceans, need them. I think I've paid my dues. I can look westward forever but still I can't be there, be in there, be safe there, be saved by water, salt or otherwise.

16. We didn't invent the 1950s family-car trip (but we might as well have). We drove from Ventura to Florida to see my Florida cousins and my Uncle Bill, Aunt Mitzi, and my grandparents with their tangerine tree and sulfur water pumped into that Sarasota cinder-block house; to New York to see older sister Judy, already out of college and on her own in a walk-up near Washington Square in Greenwich Village; to Minneapolis to see my mother's sister, Aunt Ann, before heading home, fast.

And everywhere I was disdainful—showed off my skateboard, jams, pre–Valley Girl lingo—*bitchin', mellow, spaz*—disdain for everyone yoked to *mere* land. Although I couldn't live purely for oceans as a surfer girl (too afraid) or surfer-boy's girlfriend (too boring), I was determined to be of the California kind, of mountains, fogs, new rock formations, restlessness as thick as waves.

17. It wasn't until I was eighteen that the southern California suburbanite was beaten out and the northern California backpacker eased in as Chris K. taught me that I had to keep going or get no dinner at night. I foundered in the lava-rock formations near Lassen, lost my puppy fat in the Middle Eel Wilderness, ran after him as scared and fast as I could, cheap frame backpack squeaking. When water surfaced, I would fling myself at what I needed, drenched in a newfound body as spring melt shattered down the leaf-covered hill. I wanted California to make me.

18. Marty, Laurie, Brian, boyfriends, husbands, friends, girlfriends, faces without names, names that elude the faces I'd return to them. A young baby named Jeronimo by his mother who left her lover in Spain and settled in the Olive Drive courtyard where I lived and wrote and went to college. Cindy her name. Lost and found, returned—Chris K., Chris Lee, Hans, Mary and Lee, Laurie and Nöel, and a tall skinny kid named Freak. There's enough space in the West for everyone's spirit to hover and remain, or go on, wherever it is they thought they must go.

19. Swimming in Cache Creek with Will. Changing more irrigation pipe. Riding borrowed horses into Capay Valley foothills. Writing and drinking coffee. Aubade: Driving back early in the morning to my Davis life, to change it. Taking radical right and left turns. Learning about the university by learning in the university. Making small spaces in my cottage glow with words. Meeting the moon. Learning the word *manzanita* is sometimes all I'd have and all I'd need. Reading the Beats, beating out poems on a Smith Corona correctable, a present from a mother who would some years later drown herself in a swimming pool in Santa Barbara, a city that always broke her heart.

Never trust water again. (As if I ever really had.)

Rooting my writing in the West. Rooting myself in the Central Valley like the garden Kim turned over for me one year behind the Olive Drive cottage, black valley earth and the Southern Pacific shattering through,

Laurie and I in the weedy backyard nude sunbathing and waving a slight wave at the already-gone-past engineers.

20. Two of my favorite unlost friends still live in L.A. all these years, proving it is not a mirage. Rod and Kate, who also write. But not together, though they get together when I visit, and sometimes we all write in the same place and about California. When I visit them, I feel invisible. I see how the latitudes, lassitudes, and longitudes of L.A. are inscribed on each of our inner skulls in just the same way. Go or stay? It's starting not to matter.

21. Moments of awe if not happiness, I unwrite my life in the West: look at Spider Rock in Canyon de Chelly, see the stern mountains through a snowstorm above Salt Lake City, poise myself, my friends, my car, to drive down the slippery slope of the Sierras toward Roseville, Sacramento, home. Always wondering if this trip, visit, location, incarnation, will end in a smelly Forest Service rest room or by a bush big enough to crouch behind. One summer, I had to try to teach my Florida-raised daughter that girls really can pee outdoors, her not believing me until we get to the West, blank, gut wrenching, empty enough to shake a girl up.

22. Some mornings, I'm nothing but a stellar jay at an abandoned roadside table outside Sacramento. I'm irritable (one drink too many?) and sure the crumbs on the ground are for me, so I dive the shit out of anything that challenges me, fluff my wing tips, and go along on my way, indifferent to the cars thundering along the Yolo Causeway, commuting down past Fairfield and Vacaville to the Bay. Sometimes a bird is just a bird.

23. I can't help it. I grew up there. The Earl Warren Showgrounds—black-light posters. The Bank of America bunkered down in Isla Vista. Earth Day. Parents who didn't truly know where they'd ended up, what California was, what they'd done to get there, but assumed they did. Love, peace, war, old-clothes stores, Graffeo's Coffee, North Beach, a poetry reading I gave in Cody's Bookstore when I didn't know what anything meant, either.

24. And even though I've lived some years now unhappily and happily—that is to say—normally in Florida, I wouldn't say I'm just one of the hopeful who passed by and through the West, who put California on and off like a wonderful wool sweater left by an ecstatic easterner at the Sixteenth

Street Sacramento Goodwill store who thinks she has left the snows of Wisconsin far behind. I can't unwrite my life in the West, at least not for very long.

I'm Odysseus's Penelope reversed, for as soon as I unravel these threads, they knit themselves back up into the whole cloth of memory, the visible and the invisible, everything added, nothing taken away.

Familiar Tectonics

I have stories about earthquakes. Kobe. Northridge. Los Angeles. Fukuoka.

I remember the family Japanese earthquake story where I might be a character, yet I'm thinking that my sister Linda, four years older, perhaps was the one (I could look up the date of the earthquake to find out—I was born in Fukuoka, Kyushu, Japan, January 13, 1953—I correct my spelling from a silver birth cup engraved with an intricate Japanese dog and doll in a kimono that my daughter has taken over and usually keeps in her room, returning it dramatically when she's mad at me). Yesterday in the main office at work, Rikki heard me give my social security number in exchange for my end-of-year tax statement and said: "Were you born overseas too?" "Yes," I said. "How did you know?" "Social security numbers starting with that number usually are." (Remember memorizing the mysterious number of social security, so unconnected to street or home phone numbers? Social what? Secure what?)

Live and learn, I thought, here in my forties. For someone who had to file at age twenty-one to clarify my dual citizenship—which would I be, Japanese (having lived there for three months) or American (having grown up with Japanese furniture and Japanese stories, being called Wendy-Chan by my mother, still wishing I had inherited the "Japanese plate" instead of my sister Nancy)—I thought I was the keeper of the stories, but I didn't know my own social security number could give me away.

∽

My mother told the Japanese earthquake story with some glee—unusual for her—and I think now she must have performed her telling in the same way I share my L.A. earthquake story: the family in the kitchen, the lamp swaying.

Let me back up a moment before I go on. The 1971 earthquake in L.A. Sixty miles north in Ventura, my blended family—stepmother, Audrey; and her three sons, Bruce, Rob, and Brad; my father; and myself—collided in the kitchen at 2 A.M. to watch a lamp swing slowly back and forth.

I can still feel the panicked certainty that propelled me out of bed and toward the kitchen. I can see the kitchen lamp, but not see it. That is, it was most likely brass, with four candle-shaped bulbs and a linked brass chain, woven through with clear plastic cord and suspended from the ceiling. Orange lamp shade, my stepmother—an artist's—then favorite color. Orange VW Beetle, bathroom accessories, trash can in my room where my youngest stepbrother, the sleepwalker, once peed, loud liquid hitting the orange metal. Orange kitchen, orange light–blanched faces that early earthquake morning. A group nightmare. I remember the swinging. The swaying. Six of us in a frieze around the table. Our twelve eyes.

I use this story to participate in the action of the world, whenever someone else tells *their* earthquake story. Getting us all shaken up and into the kitchen, having experienced something.

For my mother, the Mount Fuji earthquake provides a human dimension, puts her into the scene. It was her "Yes, I've been there" response, although the story as she told it really was rather anticlimactic. We're not good storytellers, actually, she or me.

During a major Japanese earthquake in the early 1950s, she explains, she ran to the door frame. At the end of the quake, the baby (me? my sister Linda?) was dangling upside down, an ankle in each hand, swinging in a mother's fierce grip. Or was it Takosan or Ruthie, one of the maids, who knew to run to the doorway, who scooped up her charge?

My parents prided themselves on the assistance they gave to Ruthie that helped her to return to the U.S. after being relocated during the war to Japan. When she finally left Japan, she left behind her infant son who remained with her ex-husband and his family, and she took up a frugal, daughter-of-the-groundskeeper existence in Santa Monica—oldest daughter, old maid almost, who refused to marry her fiancé while her parents were alive so as not to diminish her support for them.

When I was in sixth grade, a visit was arranged, and this woman who had not seen me since age three months came to Ventura. At some point as I was leaving the living-room reminiscences in order to take a shower before bed, Ruthie asked if she could help me bathe. I went very still. Showers were there for my furtive attention to my own new body, for fingering and feeling and escaping in hot clouds of steam. Not for backward memory but for its adolescent equivalent—forward memory—prediction, and dreaming. This time my mother didn't force me. I said yes myself. And Ruthie, gray hair in her black hair, scooped water and laved me with a cloth, saying quiet, singing things and murmuring.

I might mention that my mother had a habit of mentoring the huddled masses yearning to be free.

There was Labrene Limberopoulous, later Linda Leber, the Greek girl across the street whose father painted vaguely mythological scenes in medallions on the front of the house and the front walkway bright red and even painted the ropes linking the low, flower-garlanded posts into a decorative fence around the front yard. The posts painted by Nick. The rope painted red.

The Perezes, a Cuban "refugee" family next door, whose head-of-household mother cleaned for us. Years later in Santa Barbara, Ping, a Chinese man whom my mother crowed over, telling me all she had done for him. She always spoke very loudly to her charges: "This is the VACUUM." "In AMERICA we use the OUTSIDE fork for salad." "Please TELL YOUR WIFE that. . . ." "This is MY DAUGHTER Wendy whom I've told you so much about. She goes to the UNIVERSITY and she's a WRITER."

These uninvited pictures come to me with the TV news coverage of the Kobe earthquake. January 17. And with Valerie who says, "Isn't it unnerving, last year Northridge, this year Japan, on the same day?" She is a fellow teacher, and she is standing in the door frame to my crowded office, describing her own teaching in Japan.

She was on a fourth floor, teaching English to Japanese students when the quake hit and everyone but her knew what to do. The secretary, she said, was running from room to room, getting people in doorways. One student gripped her hand, she said. "Like this," she said—showing me with a tight fist on her own arm. "I knew something was happening," she said. "Ordinarily, she never would have touched me."

୧୭

My friend Kate who teaches at the university in Northridge tells many earthquake stories. She weaves them into her fiction as she has the many other disasters that she's been attracted to or that seem attracted to her: Mount Saint Helens, the L.A. riots. (I'm quite sure I opened with my earthquake *and* my volcano story to participate in our friendship in our usual way.) I tell her story all the time. A third-generation Californian, Kate understands the wildness of Western upheaval. And I, I grew up in (on) that state. The West is so deeply in me that here in the South I feel like I'm living overseas with my Wells Fargo Bank Visa credit card. When I step off the plane for a conference in San Diego or San Francisco, I feel literally that I become invisible again, indivisible. (My son this morning said the air outside was so warm you couldn't feel it at all, which is much what I feel when I return to the West, almost any tawdry, mythical, or impossible version of it.)

So I can feel/steal Kate's Northridge story not only because I know California but also because it's a mother-and-child earthquake story. When the earthquake hit, Kate knew immediately, for she is finely tuned to disasters. She and her husband, Jeff, ran down the hall to the children's room. She tells this with more sensory drama, the rolling, the darkness, the panic, the enormity, the long-anticipated expectedness. She grabbed the youngest child, Joey, from his bed and took him to the door frame to ride out the rolling, wondering where her husband and second child, Sam, were. When the quake stopped, she found Jeff had gone to rescue the same child, the youngest, and was still trying to find him in the dark, feeling among the empty bedclothes, while Sam, the oldest, was alone in his bed across the room.

Now they have a plan for earthquakes—one child each (I can't remember who takes which). Also, they have a family earthquake story.

᠔

My family's Japanese earthquake story translated into this poem, after much factional and fictional decision making. And in that sense you might say I TOO speak too loudly to unknown others, like my mother: like my mother asking Ping when his arranged bride will be ARRIVING? I speak like my mother, to myself, in an effort to empathize with her, to understand her relationship with my father—one in which he was the good guy and she was the evil mom, who became ill, who was crazy, whom he divorced, and with whom we couldn't live.

How hard it is to inure ourselves to the natural disaster of parents. I spent my twenties writing angry poems about my parents and my thirties as a poet trying to reconnect to a mother who committed suicide and left me with only the stories, with a new need to deal them into prose. Nowadays, I tend to work best with the combined deck of exploratory prose and poetry.

ℭ

SOLILOQUY: AN AMERICAN BRIDE REMEMBERS JAPAN
for L.H.B.

Your nurse had silver hair ornaments,
a brocade obi, rare sashes
pulled tightly about her waist.
You were a baby with a round face
like other babies. Your father fought
in the Korean war and brought home
presents and stories on leave.
Too often, it seemed, he left too soon.
I tried, as always, to be strong.
One day, we sat together
and he told me of the Korean snows,
compared the Japanese fogs to spring.
I thought that fog was as cold
as anything I had ever felt.

I number one dawn among my worst.
Waking from dreams, you were screaming,
your cries like small ax blows.
I grabbed for you as the floor rolled.
From the front door frame, I saw
the sunrise flaming across our horizon.
Fuji shook and the landscape floated
and billowed toward me. The nurse's tears
streaked her fine white face powder.
Fear kept us quiet in that silence
as tremor after tremor tensed
through the valley. Sirens were sounding
when I finally felt you swinging
upside down in my hands, your thin

Baby hair fanning toward the floor.
The nurse took you from me: kimono swish
and your round red face, bobbing, retreating.

We had a table made to our design
with intricate wood carvings: tall bamboo
Fuji in fog, pine branches, fluted border
of chrysanthemum and leaves, sun above
orchards of cherry blossoms. So much carved
it is almost ugly. Yet nowhere did we inscribe
the cold, the earthquake, the empty thin-walled rooms,
and I'm shaken when I clean the covering glass
and see a wailing child reflected there
who has never gone entirely away.

༄

Family earthquake stories. A pure genre about the slowly settling faults
and fissures of often unnamed and nomadic relationships, the slide and
pressure, buckle, and yield. If I ever invite Kate to Florida during hurricane
season, I know that I'll get what I ask for. Each generation must ask—it
seems—for the feel of the truth of things, the right directions to go for
safety, where the door frame is, who is standing there, and why.

Writing the Perfect Poet

Once, I married a poet. Something of a ghazal, an aubade, a deep image,
an oxymoron—well and poorly metered, consonant but competitive. We
were young, poor, and clumsy, but full of energy. He proposed outside a
Taco Bell, cars too close to the curb, the hard red concrete bench, lingering
mild-spiced-hamburger smell. I forgot my diaphragm in a Victorian bed
and breakfast in San Francisco, and, too embarrassed to call and ask,
returned again to the Davis Free Clinic to get fitted with another. We met
the night I read two poems, as one of a stream of serious stand-up poets at
Cody's Bookstore. Bold for once because I knew no one, I belted out some
quiet lines and looked up to see him in the doorway. Tentative about the
merit of what I had read, he asked to meet me again, later, anyway. On the

long drive home inland, from the Bay to our college town, Lee and Mary, grad-school friends, and I crowded the front of the Ford Ranchero dissecting "the scene" then pulled in behind the Red Top Barn truck stop's trash bins under 2 A.M. lights so Mary could vomit up her white wine before we drove on into sleep again.

He had incongruous high-school-tennis-player legs, groomed himself for new aesthetics, but had a basic sense of bad taste. His thrift-store shopping led to ten-years-behind-fashion patchwork blue-jean jeans that never hung quite right on his tall skeleton. Much pot smoked, my first bored and disbelieving introduction to bongs, such a relentless way to inhale drugs that when I would made me sleepy or made me feel lost. Yet a body that could survive Saturday mornings of frying a full pound of bacon in the chaotic kitchen of his landlord's house—and eat it up (and fry up another full pan right after) without a trace of faintheartedness. If there were no eggs, they had likely been forgotten late the night before during a supermarket amble to slake a fiendish hunger.

When we fought the last time he pounded the dining room table so hard the center split and it caved to the floor. By the time he had stopped seeing the married neighbor and started dating the veterinarian we eventually became wary friends, talking about my new daughter and his plans to go to Japan and never about the day he shoved all my furniture into a single room of our house. I went in, climbed from armchair to tall bureau, sat high and thoughtful, looking at a lamp, armfuls of clothes, a rug. Late the same month, he hugged me by the woodstove after my mother's death, but my new future-lover M. drove me to the Gallup, New Mexico, AmTrak station all the same. Once he asked for his grandmother's wedding band back. Once he insisted I keep it.

We shared poems.

We still share poems.

Sitting in Denny's one night, he said he thought we might have trouble with the proposed marriage if, as he suspected, I really didn't respect his poetic talent. The first dinner we had was in a dark college rathskeller; he pointed to the scar on my nose and asked how I got it. When we tried to get jobs together overseas, I alone had an offer from Nigeria. There were contracts available for us both in Libya by cryptic telegraph, but we would have had to marry immediately but couldn't because I hadn't yet divorced Chris K. But I would.

After Nigeria, we moved to seven-thousand-foot-high Flagstaff, Arizona, and married. He left the next week for a job four hours' drive away. Each morning, I cried, driving from my rental mountain A-frame to town for work—I'd never lived in snow and my fingers hurt. I moved into town and walked to work storm mornings, through car-high drifts of new snow, fell on my tailbone and slid downhill suddenly happy toward the university's warm brick buildings. The robber rummaged through my underwear drawers but found nothing. My poems grew, like rain tossed back and forth across the skies until hail poured out. Each weekend we'd talk about impossible futures and unmade friends. Argued free verse and form.

Two days before we had left for Africa, he walked into my apartment and I was kissing someone else. He walked out again. Who knows what writing poems did to our hearts. Once we found a way to live together, on the high Navajo-reservation plateau of Arizona, he started to refuse to let me visit with his friends. High school buddies just in from L.A. met him for freedom's sake in Santa Fe. Once in a hot tourist port town west of Oaxaca we didn't talk for four days, watched ceiling fans, found aphorisms in beer bottles, climbed the hill past chickens and thick stands of prickly pear to the pink-stucco book exchange, open for one hour a day, run by a white-haired Iowa woman. I spoke more Spanish. We had little enough to endure long bus rides.

During Arizona, sometimes happy, we'd take long car trips into winter storms and skid into safety of Southwest destinations late at night. Always a next-morning pick-up basketball game. Always a poem to be formed or just found. He was certainly *my* society—made friends over Go boards, in Laundromats, lounged tall and safely in Mexican or African bus yards, chatted us up that ride across the Sahara, filled the viewfinder of my camera.

Finding form takes such endless tinkering. My son takes after my side of the family; my daughter stakes out her father's strong genes. My ex-husbands were friends of sorts once.

My poet is not the father of any children, yet. I left him after he left me for something else, a singles sonnet, a found poem, a lyric of bearable intensity. He was a man women picked up regularly: ride to Taos, ticket to Tokyo, expatriate ennui, beers until the beers cost too much and then letter's silence in humid sudden misery. He could find a friend to share a safe joint in Moslem, north Nigeria, and I would hallucinate in fear of military police. No one more fearless on unknown roadways. In that tiny borrowed, Brazilian-made, screaming-red VW, we shopped for the college community in Old Kano town, competing with Vespas. Intent on Rammadan, residents in embroidered rigas steered motorbikes with one hand, steadied the live sheep for the feast and string-bags of groceries with the other hand. Images of frozen significance as our car shot past.

Here's one more path to composition: tall, flat ass, lanky limbs, swell of tennis calves, hand holding a cigarette but outdoors, just when smokers were moving outdoors all over America on apartment steps, fire escapes, back porches. As a TA, his women students left messages on his door and desk, small bouquets tied with satin ribbons, origami poems, things to eat. Eating big bowls of pesto and spaghetti, he learned to make it himself when I got tired and wouldn't go more heavily into garlic. Mouth. Big mouth. Wide mouth pursed in a joke, lanky and humorous as a wolf, big head-back laughter and mock stomach clutching. Hat collection—Holmes deerstalker, tractor caps, Mao cap—and Converse black high-tops, half-worn-out snow Sorrels that were too big (thrift store serviceable but never quite right). That good voice, making names particular as a handshake, indignant no-shit laugh, limbs wrapped together in hunched-over withdrawal and then a manic fling out into a jig, a gambol. Gambol? jig?—old-fashioned words, a child's dance but also a cultivated child's stance. Green eyes. Unlively brown hair, now balding, now lots of gray, white early like his mother, mother's mouth tucked in around the intolerable routine of living. Stray star in a wild night's orderly galaxy. Many, many, too many cups of sharp coffee. A temporary trance, a useful escape, but c'mon, how are you gonna live that way? It's like hiking into the wilderness at last, no tent, no matches, night coming on and feet weary. A part of you, but distant, like people talking in the next room, their words puzzle pieces, a door slamming. Escape from a circular driveway, a freeway loop going around and around my city, bridge over a dubious moat, leading away.

But let's get down to poems, poems full of bitter American irony and overworked metrics. He was loose-in-the-world versus my lassoed-by-words; yet my poems were loose and his were lassoed by stiff intention. Words were different for me, slow messages, wings. Why did all this happen? Too much to talk about and yet nothing: how we lived together, then separately, on prosody and couscous, pigeon pie and Samoan beer, word-excavated family histories, and trust in one's athletic knees or ear's internal rhyme and line. Once a poet married me. And this is some of what I have had to think about since.

Propositions on a Lost Name of a Street

My stepmother wouldn't live with my father until they were married. My mother, Lillian, never left the house. I would eat chocolate cake in the living room after midnight with my stepbrother Bruce, each of us returning after dates with someone else. My sister crawled out the window and left for college. We had no friends; they couldn't find us without a street name. I imagined a city where it was against the law to have friends or street signs. Would we have had friends if we had paid more attention to names?

For two days after coming home from the hospital, my daughter had no name. My son's name came from a list on the free bag of baby supplies the hospital gave out. It is Tait, meaning cheerful in Scandinavian. There is no such language as Scandinavian. The hospital called us back so we gave them Morgan's name for her birth certificate. Morgan's friend Lindsey wants to change her name to Courtney. On our street, the kids like to turn street signs so the names point the wrong ways. The neighbor across the street who owns three lots changes the signs back and chases kids away.

You couldn't see the street from the house. My stepmother, Audrey, planted a ginkgo tree in the courtyard. We never said the name of the street. We didn't have to. My three brothers were doing flips off inner tubes in the living room of that house the first time I met them. The other streets I lived on were Christman Avenue and Breaker Drive. In another city, I lived on Olive Drive. Then, I started forgetting street names again.

Who makes street signs? What happens when the memories of streets are too long to put on the sign? I was so in love with the names of things it didn't matter. I've never been good with names. Actually, I'm good at naming but not at remembering. I can remember my students' writings and their faces but not their names. I don't like my middle name. The name of the street that I lived on in high school means less than how I felt when I was there. I started to travel to name the world. My life was dense and interior, packed into the house like thoughts into a brain.

I was afraid of what my mother would do. At one time I was embarrassed by my family. Then I lost the knack. I felt like the biggest and smallest thing in the universe. I was obsessed with getting there. Or was I concerned with where I got to? My father, Robert, died after he remodeled the entire house. Not cause and effect. At one time, I didn't care about the names of plants and trees. Since we always drove there, we never had to speak the name of the street. The only girl, I got my own room. I thought it was better than fighting all the time. The divorce was more traumatic than I thought. I can't remember the name, but even now, I am walking up that street.

It's Not the Heat, It's the Humidity—
It's Not the Cold, It's the Darkness

FIRE AND ICE

Some say the world will end in fire,
Some say in ice.
From what I've tasted of desire
I hold with those who favor fire.
But if I had to perish twice,
I think I know enough of hate
To say that for destruction ice
Is also great
And would suffice.
—ROBERT FROST

This is my first and last five-paragraph, comparison-and-contrast essay. With a few twists, the twist of key lime in a Florida gin and tonic, the twist of an ankle on ice outside the front door in Alaska, and the twist that I'm a Californian in a continuous state of displacement. Just as everyone else drifted toward that golden state—overpricing the real estate and bankrupting the public schools—I went the other way, north, then south. I'm composed of California's irreproducible coastal mornings, light fog burning off into evenhanded Mediterranean afternoons on patios with potted red geraniums. I never saw snow until I was eighteen—this on a church-camp snow trip—and I never saw snow *falling* until a year after that in a square in Salzburg during the gray, unfamiliar gloom of a real fall afternoon. Then again, I never felt true tropical heat and persistent humidity until my Uncle

Bill sent my girlfriend JoAnn and me on a cruise to the Bahamas the year we visited him in Sarasota as college girls. In fact, until a few years ago, I never experienced warm midwinter storms, hurricane-force winds, and Spanish moss flying through the air like displaced witches' wigs. Now I live in Tallahassee and just before that in Fairbanks, Alaska, and both seem times of elected service abroad, across land and landscapes, into and out of cultures and climates—meeting Athabascans and Apalachicolans. At the same time, bringing these places together through interweavings of present and immediate-past memory produces an unexpected symmetry, a yin and yang of dark and light, dry and cold, heat and humidity. What's winter cabin fever in Fairbanks but summer–air-conditioning lockdown in Talla-hassee? At a northern All Indian Dance or a Seminole Indian Days cele-bration, fry bread is fry bread. Salmon and halibut at the Alaska Salmon Bake tastes as vividly as barbecue at Sonny's. And maybe, as Robert Frost suggests in his poem "Fire and Ice," fire is just the flip side of ice. And ice is just the backside of fire.

ᖇ

In early October, sandhill cranes that have been summering here gather in the Creamer's Dairy fields on College Road. Everyone goes down to the split-rail roadside fences to watch the cranes mass in the furrows of already harvested fields. They do what large birds do when on the ground, hunch and lurch, fold and unfold awkward lanky wings. One day they're gone, heading south to New Mexico. The Tallahassee Democrat announces the arrival of the monarch butterflies. They cluster like glisten-ing globs of marmalade on low bushes at Saint Marks Wildlife Refuge. Near me, a nuclear family in coordinated pastel shorts and polos and a biker gal and guy stroll along the grassy earth mounds at Gulf's edge, taking pictures, catching and releasing a monarch, wings and hands waving at imminent departure. *On November 1, I push in the button to engage the four-wheel drive on my Honda station wagon. Snow has been sticking for two weeks, and by winter's end (May)—when I push the button a second time to disengage the four-wheel drive—the snows will have collected up to ten solid feet deep, before melting to dirty fringes, brown earth, and a late-June spring. Winter fun is placing a bet on the date when the Tanana River ice will break up near Nenana.* On November 1, I sense a slightly crisper day, risk turning the air-conditioning off, crack the sunroof in my Honda Civic, and drive with the windows down: if I've miscalcu-lated, the sunroof's thick, tinted plastic will act as a giant lens, refracting the remaining fall heat onto my shoulders. It's still a frog night, but I try the hot tub and find it warmer, finally, than the air outside. Steam rises and seems to float across the stars that are clearer now than when under summer's broad caul of white humidity. Each star winks because my steamed-up glasses are off and the palm-tree fronds wave in a light breeze. Wind chimes clink like iced-tea spoons in glasses of sweet tea. This, I think, is the life. *The aurora borealis is out as I drive to teach a night class at the university on the hill; I skid across an unseen slow-motion mile of black ice, but once out of that danger, I angle my head to see the lights better through the scraped-off windshield. I plug my car-battery cord into the socket in the lower parking lot, hurry up some icy steps, and then throw my head back again to get a better view around the fox fur that lines my jacket hood. I'm arrested by the swirling pea greens and muted reds that veil the stars. Then I notice others, lying on their backs in parkas on a snow-covered lawn, gazing into the swirling Van Gogh night sky. I join for a moment until the cold snakes into my bones.*

෴

Halloween arrives in a gasp of autumn heat, maybe my children can wear their synthetic Walmart costumes, but more likely, they'll run too hot under a beaming moon and sweat will ruin their vampire-face makeup. Suburban parents hover like a pod of gamekeepers in a wildlife park. Cherokees, Blazers, and Explorers with parking lights on trail small herds of children up just-darkened streets. There are offers to scan candy at the police station for needles or razor blades, and the week commenced with a spate of annual letters to the editor about fundamental fears of witchcraft and demonology. There is something demonic to me about the swamps and cypress trunks, the bats flying out of the moss-strewn live oaks, the uncanny way I can perspire—as if with fear or guilt—at any time of the year. Who but a demon would invent insects that grow the size of horror-movie props? Who but a witch could guarantee that anything planted will grow so rampantly and then mold so insidiously? There's an impressive breaking down going on here that has to do with an invoked earthiness beyond my understanding. Halloween can end in a tumult of eggs drying on stucco houses or Batman in shorts finding himself stung into silliness by red fire ants. *Outside the Fairbanks Safeway, half the parking lot is filled with empty locked cars and trucks, all engines idling. The sky fills with exhaust—this is a dark sky, mind you—now dark from about 4 P.M. to 9 A.M. and losing six minutes of daylight each and every day. Commuting to the preschool with a three month old in his baby seat and a three year old in her child's seat takes on a sense of a transarctic journey. Frankly, I'm terrified. There are vehicles in slow motion negotiating the ice-fog—particulate exhaust that obscures vision and hurts the chest like inhaling a sharp poison. Overall, each day's (night's) drive feels like I'm stranded in a bumper-car concession filled with metal dinosaurs that loom up into sudden vision. Headlights fracture into disorienting diamond-cold facets. One car skids around me, pirouettes three times through a gloomy, fog-filled, street-lamp-illuminated intersection and skitters to the side of the road. I pass, then eye the school buses coming toward me in an eerie procession, strobe lights seeming to make emergency where there is not, as yet, any. Each passes, each driver in her dark maw, looks intent. Eighty below and a spare sleeping bag and gallon of emergency water that will freeze in the parking lot today make me feel less than secure. The baby is oblivious, bundled into the shape of a basketball for the five-yard dash into the preschool. Two years later, the children are, respectively, a white rabbit in a one-piece rabbit suit and Wonder Woman in her outfit from the Fred Meyers store. It's five P.M. on the way home, and we decide to trick-or-treat in town, away from our isolated street of two houses on a mile of dirt road. In a random housing track, we prepare, then, leaving the car idling, run together to the house, enter the first door, hit the marginally warmer chill of the snow porch, fumble with zippers; the parka comes off, the rabbit hood goes up, the sweater is unbuttoned, the gloves—attached by strings—are pulled off long enough to grasp a bag, the doorbell is rung, the homeowner flings open the door in a rush of hot air. Trick or treat. We manage five houses before our heat exchange results in a net loss. Later that evening, the only two neighbor boys from the other house down the road plunge and play their way down to ours at 8 P.M., delighting my five-year-old daughter who heaps candy into their pillowcases. The boys whoop away, their feet leaving great holes in the snow on the front porch that are healed over by morning by new snow.*

༈

Enough sun to grow all year long. Ground that can be dug. By July the tomatoes are rotting in the heat. In September, time for a winter garden. Over time, I plant twelve cabbage palms, five rose bushes, eight pampas grass, twenty-two Mexican-heather plants, assorted crepe myrtle and oleander, holly and wax myrtle, azaleas and more azaleas. I dig small holes in warm red dirt for more than three hundred daylily roots in a frenzy of expectation. I have two cats, a dog, a swimming pool, two children who play outside until late in the warm evening dusk. Ready or not, everything grows. I learn to put tulip bulbs in the refrigerator to fool them into thinking there has been a winter. *Even in July, ice shards remain in the shadowed banks of streams and road cuts going north out of the Tanana Valley. Spring is brown mud. Late spring is first fast grass. Midsummer, flowers—wild iris; wild rose; vetch, purple and white; dandelions and fireweed, and more fireweed flaming away. Emerald-green grass and garden vegetables grow by leaps and bounds in twenty hours of summer daylight, like time-lapse photography. This short but fierce growing season produces elephantine squash for judging at the Tanana Valley Fair. Potlucks always feature someone's experiment with moose or bear stew, dark dark meat in broth. Pots of beans and vegetables, lots of carbohydrates and brutally heavy homemade deserts. Alys and Pete and other friends who live in unplumbed cabins on little money experiment endlessly with whole grains. And lots of beer and cheap wine. Coats shed inside a too small apartment or cluttered house take up more room off than on, become part of a wall-to-wall quilt where, once served, we sit on parkas, mittens, seven-foot-long bulky knit mufflers, rock back on Sorrel's or Bunny Boots used by workers on the Alaska pipeline and found in the Salvation Army stores. Teddy Bears' Picnic writ large—eating commences immediately and continues until every pot is licked clean; then we trundle out, talked out, not 'et out, into the cold.* Covered dishes arranged with care on long tables. Everyone waits before arriving and before eating, tastes, shares recipes, greetings. There is order. There is a silver set out. Children are dressed up and shooed outside to the humid, leafy oak-tree shade in summer or to dash through a few fall leaves in winter. The reason to gather is to share food but seemingly not to eat. At the end of all the talk, knives chink on porcelain, food is scraped into the trash. We find our dish, cover it, and leave. The evening air is lovely, sixty-five degrees. I twirl in my long skirt. Want to drink another glass of wine. At home, I dig into the leftovers like an animal. On a brilliant eighty-degree day, after Thanksgiving dinner, we take a walk around the neighborhood, swimming against kids on rollerblades, the couple with two schnauzers, the woman with the blond French braid who runs seriously every day all year long. Returned, light sinking lower in the late afternoon, we watch football games to see snow on the fields up north. *Up north, far north, we watch football games to see grass left on the ground, and a sudden interest in golf tournaments is a sudden interest in seeing the earth—seeing if it is still under the snow, where we'll find it in some months, everything lost found again, garden tools, one mitten, tattered notepaper caught in the rotting stalks of plants. Every month, for six months, I resolve to start running again. Put on long underwear, sweats, another set of sweats, inner and outer mittens, wool face mask and cap, glasses, walk outside at forty below and move twenty pounds of clothes very slowly down the driveway. At the end of the Thanksgiving dinner I cook my first year, pregnant and nauseous, I watch Susan crack open the turkey bones and suck out the marrow. Each bone, each marrow. Twelve people are wedged around the table, and the house perspires inward on the glass windows like a turkey glaze; we (they) eat turkey, cranberries, potatoes, bread, and four pies, without once leaving the table until Susan gets up to bus her turkey shards; we settle into more darkness while Lynn plays flute and Ken plays fiddle.* On the first shopping day of Christmas, I see a woman in Gayfer's trying on a Christmas sweater embroidered with winter scenes. *Sweaters are ordered out of L.L. Bean catalogs, all wool, cable-knit, layered one over the other so some are never even seen. On the first day of December, we visit the ice carvings on the Chena River downtown. At high noon, there is finally enough sun to trap light and refract it through blocks of blue ice carved into life-sized moose, bear, and wolves. A stage-coach the kids can sit in. Strolling on the festive, frozen river, we warm up enough to shuck down to down vests and wiggle our toes in sock-filled snow boots.* On the first day of December, the Festival of Lights—spring, summer, fall, and winter leftovers of light fill thousands of small bulbs on the downtown trees in Tallahassee, arc from the excited eyes of my children as they help wrap presents in bright foil, leap from roadside decorations and reflect upside down in fenders and hubcaps; Christmas beams from the miniature bells on sweaters. Friends—Elsie, Lizanne, and Devan—join hundreds of men, women, and children dressed as elves, Santa's helpers, and ma-and-pa 'Clauses, for the Jingle-Bell run. Christmas in Leon County can't come soon enough and can't stay long enough. *In Fairbanks, Christmas trees shipped north from Seattle are stored in a huge heated warehouse. If an outdoor tree is brought in from the cold, all the needles fall off.* In Tallahassee, we ransom our tree from a tree farm up Havana way; Bonnie takes me and Morgan and Tait on an energetic trip of misdirection along highways and around false corners until we wade with others into the long grass and choose our own. By the second week, the tree is dropping hundreds of tiny dead black insects on the presents; I Dust-Bust until Christmas Day.

༉

For my friend Don in Pennsylvania, I collect moose stories—urban legends of slaughter and silliness and awe. Moose maimings or moose being maimed, moose ambling where they ought not to amble given this North Star Borough of ornery 1960s individuals who have floated up from the Lower Forty-eight, each to have the inalienable right to keep fifteen snarling, barking sled dogs outside their houses. A man tries to ward off a moose charge with a machete and ends up "riding" the moose through town. A moose cow and calf spend six months in the leafless woods outside our house; we the zoo animals on that empty slice of their land. I send Don a series of incriminating alligator stories from the newspaper to tell him I have arrived south. Alligators with many shades of the same personality—overly friendly, terrifying, hoary. Alligators who walk into houses through the open back door like an unwanted neighbor bumming some sugar. Alligators who when killed disgorge six dog collars. Alligators who gaze at me complacently half submerged in the marshes of the wildlife refuge, having been here longer and adapted better. As I near the end of my essay, I start to see that the long AlCan highway— ten days times twelve hours of steady insistent driving, two adults, two toddlers in the front seat of a U-haul towing all their cold memories and a car without air-conditioning toward all their hot hopes along an endless interstate—provides a concrete link between these two landscapes. They are part of the same whole. The cup is half empty *and* half full. The football field is half full of snow and half full of grass. *On certain days, we can see Denali from Fairbanks, and the whole Alaska range;* on certain days, Tallahassee has the highest mountains on earth in the tumbling, building, vast cumuli that gather before summer storms. Closed-window seasons and hot, window-open seasons; growing seasons and waiting seasons. Armadillo, opossum, gray heron, bass, manatee, owl, hummingbird. *Moose, musk ox, brown and black bear, crane, owl, hummingbird. Spruce, fir, tundra, and fireweed.* Cabbage palm, magnolia, and daylily. Hurricanes, tornadoes, heat lightning, tropical depressions. *Volcanoes, earthquakes, blizzards, and ice storms.* Crane balances with butterfly, and moose partners alligator. To have hot we have to have cold. I see how my Mediterranean self has been taken to extremes. Fire and ice will both suffice. I bind them together into one life. And luckily so.

Hummingbird in the Garage

In the life-supporting shell of the garage:
pool chemicals, fertilizers, garden tools
standing against blank walls, dark hole of attic
access ladder, wasp nests and Florida decay.

The broad door opens at a pulse of electricity
like the lid coming off a TV and all life

glaring in—hot concrete of the day
with pampas grass in full bloom at vision's rim.

In the house-to-garage-doorway, finger
on the pulse—having raised the door,
ready to kick the motor over and drive off—
I duck because of a large insect, heart stopping

the size they grow here in the south,
(I never look at a floor straight on, wait
until cockroaches scuttle into their seams,
watch banana spiders grow *outside* house screens).

I breathe—I don't know in or out, but
breathe big and wince, and then watch
the unexpected arc, thinking wasp, not bird,
no, hummingbird in the garage.

It's like a little god or goddess, a scarf dancer,
a bit of fairy dust, a Pinocchio of beak, a flying
pincer, until it pauses, on an empty speaker box,
and I'm at a loss, knowing no hummingbird talk.

Sheer wall of light before us, but it rises to beat
against the back shelves, ting into shovel, nudge
tarp, rest on a wire rack, float up toward attic dark.
I think of getting the pool scoop. Could I bear

to take it into the net? Would I manage to scare it
into an even faster blur—charcoal mark
across the white paper of the walls? And so it has me—
every dip, I dip, every pause, I breathe,

and hope, still in the doorway, neither in nor out. Get
greedy. Jealous. It's mine, uninvited. Could I keep
it and how long would that flight hold up?
And now it finds the light. Goes out. Oh, my heart.

An Etiology of Endings and Beginnings

ONE DAY

It all goes wrong. Again.

ↄ

DAYS TURN INTO OTHER DAYS

When a grown man starts to lift weights to improve himself, he's probably having or wanting an affair, especially if this has happened before. A person either cares for himself all the time, or cares suddenly for the wrong reasons—outward into proving to the world/the body instead of inward, into accepting the world/the body as it is.

I asked him to move out, again: to take his restless movements—from the swimming pool to house to computer to weather and sports reports to computer to the *Wall Street Journal*—to her.

In return, I am no longer waiting for what won't happen right—his not getting home from the supermarket on Saturday or in the evening "on time" (on my time), his not being in a good and/or understandable mood.

My month-old hysterectomy remains unprocessed—the griefs and understanding and new physical body not yet felt, savored, mourned, or written about. My love life terminated unhappily, coincidentally, with my uterus, ovaries, and appendix.

I have lost the security of a live-in lover (also ex-husband M., my children's father, trying "things" again). Though we made love maybe once every seldom weeks, I have lost my sense of being "partnered" and not alone.

The best kitchen knives. Other utensils. The special orange juice container. His insistently precise way of shaking the container that foams the juice in a way the children don't like.

Someone to blame for my day, my health, my work, my major and minor irritations.

The imaginary but comforting sense my children and I had of family—of everyone in their appropriate nuclear role. Their sense of walking out into the morning, knowing everything and everyone is in his or her place.

Someone who in tight anxiety cleans very well—the swimming pool while I make breakfast, the breakfast table while I eat, his teeth while we talk.

The children, the cats, the dog, the yard, the house, the daily chores—remain the same. Wonderfully the same.

I whisper: This is it—this is the life you get, this is what it will be. Some peace at deciding finally that this is inalterable.

The children are surprised that the phone man is a phone woman, a point for the evolution of our world that they don't mention that she's a black phone woman. She switches the line back on and asks how long it has been off.

"Three days."

"What?"

"He left and had it turned off; I'm turning it on."

"It didn't have to cost and have new orders," she says.

"Happens that way sometimes," I say. "It's probably worth the cost."

"How did you do that?" she says. "I've got one I can't get out of the house; he just moved to the other room."

"We did that," I say. "For nearly two years."

"It will work out," I say.

She shakes her head and leaves me—my kids and three neighbor kids yo-yoing in the front yard.

It's seven P.M. A long day.

The school lunches still have to be made. My children get mad at me in their own right, and we learn to live with each other.

I'm learning to take pride in my newly functional ways—calling the air-conditioning repair people, taking out a loan, repainting the house, paying my surgery bills.

The quiet of the long writing working day was always empty despite my fantasies of a partner who might find it (me) irresistible, who might drive across town to surprise me at home, and after lunch and we'd . . .

No more tacit accounting *of* and suggestions *for*—less need, no need, to get my decisions confirmed by someone who seems to work by whim, by the tightening or loosening of facial muscles.

A dog instead of a man. A dog breathes loud too on a hot night, rests happy on the floor at the foot of the bed, rises eager to meet me (even if selfishly) for her walk.

Last night, retrieving my children from summer camp, feeding them, settling them, going out to give a short poetry reading, coming home, helping them to bed, falling asleep after the *New Yorker,* a bit of mystery novel, white wine. Nothing had he been here would have been much different—or any easier.

Under the promising sight of a new moon on an early June morning, the entire neighborhood is asleep.

Here's to the end of false hopes: the expectation that someone who loves me will listen with pleasure-attention-support to the small events of my day—will understand that getting a twenty-dollar check from the journal *Crazyhorse* that published one of my poems is both rare and pleasant and to be celebrated.

I now have an extra closet for my clothes.

Grasping for insight?—that I should not blame him for having an affair and leaving when it was equally my decision not to let him stay.

No more periods, endometriosis, PMS, and/or ovarian cysts, no more sanitary napkins in every shape and size. Knowing, on the other hand, that he has reenlisted for up to twenty years of the same with a younger someone else causes an unexpected smile.

No more fear of being left abandoned and lonely because I am alone and lonely.

Possibly gone with the moving van, some unframed posters bought on last summer's "try to save things return to our past places of romance but with children" trip where I "ruined" his spiritual/natural spots with illtemper and he jumped out of the car on an empty road near Chaco Canyon and told us all to walk home because "he'd had it."

Let me put it this way, she's got her work cut out for her.

৶

A WEEK PASSES

A long night's sleep—air-conditioning fixed, I walk the dog in the muggy June morning and compose letters and explanations.

I'm no less a child than my children, they yell at me, I yell back, they hurt me, I hurt them—shock, stimulus, response—"You don't understand how I feel!" I tell them bad things about their father before I stop.

I welcome the need to grade summer-school students' writing portfolios, to roust the children for breakfast, to do in the world chores.

Less and less seems the same. I'm aware of my overtaxed back muscles. The sad draw of my cheeks and eye sockets. Depression, situational or not, rests on my body like a mantle of mud or like moon boots—every step difficult, the brain barking out orders like a hysterically tied-up dog on the top of its doghouse in the middle of the night when I walk by.

Images—clipping my son's finger- and toenails, skating after this T-shirted child who won't go to bed as the black dog pants faithfully, fruitfully, for her walk.

I tuck my son into bed, saying, "I love you more than you love me." He says, "Impossible, I double your love, I eternity your love, I love you plus one and one and one and . . ."

My daughter sings body-songs in her shower behind my back, and I can still be happy for her.

There's something about last fucks: I resisted, and continue to wonder—in that impulse—what was won and/or lost?

I've lost the ability to move freely around my own town, afraid of my shadow, of him, of her, in the grocery store, driving away from the gas pump, in the theater lobby. Luckily, I rarely get out of the house, fold baskets of clothes or conference with writers in my office, shivering in the overenergetic air conditioner.

I lose this intricate structure in my brain, constructed like a labyrinthine anthill over thirteen years, a maze that loops toward some mythical center called "us."

I make the resolution to fight but fight fair, to change, not to accept despair.

I gain a new knowledge of air conditioners—eighty-nine dollars to learn how to clean filters, flip back storm-tossed electrical breakers, but once learned, never forgotten.

I gain an understanding of how elemental I can become and still come back—can feel like bone has been torn from bone, brain molecule from brain molecule. These things help, writing, walking, talking.

Here—a moment of peace and comfort, putting chlorine in the pool, sweat dripping off my nose, flipping the switch to the pool pump, thinking, "this is all a hell of a lot of work, but . . ."

No tears for a few hours. Why? And of what am I suspicious?

I am learning where pain and sorrow go—folded away like fragile, precious clothes, peacock shawl, bat-wing vest—in a very small cupboard, to be pulled out later, perhaps, by a magician as part of a performance I can't yet imagine.

This summer I had a hysterectomy. It's hard to talk about. This summer I had a hysterectomy and an oophorectomy. It's hard to talk about. This summer I had a hysterectomy, an oophorectomy, and an appendectomy. It's hard to talk about. Not the violent-red stomach scar, now healing into a thin lip. Not the place deep in the first night where the morphine took me while I slept. Not the way the body swings like a shutter at the hip as I take the first step. Trading an old world for a new, an arterial highway for a cul-de-sac, a vagina becomes a virginal sleeve, and I wait to see what it means.

When I received the e-mail message that he still loved her—copied by accidental (?) new technology to me—I understood, that in their affair-past months, there had been clues to this future to be read: I just didn't know how to read them.

"Doing his part," he would shop for groceries for us from a list I'd prepare. His Saturday-morning shopping trips took time, a long time. I imagine his after-hurried-sex hurried shopping. What I thought took too long, took too little. When the affair first ended, he must have shopped more slowly, with memories, up and down the cereal aisle, hoping to find her as he turned into the dairy section. In fact, once, I now know, he saw her move away from him at the checkout stand. In longing, he shopped wildly, forgetting the list, falling back into his past desires. The next morning, our refrigerator gleamed open with six gallons of milk, fresh produce wedged into every cold, white space, a rank of brown eggs full of his secrets.

⌘

TWO DAYS LATER

Our son's ninth birthday. Walking around the house, I find unexpectedly missing: a quilt, the camping gear, a plastic wastebasket, and a bottle of olive oil. Small change in the scheme of things, but each calling out its bid for attention—this was how it was, this is how it is now.

He brings the pizza to the birthday pool party. He asks what I had to do to fix the air conditioner and how much it cost. I say we're not having this conversation. I walk in the kitchen and find the egg whisk on the counter—one he thinks is his—he asks to take the wind chimes and his swim goggles. I say he was invited here as a guest. I lose my temper. Before long he leaves. This birthday party, alone, I clean up after and tired go to bed. There is an alright singing hidden in this.

Before morning, I pack up the CDs, the egg whisk, the wind chimes, the swim goggles in a bag by the garage door. Happy Father's Day tomorrow. The kids are yours.

᠁

ONE DAY LATER

An old mattress and bed moved from the study back to the bedroom—I sleep better, firmer, wondering why I slept soft in his for so long at all?

My children are asleep in my daughter's new bed. Peace. I walk the dog after the last night's thunderstorm, air heavy, grasses wet and littered with patterns of windblown oak leaves and Spanish moss, footprints of air.

We'll eat pancakes and bacon and eggs and milk and juice and I'll send them off to father, for Father's Day. They are clean, full.

Was it only yesterday, I was composing a prick-curse (the Viking in me believing in wrath?) that went something like: may it fall off, never fill, may the seeds of illness strike you as one who deserves such, may you miss me right when you most shouldn't, may you be reborn as a woman and learn what you've done and what you've missed.

Walking and thinking about karma. I am not without fault(s). I try to decide if all the pain in my life that I've delivered to others I now deserve. Or is it just accidental? Three days ago, the squirrels in the road, deciding to dart one way toward safety before my car, jerked, paused, and darted wrong, the other way, and for the first time in my careful driving life a young one decided to move, sickeningly, just too late.

I say my bitter things in my head and write fewer, hold them less long. Life seeps back into me.

I fool myself. Shopping to replace a toaster, I notice couples in the department store, discussing their bridal registries. I want to stop, call out— don't do it, listen to my story. I realize: it's June. And, toasterless, return home.

A fit of crying. No way to stop it except words—when my fingers engage a keyboard, water dries and I lean forward to see what I'll learn.

Shopping? Is it a madness this desire to fill in the gaps and the holes?

Maybe this time it's self-protection: there is now no way these two asunder households could ever be mended. Each time I lay a credit receipt in the drawer, I commit to my own life.

❧

ANOTHER DAY

Walking the dog, feeling sorry for myself, I scream inside my head all my insults, thinking, nothing, nothing could be worse than this. Then I watch the heron scratch the morning clouds and think, losing a child, losing a leg, Bosnia, China, Value Jet, Susan Smith, my mother, my father, and walk on somewhat sobered.

I've achieved many women's dream—safety, security, my children. Why am I missing anything? Is the hole in me or in how I see?

❧

ANOTHER DAY

Awake at 5:30—I just hurt again. It builds. Last night he calls and the kids say they'll talk later, and he says he probably won't be there, doesn't return my daughter's message this morning, and I know he's with some her (though he said it was all over, he says it never happened, he said he'd only leave if I made him, that she went after him by looking for single men in the personnel files, he says). I spend the painful dawn hours with them, voyeur of my own pains—even as I can say, I didn't want that hand, that ass, that mouth—I look at myself and wonder, could this ever have been a body someone cared about?

I'm painting the house. I'm going to visit Kate in California. I've talked honestly to my therapist. It's all going through the motions. It's all good for me. It's vegetables and sanity. It's hollow feeling, but no tears, no screaming existential grief. Can I hope after sore numbness comes something else?

Yesterday, I almost felt sorry for him, giving up so much. Then see my fixation on him has to change. Can I move out into my own world—one where I'm too busy to think, to worry, to follow, to care? Suddenly again, I'm home alone writing.

This week's fiction issue of the *New Yorker*—a story—"Adultery," by Tim

Parks. And this true sentence: "Clearly it is very exciting when you start destroying everything."

∾

AS THE DAY TURNS (INTO WEEKS)

Last night my computer went down and I went with it. A different type of bad sleep. What I am learning is that everything can be fixed—mostly with money—sometimes with time and absence. So I worked through the debugging. I tried to—and didn't—call him, the computer expert. Tomorrow—today—I jiggled and thought and played, and got it to re-boot. Bought twenty-five diskettes and copied data. Now anything can happen.

And housework—the work of refabbing—refabricating my life, suddenly filled the gaps, the absence. Small stones falling into and starting to fill the black hole.

Getting ready for the friendly painters—brothers, north Floridians—I thought of the things I might have hidden two months ago: the vibrator in the drawer; the Prozac and Premarin; and almost nothing else. Inter-esting, this fear/shame of the body, of helping my body.

Resisted for the second time copying the adultery essay and putting it out with the "to be picked up things" tonight. But I want to change. This. But how?

There's something lighter about today—I don't know what. Mailing the window blinds to be repaired, fixing the computer (at least temporarily), finding a missing receipt and returning a damaged bedsheet to the sheet store. Fixing, repairing, finding.

The loan to pay the painters messes up—I have to drive to re-sign the pa-pers, and the office turns out to be next to his apartment complex, the one I've promised myself never to acknowledge, see, visit, know where it is.

I e-mail about last house things—he e-mails back immediately, and I'm hurt, knowing he's been there a computer button away all along, not missing me. I get mad. I apologize. I put a copy of the essay on adultery and everything he wants in the garage. I take the essay back. I work harder, harder to disengage, disappointed that I'm not. That I'm not.

I read everything as augury. I'm home alone—no painters, no kids—neck muscles strained so hard from my "make do, can do" posture of days, that I think *sleep* but can't.

This noon, went to the pizza place around the corner—ate and drank two glasses of wine. Listened to humans, myself immersed among them, watched the rain. Imagined myself happy. Between the drops I think I was. The sense of freedom floods across me then—why hurry? Everyone else is wedged into their lives, you have a chance to examine yours, I say. My head understands. Two hours later, my visible woman, interior self starts to pick up its slow ache.

ໃ

AND WEEKS

Little machine-gun repetitions of the whole week. I plan dates—imagine myself in a busy life—I think of sending her something brilliant, cutting, convincing, life-changing, that I've written. I recognize harassment for what it is. I feel incredibly frail and strong at the same time.

I make a pattern of his last things taken—the two kitchen mixing bowls, one metal, one clay. One will hold fruit. One is the only one (with the infamous egg whisk) that he makes his eggs with, beating them fluffy until I want to scream. The things he's taken all have to do with the body, with body rituals, certain old, chipped glass bowls we got in Peru (that I almost broke in a rage last week) for his rice cereal, the egg whisk and metal bowl for his eggs. Are the many weeks before this time, times he was at the antiseptic health-food store—buying body-building food and vitamins—are those times all just a familiar tale of trying to stop the tides of age? Why not have just walked into these waters—toes, ankles, knees—falling into warm, swirling, sandy shallows?

It sweeps over me at quiet moments—this is the saddest time of my life.

ໃ

TAKING IT THREE DAYS AT A TIME

Coda: Two days ago, I sent some of these words to him by e-mail. By e-mail he thanked me. "After all," he said, "you're a writer. You have to write."

There is no right answer and I was continuing to ask for it. For too long I've used my words to seduce, to please, to make up (for) my self. This journal ends. These words—when/if you read them—are for you to do with as you please. After all, he's correct. I have to write.

Where the Hummingbird Sips, There Sip I: An Appreciation

I send you withal a little Box, with a Curiosity in it . . . the curiously contrived Nest of a Humming Bird, so called from the humming noise it maketh whilst it flies. 'Tis an exceeding little Bird, and only seen in Summer, and mostly in Gardens, flying from flower to flower, sucking Honey out of the flowers as a Bee doth; as it flieth not lighting on the flower, but hovering over it, sucking with it's long bill a sweet substance.
—THE HONORABLE JOHN WINTHROP, GOVERNOR OF
    CONNECTICUT, 1670

She dances messages
beyond my writing-desk window-pane,
raises questions,
yanks them away again.
Flying forwards, backwards,
picaflor, beija flor,
huitzitzil, chuparosa.
Blossom-picker, flower-kisser,
rays-of-the-sun, rose-sucker.
Weighs as little as a penny,
or not much more. She's
Buff-bellied, Lucifer, Roufous, Ruby,
Violet-crowned, Broad-tailed, and Calliope.

She's what I want to be.

She navigates my stanzas.
She takes my words away
to throaty scarlet penstemon;
to meaty trumpet flowers,

calls on hibiscus, sinks
into summer's columbine,
pollinates a cactus blossom.

She's catch as catch can.

Truth is—
she's a whore for red,
scavenger of nectar, syrup, honey,
maintains the metabolic rate
of thought. Her wings long hands
in service of her tongue—
even as she begins,
she's at top speed,
rising phoenix-like
from another flower-flame.

I invite her
to inhabit me.

She takes after my own heart.
She's my cross-dressing
dandy of a girl—
too busy to make-up
too busy to stay,
frivolous ruby for her gorget,
head crowned in tourmaline.
White and brown belly-feathers
beneath that finery.
She's dashing,
in her hurry-up way.
She is at risk—
compounded into amulets
and hummingbird soap,
powdered, or stuffed—
turned by bounty hunters
into a potent corpse
to "dominate, conquer

and attract" *amor*—
sold with a preprinted prayer
and a red silken bag.
A sacrificed bride's finery,
an Aztec warrior's
shimmering cloak.

She's insight. She's action.

She's fragile but not frail.
She failed geology—
for her bones of sparkling dust
cannot be fossilized
cannot be saved.
She is kachina Tocha,
the Humming Bird.
When the Gods required speed
and good looks, they called
on their feather dart.

I claim her as kin.

She's past the window,
she's past the garden fence
a Curiosity with curiosity,
Just out of hearing,
just out of sight—
stars and constellations
spark into fires.

Hummingbird at Heart

Before I took a recent trip to the Southwest, I sat down and wrote a
poem about hummingbirds. Well, about how a hummingbird is a writer's
muse to me. I was following this hummingbird thread for reasons I didn't
fully understand, prompted by finding an impressive illustrated book about
hummingbirds at the public library and taking it home, thinking my son

might like to look at it with me; prompted by a weekly poetry-writing-group meeting I attend and having no poem at hand; prompted, I now think, by hummingbirds in my immediate future.

I had already done the hummingbird thing, that is, written a humming-bird poem when I accidentally found one trapped in my garage one day four years earlier. I've always liked these birds, once putting out a red-plastic, sugar-water container in the backyard after making a few sightings in the garden and planting red salvia to attract even more. Sometimes, at my back-room, writing-desk window, I'd be face-to-beak with a hummer and hold my breath. There's something about such lovely stasis of penny-weight and hollow-boned body, of bright feathers and blur of wings, that makes me hold my breath. Probably you do too. And then the breath al-ways seems to go out as the bird darts away, whoosh, taking our senses with it.

≈

I've learned that these birds heavily populate the Americas, that they live on nectar and insects, that they fly sky-high, up hundreds of feet and then down like darts when mating. In Central America they appear on postage stamps and currency, sip from hibiscus plants in central-square parks where bandstands still host town bands. The largest hummingbirds live in South America. One of the mysterious Nasca lines in Peru (that can be un-derstood best from the air but were made by people living long before us, and long before air travel) takes the shape of a picaflor, a vast humming-bird outline of raised earth. I'd looked for hummingbirds while backpack-ing in Peru and Guatemala in the 1980s, but back then I was greedy for adventure and looked harder, dreamed more deeply of seeing the mysteri-ous and rare quetzal bird with its long, trailing, iridescent blue-green tail that the Aztecs fashioned into ceremonial cloaks. I never saw a quetzal; few of us ever will. I did see some hummingbirds though. And I held my breath, then, as now.

Writing my most recent hummingbird poem, I sorted through the li-brary book and found bits and pieces of information. I composed. And then only a few days later, we packed—my thirteen-year-old daughter, my ten-year-old son, and me—into a truck and took a long-planned trip to the American Southwest, to Indian country. And found—hummingbirds.

It was like the women's magazine truism, when you look for love, you don't find it, when you focus on hummingbirds, they're not there. But when it's time, the thing you need comes to you.

⌇

I lived on the Navajo reservation for three years. My daughter was born just off-reservation, in Cortez, Colorado. As a single parent on a journey to revisit these places, I needed to fold some old memories more safely away, to relearn to reenjoy things that I knew were there but I hadn't quite seen at the time. The hummingbird poem had been prompted, perhaps by some flash-forward to this voyage I had not yet taken. For everywhere there were broad-tailed hummingbirds. Spirit-filled, spirit guides, signaling to us from the first day until the last day, four weeks later, when we turned onto I-40 and headed east again to Tallahassee.

⌇

Zuni pueblo, below Gallup, New Mexico. Up a dirt-packed roadway toward the central square by the old Catholic church of the old town, we walked into and then backed out of a Hopi summer ceremonial, a kachina dance. Dancers represent spiritual guardians, monsters and warriors, men and women, clan figures, celestial and supernatural beings, and all manner of earthly ones, including animals. The dances are closed these days to tourists, because, as the man in the shop said, "someone did a bad thing a while back." I appreciated the "someone," which is the Indian way of saying, you all, you outsiders, stumbled into too many dances, too many ceremonies, and didn't act right. For that moment, we simply stared, my daughter, still as a carving beside me, my son backing into me, nestling, pulling my arms tightly around his shoulders. Twenty men dressed as warrior women. They wore loose white shirts and black wigs of thick yarn and large, featureless face masks painted turquoise and black. With bells and green plants thonged around ankles, the kachinas' legging-wrapped legs moved in unison, step, slide, step. I observed small children chasing through the quiet, unmoving, appreciative village audience, then we turned, went back down the hill, into the dusty traffic of town, quietly awed.

Later that day in the Canyon de Chelly campground, the hummingbirds also danced before us. We had seen a hummingbird carved in amber in Zuni, too expensive even for our expansive tourist pocketbook. Several birds threaded their imaginary May poles across the watered green lawn at the Thunderbird Lodge and then seemed to sew us back into the canyon rhythms at the nearby campground—tents, cooking pots, smell of butane and shimmering afternoon heat under Russian olive trees and cotton-woods where the wind rises each afternoon and dust devils take their insubstantial shapes.

᪥

From there on out, there wasn't a campground that wasn't so blessed. Though I'd lived in the Southwest for several years before my children were born, I don't remember the hummingbirds singing to me then. Perhaps I was too young, too busy, didn't feel as in need of a center, an internal gyroscope, a feeling of at-homeness-and-at-oneness. Now, I seemed to listen for them and they for me.

On a cliff at Hovenweep National Monument, in the four corners where Arizona, New Mexico, Colorado, and Utah come together in an artificial demarcation of topographical logic and myth, a broad-tail flew dazzlingly close as a friend and I did tai chi on a canyon ledge. We held a personally invented ceremony for and with a Navajo rug I had bought, unfurling its earth colors on a rock cliff. Moss gray, lichen black, sandstone red. We sprinkled sage onto it. We talked. Our children watched as my friend used a stick and showed us some tai chi sword movements. At full dusk, we rerolled the Chinle-patterned rug—now sage-filled and welcomed into our life—and returned it to the truck; it would travel home with us and be unfolded in Tallahassee where we picked the sage out and bound it into a bundle for the shelf, hung the rug appreciatively on the wall.

But the hummingbirds—I can still feel them. There like the breath of dusk was the affirmation of the Anasazi (ancient ones in Navajo), relatives of the Zuni puebloans whose ceremony we had glimpsed in the impressive movements of the kachina dance. Once, in a time my mind can hardly wrap itself around, a family lived on the Hovenweep cliffs, hauled water, ground corn, burnt juniper and pinon pine. And a hummingbird heart held them quietly to that place—like it held us on that recent summer night.

As for a family travel trip of five thousand miles—just the three of us for the remaining three weeks as our friends went another way—it continued as a time of learning and relearning who we were and are and might be, by paying attention to those things close at hand that we had come to see.

Waking the next dawn in my sleeping bag on the Hovenweep cliff, I heard the distinctive giant-cicada thrum of the broad-tails launching themselves into the morning and so launching us. By midday, at Bluff, eating our first eggs and bacon, our first bought meal in a week in the Twin Rocks Trading Post lunchroom, we looked from the cafe booth out the window to the shady wooden porch and saw hummingbirds queuing at a line of three red-plastic feeders—sipping nectar in the desert heat, their wings dynamos, shimmering mirages. Then they were gone, one after another peeling off, out, and up, into the bright canyon light. Taking some of our weariness with them.

৵

It just kept unfolding that way. Sometimes it seemed there were too many credit-card stops for gas, food, souvenirs, block ice, butane, postcards, Laundromats, overlooks, snapshots, and sandwiches. Some days were tedious with heat.

As we arrived at Navajo National Monument, travel weary, I was complaining to my children that they didn't appreciate me, thinking they didn't understand what our journey was about. In the ranger-station gift shop I was talking to the woman who worked there, who gave her name as Mary Tsosie, about Martha Jackson, a silversmith it turned out we both knew, and my nudging son said, "Look, Mom, a hummingbird fetish." And, still talking, almost absentmindedly, I bought it, the first and last I saw—turquoise, with a white shell and a red-coral band at the neck—a thin, steel pin sawed off for its long beak, and strung on a slender leather thong. And I wore it then, every day.

Zuni Indians carve the small fetish figures for their spirit bundles (and now of course they carve them for tourists). This fetish hurt me one night in the sleeping bag; I turned the wrong way and pinpricked myself. The next morning I woke, rubbing my collarbone free of a drop of hummingbird-sweet blood. Tai chi on the cliff there, by myself this time, balancing, rebalancing as a person and as a parent I hoped, and as if in answer, a hummingbird came by, breezing through my picture window, my open panorama of sunset on a Navajo mountain.

At the north rim of the Grand Canyon, at Jacob Lodge, we rented a cabin for showers and the solaces of roadside easy living and stumbled into a Sheherezade of hummers at the artificial waterfall of canyon rocks the lodge owners had built between the six log cabins. Two mornings in a row, I made coffee in my room while the children slept. Coffee in hand, I walked out to watch the broad-tails whose thrumming had taken me right out of sleep into the gray morning light. They danced—flying forward, backward, peering into a water tap, hovering over my coffee mug, bathing and chasing away warblers and tanagers, even the feisty stellar jays, with their fast pinprick aero jabs.

At Bryce Canyon, I walked down the hill to put my check in the Park Service box for the campsite, and a broad-tail's taut-string chime put me on alert until I tracked it through air, my head sweeping along its trajectory across the camp host's trailer and into the ponderosa pines beyond. It was like tuning my ear for my children's heartbeat when the doctor did a sonogram. I can't quite hear it because I'm trying so hard, so excited, so unclear as to what it all means. Then I relax and it's more than there.

The hummingbird alarums almost always caught me doing something else, preoccupied, not looking up at the juniper berries, not always appreciating the dry, blue bowl of desert sky, and then the broad-tail apostrophe would claim me: pay attention, it said, and I would. Standing straighter. Thinking about where I could go and what I could legitimately lay claim to as experience. Marveling at the speed of thought.

ॐ

I brought my hummingbird fetish home—wore her for the transition week back into the high humidity and late-August days. She's imbued with the ceremony of newfound attention, of days and nights on the cliffs at Hovenweep, of pauses in the daily chores of camping and parenting when I could cock my ear and get in tune with what I was doing. She's nearly inexplicable. A reminder. A healing, a warning, a hope. I show her to a friend or two anyway. If I put her on, my children always notice and call her by her kachina name, Tocha. Who taught us to hear and to watch, to understand that it is possible to make our own ceremonies if we listen for what our hearts are telling us that we already know anyway.

I expect one day this fall, I'll be face-to-window-to-beak with a Florida hummingbird. I'll hold my breath. Wink. Gaze, as it takes another piece of my attention out into the first fall breeze—you know, that moment when the summer heat breaks and you praise your life. And you inhale deeply. You touch your muse, your luck, the fetish you wear around your neck, the new and better way you've reimagined your life; you get back in tune with the things you care about, you walk into the garden or you talk to your children, and you sense these things more deeply. You find all along you have a hummingbird at heart—for a heart.

Someone's in the Kitchen with Wendy

1233 Olive Drive No. 7. I lived there for five years—1974 to 1979. I called it home, the place I lived, a shack, a cottage, a little house. It's one on a court of six little houses. Mine—of the six—is the closest to the Southern Pacific railroad tracks. Yards away. So close that the needle on my record player skips on the long-playing 33 rpm records I have—then.

$\backsim$

Callori Court we call it, too, after Fred Callori the landlord who lives farther down the road, who rents to various college students and eccentrics. Leonard the recluse has the house to the right of mine, away from the tracks and toward Olive Drive. Older, wearing a long-sleeved shirt, a hat pulled down, he parks his car four feet from his front door and ducks inside. His cottage, it is rumored, is wallpapered with collages he's made using magazine photos of flowers, kittens, and young girls.

A Native American woman lives for a while in the front cottage on my side, nearest the street—I've see her talking to the air and waving an elegant eagle feather around near her backyard clothesline to the accompaniment of burning leaves; all our backyards on my side of the court are part of the same grassy field. Olive Drive is a one-way exit off I-80, westbound from Sacramento to San Francisco into the college town of Davis, California.

Cindy, a blond woman, has just returned from living in Spain with her bronze-skinned baby boy, Jeronimo. She and her son share the street-facing house across Callori Court's dirt-and-gravel drive with a woman, Laurie, who becomes a good friend of mine. A fellow English student, Laurie will move into an across-the-tracks, in-town apartment with Noel the Nicaraguan, and then leave us all behind, disappearing to an East Coast homeopathy school by decade's end.

Dennis, overweight and a salary worker in Sacramento, lives across from Leonard—he's built a fence around his front yard, lined it with Christmas lights, and let it run mostly to weeds. Directly across from me near the tracks—Richard's cottage lies half hidden behind tall overgrown bushes. He greets all newcomers, permanent or transient, to Callori Court, with mayoral aplomb, wandering from his front door whenever he senses movement in the courtyard. Richard is small, freckled, sneaky looking, and feral but friendly and eternally almost done with classes at the university.

ဆ

Everycollegetown USA. Olive Drive cottages.

I'm perplexed again—is this word too formal for the wooden-floored, wooden-walled, gas-stove-heated, room-tacked-on-here-and-there con-structions we called home? I sometimes called mine "my shack" in affected indifference, affected because I knew I was privileged poor, not poor poor. I chose to live there for the low rent and the not-an-apartment-complex freedoms of the, at that time, almost-rural road. No palm trees, that would be southern Californian, but a roadside motor-court feeling, with walnut, sycamore, and cork oak trees. Still, the cottages on Callori Court were shack-like in their disrepair and flimsiness, in their individual and tiny floor plans; in the transient and transitional way they were always passed along from renter to renter. For instance, my then husband Chris K. and I finagled ours from another Chris, Chris Lee, a half-Chinese young man we met in the university music school where I worked part-time clerical for many years, where Chris K. reincarnated after his biology B.A. degree to study viola.

Chris Lee had long, black lustrous hair tied back into a ponytail, played in an early-music ensemble—was one of its galvanizing members, really—viol da gamba, countertenor, billowy silk and satin medieval clothing. He'd take up playing sackbut if the group needed a sackbut. He lived in No. 7 where he did leather work in the back, added-on, lean-to-style, low-roofed room (the cat door I inherited retained his hand-tooled leather flap) until a slip of a leather-shaping knife stopped his playing indefinitely and he dropped out for the next term.

ဆ

It is 1974. My formerly-a-surfer Chris K. and I walk halfway down Olive Drive to Fred Callori's house to pay the eighty-five-dollars-a-month rent, to announce that Chris Lee has been gone a month now, but not to worry, we are comfortably in residence. Fred is a short, probably hard-drinking Italian man who cultivates the acreage he owns up and down Olive Drive, on this side of the car-repair shop and that side of a real, though small, apartment complex. Fred looks up at golden-haired Chris K., down and across at me, squints and pockets the money and turns to go back into his suburban ranch-style house where I hear the TV and the sound of dishes being thunked onto a table.

There is never a lease. I don't think I ever miss a payment after Chris K. moves out (for two months into the front cottage that Cindy, Jeronimo, and Laurie have vacated and passed on to him) and I stay on, but I do borrow here and there, this month and that month, to make the rent over the years. Richard, my neighbor, tells me that Fred told him that when first married, before they built the suburban ranch house down the block, Fred and his wife had lived in No. 7, 1233 Olive Drive.

❧

Just as we accessed No. 7 from Chris Lee by sleight of hand, I did the same to get the shack to myself from my surfer-biologist-now-viola-playing Chris K. though I didn't know I was heading that way. He and I had lived together for five undergraduate years in a variety of unsatisfactory apartments and were headed in a stop-and-start way toward marriage and then divorce in the early 1970s (it wasn't just a love-the-one-you-were-with time—it was a live-together-and-then-decide-you-should-do-something-else time. So we did).

We moved out of a married-student housing and onto Olive Drive and day by day we were changing, like the people who passed into and out of the other cottages. Graduate school (for me), the mid-1970s (for us all), had elements of a cosmic shell game, people inhabiting this and that shell in this and that relationship to one another.

❧

Now, the floor plan. A subdivided rectangle: front room and bedroom, backed by a kitchen and bathroom, backed by a later addition: workroom and narrow-passageway storeroom into the shell of a garage. The front of the cottage facing east toward the Sierra foothills, not visible through the cork oaks that line the road. The back of the cottage facing west toward the university campus, then the western foothills, then the Bay Area and the wide Pacific.

Again, in more detail, come to the east-facing front door up a narrow, broken-concrete walkway; wooden boards nailed together in a platform for a small deck to the left. The whole shack painted whitewash white, the door white, the door frame, though, painted royal blue. Hobbitlike, I suppose. (I've just read the first chapter of *The Hobbit* to my squirming ten-year-old son this month and now he's hooked and lost, reading about Bilbo Baggins instead of doing his homework.)

Enter the house and lose your foot through the rotted boards at the front door—bam! The first week we live there, the boards give way under Chris K. He rides them, falls off the wave. Fred and his son come and replace a few boards. Underneath, we spy dirt six inches down, heaped with empty walnut shells the mice have scattered there. Wordless Fred and his wordless son gouge out the rotten section and patch it with new old boards and then roll out a new scrap roll of linoleum, ugly brown and mottled gray or mottled brown and ugly gray, loosely laid across most of the eight-foot-by-ten-foot living room.

Bedroom to your right. Smaller. Look around. Two large windows. One step back into the living room. One window by the living room front door, a second on the wall to the left and a small, black gas furnace in the corner, raised up on squat metal legs with a black metal stovepipe that travels up and out the roof through a flange painted the dirty-white color of the ceiling. I spend years hoping the roof won't burn and lighting the stove's pilot with long matches and jumping back from its familiar whoosh.

Front door lines up with the door frame (no door) into the kitchen that lines up with the door frame (no door) into the late-addition back room where Chris Lee used to sit at a low, custom-made worktable, smoking pot and pounding leather. The back door can be wedged open to let me pass out into a train-filled evening. Even now I hear the black cat leap through the leather flap with its customary one-hand-clapping sound.

ॐ

The kitchen, at first, is less a room than a passageway from the front of the cottage to the back of the cottage, a walkway. It holds a slump-shouldered, arctic-blasting Fridgedaire and gas four-burner stove. The stove lists against the wall between kitchen and back room and has two legs wedged up with paper to make them even with the others along the buckling floor.

One window above the sink. Shelves over the sink to the right and left both, but without doors or curtains, just shelves upon which I arrange packages of noodles and grains—Contadina giving way to Arrowhead Mills—as I learned how to cook, and later still how to appreciate, whole-grain food.

Until last night, when redreaming about this house, I had forgotten the kitchen table. Easy to do really since it was half a table, sawed roughly to fit the narrow, turn-sideways-to-walk-toward-the-sink space between fridge/stove on one wall and living room wall two steps over. The half table was nailed to the kitchen wall. It was painted the same royal Hobbit blue as the front-door frame and was quite substantial—all legs and a half yard of scratched surface. Sitting at it was problematic, though, because a chair would barely fit between leg and wall and because the row of bracket-and-board storage shelves overhead would catch the hair of any but Hobbit-sized diners.

When eating with anyone else, I took to sitting at the cross-legs-low, wooden, carved Japanese table I'd inherited from my mother and placed in the front room. The bas-relief scene of Mount Fuji was covered with glass and then covered with Goodwill plates.

⌇

Still standing in one of the kitchen doorways, to the left, another fairly flimsy door led into the bathroom—boards nailed to boards, metal question-mark latch from the inside. Lion-footed bathtub. Free-standing sink. Toilet. No window. The room a scuffed, rusty, blood-colored red—red painted floor and walls and the underside of the lion-footed tub, also painted red. As if the room had put on trousers of red or as if I had fallen into a large sleeping giant's meaty-red mouth. White but chipped and black-stained porcelain tub interior. White commode and sink. No shower. Imagine five years with no shower. Heck, I still can't.

The back room is first a workroom, later a bedroom when bedroom turns to "study." Leading from it to the right is a very narrow passageway behind the bathroom (also windowless) that opens at the rear of a dirt-floored, spider-filled, garagelike addition. No front garage door. No double walls or insulation. No lightbulb, no light switch, and no car to park in it. I'm living in a bicycle-proud city and I own no car; at least not after Chris K. drives ours away.

၈

Fred and his son also relinoleum the kitchen with another scrap roll. Cat hair catches easily in the unglued-down corners. Chris K. and I buy fresh paint. Sometimes I imagined the paint of each new owner was what actually held up the walls all over Callori Court. We chose mauve for all the rooms except bathroom (which we left alone) and kitchen (which we didn't). Purple-corduroy curtains, unlined like the cottage walls that were uninsulated. And the kitchen a gleaming school bus–yellow enamel that soon chips and peels because I don't know enough first to wash off the previous cooking grease and dust. I just slap on brushfuls of thick, bright yellow. Very nice. For a while.

၈

While painting the walls mauve one day shortly after we move in, a former professor of mine, Will, calls me up on the phone to ask how I had enjoyed a writers' conference in Squaw Valley that summer. Phone call leads to beer at the bar around the corner, leads to a visit to his farm in the Capay Valley, thirty miles away, leads me to emphasize my already growing restlessness, leads to Chris K. moving to the front cottage when Laurie and Cindy turn it over to him. He trades our Volkswagen in on a motorcycle and a leather jacket and then, tiring of watching the professor drive his truck up to my cottage, he moves to Oakland, waits tables by day, plays electric viola in a rock band by night. Once Chris K. calls me, having taken one hit of a two-person acid dose he said he had hoped (for some reason) to share with me. I talk to him while he flushes the hit he had saved for me down the toilet in his Oakland apartment, while I try to calm him with words at a great distance and from the same wall phone, looking into what had been our short-marriage bedroom and was now the desk room. That is, the place that now held my achingly stubborn and poorly spelled and desirous and immature sheaves of paper and Smith Corona correcting typewriter.

I shuttled away at my master's thesis of poems there by day and continued to work as a night clerk in the music library on campus. I'd walk home at 10 P.M. along the Southern Pacific rails. I could tell from vibrations in my feet when to hop off the rails to let the trains thunder by, filled with sugar beets mostly and with passengers waving sometimes. I'd approach Olive Drive and my own shack in an owl dark, my head echoing with classical music that I'd play loudly as I worked, typing up record orders for the music department and checking out equipment to music students.

These days, as a single mother, I'll go to sleep tonight just after my kids (if I can stay awake that long) and get up at 5:30 to wind the key of the day tightly, but then, on Olive Drive, I would be exhilarated and almost only just waking at 10 P.M. I might sit on the stove on a cold northern California night and read. I might take a bath by candlelight in the red-painted bathroom.

႟

Not one of the visitors to that house could have avoided the red bathroom. Will used to take a bath, sloshing water over the tub's rim, smoking a cigar and enjoying a shot of whiskey or beer on the nights when our affair was harmonious. I'd stare at myself in the carved, old wooden mirror. It was oak, I found out after I had the paint stripped—four years into my five-year residency—and enjoyed more clearly the carved flowers that vined across the top and considered how to resilver the beveled reflecting surface that most often threw back the bare ceiling lightbulb and my wide-eyed, wanting-to-have-a-crystal-ball gaze. I washed my face clean there, staring as I dried it at the necklaces I had accumulated in various trips to Ba-zerkely, always falling for another variation of reputedly water-buffalo-bone and/or hand-carved this-or-that necklace.

႟

These days I wear no necklaces though my hair, twenty years later, is again as long as it was then. I had a single turquoise-stone necklace from Chris K., and Will gave me a piece of sandstone he'd had set in silver. With those, I treasured a black bead necklace made from ground and compressed rose petals, concocted with the help of my high school best friend JoAnn's mother, Doris, from her family's recipe before JoAnn and I went away to different colleges. There was something out of macramé of course. And I remember a red bead necklace from Africa like those I'd see there when I taught in Nigeria a few years later. In a travel journal I have a detailed list of these, my favorite necklaces, stolen with my backpack in a

Belgian youth hostel in 1976 while I slept. The next day, I recorded each one in this journal with the despair of a young woman who thought such losses mattered more than almost anything.

I don't wear necklaces now, but I still collect them.

On Olive Drive one day, I pound nails into the tongue-in-groove bathroom wall and hang the necklaces in decorative patterns on the left side of the sink. I stare into the mirror. Wash. Dry. Choose one to wear.

⁌

Laurie L., my girlfriend from that time, sits on the floor between kitchen and back room with me. We're experimenting with the black walnuts we've gathered from the tree outside. We're using a hammer and smashing them open on the scratched linoleum and thin wood floor (this is hot Sacramento Valley summer—at Christmas we'll cover the house with potato-print Christmas cards that we make together—raw potatoes, poster paint, white butcher paper). I'm astonished that we were cracking the nuts that way for the floor was not that strong and the black-walnut shells were. And Kim, a new graduate student, has come by the cottage, the shack, for the first time and is standing and talking—about his years in Bolivia in the Peace Corps, growing potatoes, and we're drinking beer and slamming those nuts open. He said later it was an enchanting sight. But he wanted to be enchanted.

One night outside the music library where he has stopped by to talk to me, he grabs me in the dark and kisses me on the cheek, missing my mouth. I tell him I'm seeing someone else (Will), and he says I should give him a chance. He had arrived in one of my graduate classes one day, in logger's boots, a long-sleeved green silk shirt I'd later found out he'd inherited with several others from a dead uncle, wearing a red bandanna on his red hair (red beard, too) and a multistriped poncho, like Clint Eastwood's in *The Good, the Bad, and the Ugly*. One of five children of a rural northern California doctor, he carries everything he owns with him when he returns to college, tan Datsun pickup truck, a desk chair, a box of books, a handmade-by-him deerskin bag, and the curiosity of someone who has stopped time for three years in the cold Bolivian altiplano and arrived back on a wildly active college campus.

Kim drinks the beer I offer him in one enthusiastic head-tipping. He watches Laurie and me, talks, and leaves. But surely one of us had enough beer and went into the red-painted bathroom and considered it. And one of us put the empty beer bottles on the kitchen counter—for it was only three feet in different directions at that moment for either action.

❧

After my second writers' conference in Santa Cruz, California, Kate and Bill (two new friends) and Jeff (a writing-program friend from Davis who went to the conference too) and I sit late into one evening on the front deck (if it could be called that) of 1233 No. 7 Olive Drive playing truth or dare until Bill is wearing only a towel across his lap. I tell this to Will later as a funny story and he glowers. Bill becomes (or maybe is then for I know him later as) an alcoholic. Jeff leaves for the East. Kate was, is, and remains now (even as Laurie has gone somewhere unaccountable) my dear good friend. She starts at Olive Drive and has not ended. Bill probably peed in the weeds by the railroad track, and the rest of us probably contemplated our futures in the wooden, beveled bathroom mirror with the sharp light-bulb glowing above us. I don't remember ever changing that lightbulb but I must have. I don't remember using the bathtub though I know I did every day for five years; that is, I don't have a persistent image or an insistent story of me in the bathtub. I can't see myself there. I remember Will sloshing water out and smoking his "ci-gar"—because that was out of my everyday experience. I remember hanging the necklaces on the wall. I know the bathroom otherwise was relatively empty of clothes or bottles or clutter.

❧

I spent five years with a bathtub and not a shower. I can't imagine doing that now though. I'm overly fond of the hot tub in my Florida backyard and keep it (others say) overly hot. Surely I must have bathed in my own red-painted bathroom and walked out to the lean-to bedroom, lain down on the quilt-covered mattress, looked out the Indian bedspread–curtained window to the sycamore tree. I wrote a poem about the tree. About the Native American woman when she lived in the front cottage. About people who left and who stayed. About Laurie. Stories later about her and Noel, about Cindy and Jeronimo. Nonfiction lately to understand Will whom I didn't quite stay with (or with Kim) for five years but still e-mail today.

I didn't know how to cook when I arrived at Olive Drive. We were three girls (still at home) growing up with a mother who fussed over each bland meal. An army family (my father the major was an army recruiter in Ventura, a reservist) with a meat-and-potato Midwest palette of tastes and options. We'd buy six half-gallon cartons of milk packed into brown cardboard boxes at the navy-base commissary. To do this, we'd drive thirty miles, a long way then, from Ventura to Oxnard and Port Hueneme to shop for our groceries. The four-foot-long Seabee bee mascot atop a tall pole at the entrance to the navy base—holding angle iron, wrench, and other tools and wearing a jaunty sailor hat—became my symbol of American can-do. And food came in prepacked units—in groups. Rarely fresh. Shippable, manageable. Butter in pats. Meat in tins. I developed the heart of a commissary sergeant—I love cupboards full of writing supplies and a shelf full of emergency rations.

Chris K., whom I met in high school on the beaches above Ventura and followed through our undergraduate years from college to college, taught me to eat health food. My senior year in high school, he was a freshman at UC Santa Barbara, surfed, walked over to the Sun and Earth health-food store and restaurant in Isla Vista for fresh stone-ground raisin sticks and hand-ground peanut butter, for rice and steamed vegetables and cheese under a geodesic dome in the back garden. I put up with Chris K.'s ability to take up the next fad before it became a fad while I was cautious, waiting twenty years to wear Birkenstocks though Laurie worked for years in the Davis Birkenstock store and I admired Laurie and I would visit her there, watching her resole shoes and sip comfrey tea from a large mug.

I learned to put up with health food—so alien to my home upbringing. By reading the *Moosewood Cookbook* and *The Vegetarian Epicure* in the music library at night. By gazing at pasta and grains in the bulk glass jars in the health-food store in this college town and that college town. By backpacking when I was eighteen with Chris K. to Britain and Europe and Turkey and Israel and hesitantly tasting what he ordered and coming back "civilized" enough that I now scold my children for their Kraft Macaroni and Cheese taste buds, inherited naturally in a middle-class white progression of some magnitude.

Olive Drive kitchen—I have a photo. Black cat collecting dust motes on the windowsill and me in cut-off Osh-Kosh overalls, bending over a cutting board. The angle of my head, the intensity. The not knowing who took the picture, what was being cooked, or who for. This photo makes me emotionally weak-kneed.

༄

Once I made an East Indian food feast for twenty—we sat crammed in the living room and the writing room, immobilized under the weight of the courses I had to pass around from too few cooking pots with borrowed-from-other-cottagers utensils. I had cooked for five hours. I had begun by buying all the rare-to-me ingredients on the introductory advice found in an Indian cookbook: Madhur Jaffrey's *An Invitation to Indian Cooking.* The pages are still turned down at Seekh Kabab, Cauliflower with Onion and Tomato, Rice with Whole Spices, Cold Chana Dal with Potatoes. I remember the array of spices—cardamom, cloves, saffron, ground and simmered and seared and sifted together. I don't know who I invited or why or where I got the money, that month, for the feast. But feasts were a fact and a facet of that time.

In the garage—if it could be so termed—was an immensely heavy, metal ice-cream-vendor's freezer. It had six-inch walls, a double flip-top lid. Kim and I picked it up at some yard sale, and he kept it ever after filled with venison for me (I learned to prepare venison stew, spaghetti sauce, and shish kebab) from deer that he hunted on his family's Humboldt County ranch where his brother grew a modest hidden garden of hemp, sinsemilla plants that staked that brother some years later in life to the purchase of his own ranch. I remember the awe we all felt for those six-foot-tall resinous plants. They glowed a deep, illegal, healthy green on the rainy hillside when we visited the brother's operation one year, driving past the hippie, re-painted, broken-down school bus parked to block one side road and manned during police alerts with houndlike long-haired pot farmers with rifles willing to protect their investments.

༄

I stayed longer than most. Longest place I've lived until this year, when my years in Florida threaten to double my years at Olive Drive. I took the mirror with me when I left, and that leaving unleashed a long set of interlocked stories that are not usefully shared right now. I stole the mirror from Fred Callori—replaced it with a cheap drugstore mirror. Took it. Took it with me. I took the mirror to Arizona, to Alaska where my then husband M., father of my children, argued against hanging it on the wall. He didn't like mirrors outside of bathrooms (imagine how he would have felt about red-painted bathrooms), that is, hung on public walls. He didn't like catching sight of himself, I guess, in the frame. While I imagined the mirror was a well, a record, a pool of my past experiences. I just saw desire and hope and leaning forward in it. I saw the other side of a room reflected. I didn't see age—which I now suspect he saw—or fate or fear.

～

In the Olive Drive cottage, shack, home, hideaway, there is a reproduction of Vermeer's painting of a head of a girl with a gold earring on the wall. There is an Indonesian batik on another wall. There is a quilt I made. Now lost. It's on a bed. Now gone. There is a wall by a bookcase with the phone where I took that life-changing phone call from Will. There are purple, poorly handmade corduroy curtains letting in the light of poems. There is a rusted 1940s cheese grater and thick clear-glass lemon juicer on one kitchen shelf and some handblown blue jars with metal lids found at the Sixteenth Street Goodwill. There are two huge Sacramento Valley squash Kim brought by one day still sitting on the front deck by the front door. There's a stray hollyhock growing bright purple in late-summer light. Under the sycamore tree in the back is a sagging bench that the black cat leaps over on his way through Chris Lee's hand-tooled leather cat-door flap.

There's a copy of *The Joy of Cooking* open on the young woman's kitchen counter. In the bathroom, water has splashed out of the red-painted, lion-footed bathtub and she's absentmindedly or perhaps irritably sopped it up, the wet towel kicked into a corner. Later, she'll have to load the laundry into a wire basket on the back of her ten-speed bicycle and wobble down Olive Drive, across the railroad tracks and into town to the Laundromat. Sometimes she'll stop by the Bank of America and get out enough money, she hopes, to pay Fred Callori for the borrow of his house, her home, at No. 7. The bathroom mirror was sold—in a placating gesture—at a garage sale during a marriage now ended. But she's not afraid to look in it again. To see the red walls. To see the necklaces gleaming cheaply on the wall beside the basin. To dry her hands on the towel. To walk out into the small outer rooms and meet her friends, and—if they're there—they're right there, because that shack is so small. And, of course, each time she walks out of the bathroom and into the kitchen, she remeets her self, just as she is going somewhere else.

(Mainly) Middle-Class Suburban (Mostly) White, or Making Sense of Suburbia

It is . . . very difficult to escape, culturally from the class into which you have been born.
—GEORGE ORWELL

Some of the most assiduous class climbers are university professors.
—PAUL FUSSELL

My next-door neighbor Reba asks me to drive her to the Tallahassee Regional Airport early Sunday morning by leaving a voice-mail message on my answering machine the Saturday night before while she's taking her two children to Taco Bell.

It will be the only morning all week when I don't have to get up at 6:30 A.M. to get my son and daughter—ages ten and thirteen—in motion, ready to take their school bus or geared up and delivered to the soccer field. I don't want to do this—get up that early—but I will (and say so on the phone message I leave, in turn, on her machine) because she's in the process of getting a divorce. Like I was three years ago, though not at all really like I was. In fact, before she started preparing for a divorce we didn't talk at all and didn't like each other much—and probably still don't, if we were to reflect on it.

Reba never took me to the airport while I was turning into a single parent. She's local, married to a local man, a high-school sweetheart. I'm not local, but find myself slowly if not accepting of—then at least expecting— north Florida's south Georgia ways, understanding parties will begin at best an hour after the announced arrival time, that fall disappears between the end of a long summer and the start of a mild winter, that women wear foundation in the highest of humidity and dresses with lots of fabric and even with bows, that vowels and smiles are as drawn out as glasses of tall sweet iced tea.

Last year about this time, Reba came over to my yard with her husband to give me a bill for refinishing an antique nightstand of her daughter's that my daughter, in some fit of preadolescent pique carved her initials into— MB. Reba, who is petite and blond, has a sharply angled jaw, deep-set eyes, and a fixed smile. She had been trembling with indignation on that day six months earlier when she told me how she had discovered the initials. At that time, I did the neighborly suburban thing and got mad at my daughter and offered to pay to fix the problem. By the time the bill was presented, my ex-husband who had been living with me for the better part of that year had moved out, again (I found out later that the across-the-street neighbor had called the police while he was here with the moving van loading up his possessions).

I was broke and living alone, having bought out my ex-husband's equity with a loan from my retirement account and spent more than I had to hire two brothers to paint the house—completely. I went into debt to remain in a neighborhood I had been originally ambivalent about moving into (I cried at the mortgage closing of this, my first house). I had cobbled together my salary, child support, summer-school teaching into an economy of my own that I had barely adjusted to, much less recognized, having paid off my own student loans only the year I arrived in town. I painted the house because my ex, M., had been looking stormy about the way I had let the house go. By the time I got around to hiring the painters he had moved, and I found the sharp dizzying smell of the paint a tonic, a kind of "I'm going to paint that man right out of my hair" relief, coming, no doubt, from my *South Pacific,* Mary Martin childhood.

In any event, I was outside cleaning wasp nests from the garage when Reba and her husband, Wes, he standing back a ways, she in a yellow twin set and flowered skirt and heels that sank into my centipede-grass wide front lawn, hovered at the edge of my vision. "Wendy," she said, "we finally got the bill for refinishing Courtney's bedroom nightstand," and held out a piece of paper. I looked down at a bill for ninety dollars. Family antique my ass, I thought, but was too discouraged to say this aloud. I would put this bill in the bill pile. Wes said nothing, having been brought along, I assumed, for moral support. Reba was trembling this time too— she held on to each day it seemed to me with the petite-woman's pit-bull tenacity. And, she was within her rights by suburban standards. "Thou shalt not do wrong to thy suburban neighbors" is engraved in the air over the main road into this housing area of $100,000+ structures and near one-acre lots . . . "or they will sue you or use your homeowner's association dues to sue you" (should you want a fence here, or an outbuilding there), I had learned. I took the bill wordlessly, unable to muster a neighborhood smile, and went inside. They left. I wrote a check. Put it in their mailbox.

These days, Reba's husband, Wes, is playing tournaments with his tennis partner and unable to take his soon-to-be-ex-wife to the airport; his tennis-partner girlfriend is herself separated, mother of three—the wreckage of their affair encompasses five children, the quiet propriety of their corner lot (painting its wood blue was the only eccentricity they displayed of any note in a neighborhood of brick and, like my house, stucco). Reba's world(s) have collapsed. Ninety dollars could not now make a dent in the problem. Having "been there," I'm as friendly as I can be to a woman whom I too couldn't have lived with—dinner was, my children reported, often at 8 P.M. and included not just one but more than one vegetables. Rules were many and enforced. Reba's husband was often in the garage or gardening or playing basketball, thunk thunk thunk on a driveway court too close to my bedroom window where I drank gin and tonics and read and wondered what had happened to my own life.

My marriages to Chris K. and then Brad were in some ways self-forgivable. After getting a biology degree, Chris K. took up viola at age twenty-two and I took up writing, more seriously. He became a Bay Area new-wave electric-viola player, I went on into poetry and teaching writing. Brad was a poet and I fell for the poetic party line that a poet should marry a poet. Forgive me. Forgive us. We have forgiven each other. But M., a librarian, eventually a computer guru, came along as my biology burned brightest in my thirties. He was more stable, fully upper-middle-class to my lower-middle-class aspiring bohemian, and we were ready to have children though not (like so many before us) to raise them.

"Even if their husbands perform a fair share of household tasks, working women still take responsibility for seeing that the work gets done," comments psychologist Kathleen C. Light of the University of North Carolina at Chapel Hill School of Medicine. "[The working woman's] sense of vigilance and being on call is virtually constant, whereas her spouse more often does his assigned chores and then relaxes," Light contends. ("Working Moms: Stressed to Excess" *Discover*, August 1997)

I am rarely relaxed and I am reclusive. I don't offer hellos or gossip or covered dishes or discussion about the school districts. In seven years, I've never been invited inside Reba's house next door though she's come to mine several times, particularly recently to get some advice on questions to ask a lawyer. I don't know if this is me or her or suburbia. Probably all three. I note this as a fact, not as a complaint, as a symptom not as a problem, if there is one. I expect, like me, Reba is in her forties and her husband, like my ex, is arriving a little faster and no less reluctantly at fifty. Thus, we're both middle-aged, middle-class white women living in suburbia. I'm single. She's soon to be. I've held on to my place here—as I described it irritably to my daughter one stressed-out day—by my fingernails. Reba and her husband are probably going to sell their house.

Neglect of one's lawn in middle-class neighborhoods can invite terrible retributions. (Paul Fussell, in *Class,* p. 82)

Lawns here are wide and green (I've learned about mowing and the allergies I never knew I had, about lawn services and sod webworms) and houses are large and generally very well maintained (I've learned about weather-stripping and keeping the pool chemicals in harmony, about new methods for termite control and the need every month for replacing things I never before dreamed I even had). Most homeowners, from a glance at the neighborhood directory, are dual-career couples whose wives—if they once stayed home—are reentering the workforce as children are now turning from toddlers to teens, like mine are (Reba has an eleven-year-old son whom my ten-year-old son admires and a thirteen-year-old daughter whom my thirteen-year-old daughter has a more complicated, on-and-off-again friendship with). It is a neighborhood of surfaces and reflections.

In his broadly satiric book *Class,* Paul Fussell anatomizes the unspoken American classes. In ways that hit home. For instance, one of my strongest childhood memories includes being told by my mother that I couldn't go three houses up the street to my friend Vanessa's house to watch the color TV—the first on our block—because her mother was DIVORCED. Her overweight brother lived in a back cottage. Her mother's boyfriend wandered in and out of a house that was fascinatingly free of regular eating hours, and her mother's large-finned Caddie was always parked at an intriguing angle in an unkempt driveway. She was the most-mentioned "bad influence" on our block of California stucco houses, followed by the family who painted their stucco house a bright purple, causing a need for an unusual public meeting while the Limberopoulous's outrageous Greek redecorating (painted murals, bright colors, strange music—loud) was tolerated in a rare expression of clench-toothed, cross-cultural diplomacy.

Vanessa was a memorable friend (allowed to swim in the wading pool at my house) and a funny reminder to me of the fragility of social strictures as, ten years later, my mother was divorced and later still, I was—too many times for middle-class comfort. Perhaps it *was* that color TV?

Fussell divides Americans into nine classes:

Top out-of-sight
Upper
Upper Middle

Middle
High proletarian
Mid proletarian
Low proletarian

Destitute
Bottom out-of-sight

At the end of his book, he adds Category X: bohemian, self-cultivated, intellectual, etc.

> Entering category X often requires flight from parents and forebears. The young flocking to the cities to devote themselves to "art," "writing," "creative work" anything virtually, that liberates them from the presence of a boss or supervisor—are aspirant X people, and if they succeed in capitalizing on their talents, they may end up as fully fledged X types. . . . Being an X person is like having much of the freedom and some of the power of a top-out-of-sight or upper-class person, but without the money. (213)

I've always liked to think I'm less compromised by class because it's a comfortable aesthetic stance, and because I'm a college professor/writer I hold to such aesthetics. That is, until Fussell pointed out my aspirations to Category X—aspirations that have always made me uneasy even as I continue to pursue them. And I'm not alone, as evidenced in this e-mail from a former graduate student in his second year teaching at a Northern university who is talking about another former graduate student, and mutual friend, who is in his forties and his first year of teaching in the same large city:

> I always catch him giving himself shit for being able to have "stuff" now—new TVs, he's talking about a house, and so on; he's apologizing for having cable. No sin there! Like me, he tends to define himself in opposition to "the dominant." That doesn't work out too well in the end: I'm like 35 years old and I live like a 20 year old. Where are my wife and kids, my house and my TV, my car? Instead, I have a dog and 61 Simpsons episodes on videocassette.

I give myself shit too, but I admit to a passion (and some ability) for consumerism if it runs to interiors—generally Western-inspired—and gear-laden sports like camping and bicycling and nothing but the best, from recessed lighting to a new bank loan for a sports-utility vehicle.

> Child care is the biggest job at home for both men and women, but women spend more than three times as many hours tending the kids. Though men cook and shop more than they did a decade ago, they still lag behind in those chores, too. (*Newsweek,* May 1997)

I also have a more flexible schedule than most, writing at home two days of the week, adjusting my activities to my parenting while my neighbors generally have to adjust their parenting to their schedules. For instance, Reba used to alternate morning and evening child caretaking with her husband; now she leaves before the children at 7 A.M. and comes home after them at 5:30 or 6 P.M. That's not the way it's supposed to be in the suburbs.

> New houses are three rooms bigger than they were 20 years ago, even though families are smaller. The venerable bathtub is giving way to the "soaking tub," with jets. (Brigid Schulte, "Big Has No Boundaries in the New America," *Tallahassee Democrat,* October 1997)

I have one of those tubs and have continuously tried to "rise above" its predictability as a class marker by decorating around it—putting plants in it, taking measurements to cover it with plywood and create a sitting space (this didn't work), trying, trying to do something with the (essential for re-sale value) enormity of it; it's only recently, when my children and I all had strep throat in a family cacophony of distress that they decided they'd try the "big bathtub," filling it with expensive gallons of steam and glee.

I've always gone a little nuts in suburbia and I've always returned. I'm like a nesting doll—I've lived out of a backpack, a cottage, and now this 2,000+-square-foot house—too big for our three-person family needs, too expensive and expansive, yet too good to give up.

ᑫᑭ

Yes, it's too good to give up. And if I examine my worries, I can see they come from my family and offer a salute to my gender—my mother was a frustrated, manic-depressive, middle-class agoraphobic, and I reacted by climbing my way onto the class ladder in the only possible way—through Category X—but Category X requires that I succeed in a hierarchical, still male-dominated academy. Not surprisingly, every move I make worries and maddens me.

A tendency to get very anxious suggests that you are middle-class and nervous about slipping down a rung or two. (Fussell, in *Class*, p. 2)

In a magazine, I read that only one woman in ten in America makes more than forty thousand dollars a year. I'm one of those women, and it continues to astound me. By what it means about me and about other women, too. My mother was an army wife, a social worker (on-the-job training and only for a few years), a substitute teacher, a live-in house-keeper for wealthy people in Santa Barbara near the end of her life; an intelligent, unfulfilled woman who was constantly disoriented by the moves and demands of army life. Any sense of career she had after some spirited years working in a shipyard during World War II was put on hold by four pregnancies and a marriage of absences and infidelities and 1950s propriety. She would obey at the price of her sanity. She conformed even as conformity broke her: We were told never to say she was getting medical help but was "visiting the relatives." We made a big show of family din-ners, of house and home, but no one was ever comfortable there, and food made predictable negative inroads on my sisters' and my psyches. This is to say, we were relatively normal 1960s middle-class. Our portion was not alcohol or incest or stifling of personality (my sisters and I all have personalities by the fistful), but we had our lot of madness, insularity, debt, and small disasters.

Enter the bohemian escape, ascent, attitude. I more easily took to my stepmother who was an artist, and I blended more comfortably into a blended family whose quirks were on the table at the outset than I had ever entered into my own. I was terrified of the '70s like my mother's daughter but therein found freedoms and friends and arts of my own, wreathed around by the freedoms of the time, the occult, sex, aesthetic discussions, funky clothing, health food, junk food, tried-on personas, and part-time occupations. I avidly pursued Category X when I realized it offered me succor from my mother's failures: work, flexible hours to nurse my inherited phobias, enough stability to help me keep a cap on family demons, and the challenge of work and family in a new decade, a new key.

> Many stay-at-home moms in the '50s, for instance, had sky-high cleaning standards, such as insisting that cleaning the kitchen floor entailed scrubbing the grout between the tiles with a toothbrush.
>
> Those kind of standards, though, don't work for today's two-income families. (Kathleen Laufenberg, *Tallahassee Democrat*)

But we don't change our pasts that easily. Neither by succeeding as a woman in the academic arena (it's still damn hard) or by trying to marry (too?) rationally. M. as an upper-middle-class man was able to dabble in Category X but had the soul of a 1950s mother—his own. He did clean the tiles with a toothbrush, and it took, has taken, three years at least for me not to feel guilty with clutter, with chores left for tomorrow, with meals eaten when hungry, with sufficient rather than perfect.

But believe me. I accept this as my baggage. I grew up in suburbia and I returned here, with M. And now without him, I remain. I dwell here. It's a good place to write. It's essential for someone of my ilk. I pace the rooms of this big, well-lit house. I walk to the front glass window and safely observe the world. I walk to the back writing room. I finger souvenirs from my forays out—insistent travel that I took over time to map a world that I didn't quite believe in (how could I—I was locked in mortal combat with make-nice imperatives, with a monoculture). One of my friends on e-mail put it this way: "i'm not looking forward to another winter here. the first month or two is okay—kind of bracing. but, man, i miss april! and suburbs: yech. i grew up in central california suburbs that are so much like these, i feel i haven't gone anyplace. just died in sacramento and my corpse is rotting while my spirit leaches into the earth." Do I need to add that he's a poet, a college writing teacher, met in the poetry circuit?

༄

> Suburb—a district, esp. A residential district, on or near the outskirts of a city and often separately incorporated city or town. Suburbia—the suburbs or suburbanites collectively: usually used to connote the values, attitudes, and activities regarded as characteristic of suburban life. (*Webster's Dictionary,* of course)

Cultures. Cultural. Cross-culture. Certainly there are black suburbias. And Asian. And Latino. Though I've lived long enough in one of my pasts on the Navajo reservation to be pretty sure there are no Native American suburban landscapes hidden in the four-corners region, unless you consider the BIA-built subsidized housing an incomprehensible equivalent. Does it bother me that there are only two black households in this neighborhood, neither of whom I know by name? Yes. Though the function of suburbia—as I can see by my having never been in Reba's house—is to keep such distances. In fact, I know the names only of families my kids play with and then by the designation, usually, of Jim's mom or James's dad. But then, my kids aren't playing with Latrell and I'm not getting to meet Jamal's mom. My African American friends, like me, like my white friends, are in Category X—writers, dancers, teachers. Like me, they live suburban/bohemian, and probably have high levels of cortisol for, in fact, my many women friends generally have marital and child-raising trajectories more like me—remarriages, time-out-of-mainstream-life exploring the world and now returned, to write and roost.

> Women who had at least one child living at home excreted substantially more of the stress hormone cortisol in their urine than did their counterparts without kids at home, regardless of marital status or number of social contacts. Independent studies indicate that

long-term elevations of cortisol contribute to heart disease, the Duke scientists note. ("Working Moms: Stressed to Excess," p. 44)

Stressed to excess. Sorting out surfaces and reflections. Looking for the true depths in mundane despair. One of my students reading a draft of an essay where I took the Category X intellectual stance said, "Although you may be wiser now, I don't like you belittling yourself then. Despair is despair," and I've reflected on her observation for I've come to understand I can do my best in suburbia. On that walk to the front door, I see the un-fixed front-porch column is still rotting away because I haven't gotten it to-gether (so help me M.) to get it repaired yet, but work is getting written and the children are safely at school. At the back window, I look out at the swimming pool with its embarrassing rafts of drowned oak leaves (the lawn is cared for but it's like squeezing a ball of flubber—something always gives and this time it's the pool that nags).

I'll study the South. I'll dream of the West. I'll sign only the petitions that I believe in re: the neighborhood. I'm a little less inward than I used to be—I say hello to the neighbors who walk by. I'll keep fondly in mind the intense education of a romantic biracial interlude and remember how marked I felt when my ex threatened to fight to keep the kids from me be-cause I was dating black and how sobered I was in the supermarket and cinema accompanied by this handsome man in this New South. Luckily, I know it ended for multiple and not for miscreant reasons. (He now lives in northern California. M. moved to Orange County, California—the con-veyor belt, cocktail-shaker movement that [re]constructs that state contin-ues.) I'll learn to accept the compliments of students who arrive for meetings at my house and admire it. I'll learn to find myself here, in my work, my children, my words, the (tea) leaves of the swimming pool, the challenges of relentless summer heat. I'll teach good classes. I'll start run-ning again—I promise—and maybe all this will help control my cortisol levels. And I'll try to pack away as many satirical inverted commas as I pos-sibly can. I am learning to do unto others.

And that is where the story of Reba comes in. Reba is moving. She's told the eldest daughter. Not the younger son. My children are sad, but sup-portive. We're going to try to help however we can. But for now, we're staying in the suburbs.

Souvenirs

In a certain sense, I'm a souvenir—born in Japan and returned to the U.S. three months later when my army parents began their slow settling to the West Coast. First Washington and then California where I grew up—surrounded by souvenirs and talked about as if I were one myself. I have inherited family souvenirs and with them caretaker's rights and storyteller's freedoms. Souvenirs are the pentimento of my life, the underdrawing. They're the skeleton around which my muscles grew and flesh formed. They're the speck of irritant that conjured the pearl of these thoughts. Or, perhaps they're what remains, as I remain—a human falling through the hourglass of my genealogy.

GETTING THE SILVER FOX

THE MINK SKINS IF I GET THEM WILL BE THE WHOLE SKIN.

I AM GETTING SEVEN SILVER FOX SKINS FOR SURE.

THE FELLOW THAT WAS GOING TO GET ME THE BABY SEAL SKINS GOT THERE TOO LATE.

BY THE WAY, I CAN GET THE BABY SEAL SKINS AFTER ALL. AS SOON AS THE SKINS ARE TANNED I'LL SEND THEM TO YOU.

ABOUT YOUR SEAL SKINS, THEY ARE ON THE WAY, AND YOU CAN HAVE THEM MADE INTO ANYTHING YOU WANT.

I AM QUITE SURE THAT I CAN GET ENOUGH MINK SKINS FOR A COAT. IF YOU WANT THEM SAY SO RIGHT AWAY.

BY THE WAY, IF YOU CAN'T USE THE SEAL SKINS FOR A COAT OR IF YOU DONT WANT TO, JUST KEEP THEM UNTIL I GET THERE AND WE WILL FIND A SUCKER TO UNLOAD THEM ON OR TRADE THEM FOR SOMETHING YOU CARE FOR.

(FROM "V-MAIL")

From my father, I've inherited a collector's avidity. Besides being military, he was a hobbyist, tourist, self-educator—he was a collector of house tools, leather-tooling implements, photographic equipment, coins, army medals, bomb casing decorated with mother-of-pearl in Korea and currency and coin from Germany and the Far East, furs from Iceland, footlockers full of goods from every site of army occupation—Iceland, Germany, Japan.

> He set the vase back beside the bed
> And waited hours for dawn.
> When he got up, rest at an end,
> He put his souvenirs
> Into an army trunk
> Stenciled with his name.
> (FROM "SOUVENIRS")

From my mother I've inherited attitudes about souvenirs. For her, they either had to be bargains, jumble, yard sale, church sale, bargain days. Or they had to be perfect, unblemished, schlock or not (quality was worthwhile but often braggable gaud and glitter was even better). Hummel figurines, silver spoons, cut-glass bowls, just-postwar Japanese-made, Western-styled furniture, vases.

> I never saw her cry, until the day,
> vacuuming behind, she tripped the entire
> hutch of wood and a rain of souvenirs fell,
> pieces and fragments on hardwood floors
> of that, our final house.
> (FROM "BEFORE WARS")

The Japanese allotment made the most lasting impression because I was one, born in Japan, a war brat of the Korean War, youngest child, last family posting overseas. And with that posting, souvenirs. Family stories. Family furniture. Chinese lacquer cabinets. German slipper chairs covered with Japanese brocade. Child-sized kimonos worn by my older sisters and then me at Halloween until the lovely red silks disappeared into some local disaster—spilled on, torn, tossed in sorrow, tantrum, or tears.

> The souvenirs, unsheathed, escape
> Icelandic wool and fox fur lined

footlockers. Newspaper shrouds
proclaim old columned news
in codes of Japanese.
For years, the Hummel figurines—
clean-limbed imitation Aryan forms
danced across lacquer tables.
(FROM "BEFORE WARS")

My father acquired more than thirty army footlockers to transport us
hither and yon. He built special storage shelves in the last family garage and
lined them up there. I kept one, spray painted it royal blue, took it to college with me. The metal top drawer would lift out to display an equivalent
space underneath. By the time college was over, I kept my inherited darkroom in it and eventually sold the darkroom equipment—well stored in
the scratched footlocker.

THE MAN AND THE BRONCOS

The most mysterious negatives were found
while clearing out the darkroom when he died,
a hundred murky black and white transparencies
of broncos bucking under spur and rope, all taken
at the rodeo by a man who seemed never to like horses,
who found no use for anything outdoors.
He would have taken up photography
as the smallest sanest form of alchemy and wonder
he could force into a life of regularity.

But a hundred times he held emulsion to his eyes:
Horses in their raw arc pulled toward sky
and light scraped wide crescents from each underbelly.
This he sought, and small illuminations in the dark.

When I think about it—I lived my parents' life like a hermit crab. I
found a shell—this family—and crawled right in. Then I picked up one
object or another, and kept it, dropped it, nicked it, tore it off going into a
shallows, decided to trade in, or up, or out. There was an exhilaration
about having acquired one of the family souvenirs—for of course none of

us gave up possessions easily. My mother would give us her things readily in conversations and take them back in the next breath, the next day, at the first real asking-for. When she wanted to gain leverage, she came at us, literally, with something held out—releasing first what was already our own. For me, acquiring my Japanese silver baby cup was a major coup, accompanied by a severe teenage rhetoric of demand and recrimination. She let it go reluctantly. When, divorced, and moving from house to apartment, she had to diminish the furniture hoard, we played a shell game of give-and-take. I couldn't ask outright for what I wanted, or that was withheld. Interested indifference might turn up something though. But with things, I inherited responsibility. No ideas but in things, claims William Carlos Williams. I have lots of ideas. And conversations regarding them, around which I almost built an identity. They were lingua and lingua franca. My mother could call me about the furniture more easily than about anything else in her or my life.

INTO AND OUT OF GILLIAN

Soap and German goblets and Japanese brocades, self-help books and trashy scenic paintings—heavy with green heavy with yellow—and sweetly sour red wine on Sunday, late, and seersucker bathing suits and empty lipstick tubes, go into Gillian.

Wishes and cheese casseroles, some 1950s acceptable behavior for unknown neighbors, some late night terror—blankets that smell pink and leaden at the same time—and a way of reading any print—signs, contracts, cereal boxes, menus, church bulletins, inoculation and report cards, billboards, and TV evangelists' phone numbers repeated twice—and a way of sitting very very still, disallowing sharp hand movements, before the opinions of doctors, come out of Gillian.
(FROM "GILLIAN ALONE")

My father changed hobbies, remarried, consolidated, went on. He left the furniture with my mother who held onto it fiercely enough for both of them. But he took his tools and talents. And memorabilia. When he died, the Mason ring and Army Officers' Training School ring went to my sister who nursed him. To me, of course, the photographic equipment. I have his dog tag and a broken silver ID bracelet. A framed set of army medals went

to one of my nephews. I don't know where his mother-of-pearl inlaid service revolver is now. My stepmother kept the coin collection. She and he
had consolidated happily and remodeled her house—another of his
skills—to change each place he lived, to tailor the walls and doorways and
cupboards to the needs of the family. There was something of the busy,
householding hermit crab in him, too, I see. But they bought new together,
mostly. Fewer footlockers. New horizons and hobbies.

～

Responsibility is weighty. There came a time that my place in the world
was defined by what I had salvaged—the Japanese-crafted wooden dresser
that my sister carved my other sister's name into to get her into trouble,
which backfired for the name was misspelled. The low, carved Japanese
table—my mother's favorite that always led to a story of how she had
asked that all her favorite Japanese symbols—chrysanthemums, Mount
Fuji, cherry blossoms, fir trees, and so on, be carved into the surface in a
stunning display of culture clash. A Western enumeration of the ineffable.
When my sisters and I cleaned out her trailer after her death, the closet full
of bargain clothes reverted back to the junk man. The family furniture
mostly had previously been parceled out. The prime German and Japanese
souvenirs were the last to be divided. The Japanese plate to Nancy who
wasn't there but asked for it—of all things. It had been given to my parents, it was said, for giving some friends a Western wedding cake. They
sent the valuable family heirloom back. It was returned, and they learned
that they should keep it and not insult the bride and groom's parents. A
Japanese vase to Linda. A roll of Japanese brocade to me. And to Judy
some Imari porcelain. A few things I had never seen surfaced—a small
purse and fan that I still have. Other things were remembered but never re-
found—a two-inch netsuke, ivory carved to the shape of a slightly open
clam shell with a scene carved inside the shell of women in palaces and
gardens. I took some lacquer end tables that disintegrated under hard use.
My life was as complicated as my parents' had been, "Twenty-six houses in
twenty-one years" as my mother summed it up. And what centered that life
was this and that souvenir, packed, unpacked, shared, storied-up, bragged
on, argued over.
My moves included more U-hauls and indecision, more backpacking
and student poverty, and then as a young mother, less ability to maintain

the family inheritance. When things gave in to the weight of my life or my misuse or indifference or my inability, for instance, to transport hand-joined corner cabinets that were starting to buckle with the weather changes from California to Arizona to Alaska, I sold a great deal in Fairbanks where furniture had been hauled in since first homesteaders' settlement. My family pieces joining the flotsam of the far North. And my psyche pulled loose in this and that corner, untethered by certainty and the family form of stability.

> No matter how you move or arrange it,
> The furniture takes up where it left off.
> Your rooms are changed
> And you with them. Night brings out
> The ghosts, emissaries of the past
> With whom you act and reenact the most painful
> Of childhood scenes and stages
> Until pushed out by the complacent hulks
> You were pushed out by before,
> You go for a walk.
> (FROM "FAMILY FURNITURE")

I thought. Until I thought more about how "I am what I hold." Around my house today are tips of family icebergs. Hidden under my own life-souvenirs of Navajo rugs and Nigerian handicrafts, mixed well in, is the leaven (or leadenness) of the past—is the Japanese coffee table, the last intact fan, the family photographs, the book of annual Christmas letters. Small wooden dolls. A bracelet I can't remember my mother wearing but always remember coveting. Now it's mine and I don't wear it either. My mother's passport—with my birth picture; my passport from Japan to Fort Lewis, Washington, age three months—just passed on to me with a photo album by a sister Nancy who has decided she's had enough.

Already, in this life, I've written pages of poems and stories, piecing the jigsaw puzzle of the past, of my personality. I see that I collect souvenirs with a fatherly vengeance. I line shelves with a motherly intensity. I prefer whole and perfect. I mourn loss. I feel free when I abandon the fractious weight of bits and pieces. I'm like a magnet. I have sparks shooting off of me. I think I remember things I can't possibly know. I finger bits of brocade, ivory, photographic paper. A plate is chipped. I want to throw it out and start over. I open a drawer and find a figurine I had forgotten. I pull black-and-white pictures out of albums to show my children, and find myself wandering into another room, instead, to think about them. Or I walk to a cupboard and open it, look in, to see if the souvenir I've just suddenly remembered is still there. And if it isn't, I'll no doubt find another one. A part of them, a part of me.

Autobiography

My lives look like subway cars, colliding along the rails in the dark
when electricity blows and passengers lean precariously forward.
Someone falls into someone's lap. A man with a suitcase lurches
away from his safe handhold; the lady with the white purse laughs.

My husbands meet in the back room in the TV glow, the game is
in a final inning, they jostle for remote control. They decide it is
    easier
to be friends than to be with me. They take up viola and amphetamines,
marijuana and Go games, computers and credit cards; they share
    their *whens*.

My children hold a family reunion on a soccer field, get in the
    players' way,
run hot with memories, start shouting matches from sideline to sideline.
They stand face to face in exacting symmetry. They claim: *you never*
and *you always,* trail picnic trash of torn paper, of matches and
    apology.
My lovers leave the house early, walk the neighborhood in the dark.
They head west but forget to wait for me. Those who stay lift the lid
on a cauldron that reheats on the stove. My dogs howl in barbershop
harmony. The cats stalk off. They have always known it would be
    this way.

My sisters meet my lives in the corners of their municipalities. They
    say *really?*

And *fine*. My brothers arm-wrestle my lives, waiting for surf on a pacific ocean
where they've gone to get away from their own lives. I should remind you—
my lives are giving themselves a surprise birthday party— everyone
  is invited.

My lives line up like clothes on a clothesline. A shirt billows out in
  grass-
sweet-smelling dry sun. A skirt hangs inanimate in drizzle rain. My
  lives dream
as wind rises, bath towel flapping and solitary. Why, even now, my
  lives
snap off the line and fly into the space between this place and my
  other lives.

WENDY BISHOP teaches writing at Florida State University. The author of *Working Words: The Process of Creative Writing* (Mayfield, 1993), she coedited *Colors of a Different Horse: Rethinking Creative Writing, Theory and Pedagogy* (NCTE, 1994) with Hans Ostrom. Recent books include *Teaching Lives: Essays and Stories* (Utah State University Press, 1997) and an edited collection, *Elements of Alternate Style: Essays on Writing and Revision* (Boynton/Cook, 1997). She continues to publish poems, nonfiction, essays, and stories in literary and composition journals; new poetry chapbooks include *Touching Liliana* (Jumping Cholla Press, 1998), *Mid-Passage* (Nightshade Press, 1998), and *My 47 Lives* (Palanquin Press, 1998). A poetry-writing text, *Thirteen Ways of Looking for a Poem,* is forthcoming from Longman Publishers.

DOUGLAS CARLSON'S essays have appeared recently in the *Georgia Review, Alkali Flats,* the *American Literary Review, Ascent, Petroglyph,* and *North Dakota Quarterly.* His work has also been included in the anthologies *The Sacred Place: Witnessing the Holy in the Physical World* (University of Utah Press, 1996) and *A Place Apart* (W. W. Norton & Company). Earlier essays were collected in *At the Edge.* He is currently visiting writer-in-residence at Concordia College in Moorhead, Minnesota, and serves on the editorial board of White Pine Press. In 1991–1992, Carlson was guest contributing editor for the *Georgia Review's* special nature-writing issue.

JUDITH KITCHEN teaches at SUNY Brockport and is the author of *Only the Dance: Essays on Time and Memory* and coeditor of *In Short: A Collection of Brief Creative Nonfiction* and *In Brief: Short Takes on the Personal* (forthcoming from W. W. Norton & Company). Her nonfiction has appeared in the *Georgia Review,* the *Gettysburg Review,* and *Prairie Schooner.* She is a regular poetry reviewer and an editor of a chapbook series.

DAWN MARANO is an acquisitions editor at the University of Utah Press. Her poetry and nonfiction have appeared in several publications, including

Ascent and *Terra Nova,* and in the anthologies *The Sacred Place* and *In Brief.* Her work was cited as one of the Notable Essays of 1996 in *The Best American Essays.*

W. SCOTT OLSEN, an associate professor of English and chair of the Environmental Studies program at Concordia College in Moorhead, Minnesota, is the author of a story collection, two travel books, and a textbook. He edited the special essay issue of *American Literary Review,* coedited the anthology *The Sacred Place,* and currently edits the literary magazine *Ascent.* His work was twice cited among the Notable Essays in *The Best American Essays,* in 1996 and again in 1997.

ACKNOWLEDGMENTS

W. Scott Olsen

For Maureen and Kate and Andrew, and their new stories each day.

Parts of this section have appeared in *North Dakota Quarterly, Pottersfield Portfolio* (Canada), and the Casper College (Wyo.) Writers Conference Anthology.

Dawn Marano

For Don, who believed and said the words would come when I was ready for them.

Excerpts from "Motel Mind" have appeared in *Terra Nova* and in *Where We Live: The Crossroads Anthology.*

Douglas Carlson

Thanks to Donna, who's been there since the beginning.

The epigraph for this essay was quoted in *Second Nature,* by Michael Pollan. Earlier versions of sections of this essay were published in *American Literary Review* and in *At the Edge* (White Pine Press, 1989). "On Your Chosen Site" is slated for the debut issue of *Alkali Flats.*

Wendy Bishop

This writing is for Morgan and Tait, who allow me my versions.

"It's Not the Heat, It's the Humidity" appeared in *Flint Hills Review*.

"Hummingbird at Heart" appeared in abridged form in *Journeys*, a local Tallahassee journal.

"Autobiography" appeared in *5 AM* and also in *Mid-Passage*, a poetry chapbook (from Nightshade Press). "Hummingbird in the Garage" will also appear in *Mid-Passage*.

"A War Bride Remembers Japan" appeared in *Colorado-North Review*.

"The Man and the Broncos" appeared in *New Delta Review*.

Complete versions of "V-Mail" can be found in *American Poetry Review*; "Before Wars" in *War, Literature and the Arts: An International Journal of the Humanities*; "Souvenirs" in *Quarry West*; and "Gillian Alone" in *Quarter After Eight*.

I appreciate those editors allowing me to weave them into a new narrative here.